Am-SB-c-30

ECONOMIC CONSEQUENCES OF
A LAND REFORM IN BRAZIL

CONTRIBUTIONS TO ECONOMIC ANALYSIS

67

Edited by

J. JOHNSTON

J. SANDEE

R. H. STROTZ

J. TINBERGEN

P. J. VERDOORN

NORTH-HOLLAND PUBLISHING COMPANY
AMSTERDAM • LONDON

ECONOMIC CONSEQUENCES OF A LAND REFORM IN BRAZIL

WILLIAM R. CLINE

Department of Economics,
Princeton University

1970

NORTH-HOLLAND PUBLISHING COMPANY
AMSTERDAM · LONDON

© NORTH-HOLLAND PUBLISHING COMPANY – 1970

All rights reserved. No part of this publication may be reproduced, stored in a retrieval system, or transmitted, in any form or by any means, electronic, mechanical, photocopying, recording or otherwise, without the prior permission of the copyright owner

Library of Congress Catalog Card Number: 73-126500

ISBN: 0 7204 3167 0

PUBLISHERS:
NORTH-HOLLAND PUBLISHING COMPANY – AMSTERDAM
NORTH-HOLLAND PUBLISHING COMPANY, LTD. – LONDON

PRINTED IN THE NETHERLANDS

INTRODUCTION TO THE SERIES

This series consists of a number of hitherto unpublished studies, which are introduced by the editors in the belief that they represent fresh contributions to economic science.

The term *economic analysis* as used in the title of the series has been adopted because it covers both the activities of the theoretical economist and the research worker.

Although the analytical methods used by the various contributors are not the same, they are nevertheless conditioned by the common origin of their studies, namely theoretical problems encountered in practical research. Since for this reason, business cycle research and national accounting, research work on behalf of economic policy, and problems of planning are the main sources of the subjects dealt with, they necessarily determine the manner of approach adopted by the authors. Their methods tend to be 'practical' in the sense of not being too far remote from application to actual economic conditions. In addition they are quantitative rather than qualitative.

It is the hope of the editors that the publication of these studies will help to stimulate the exchange of scientific information and to reinforce international cooperation in the field of economics.

THE EDITORS

PREFACE

This study was submitted to Yale University in 1969 as the author's doctoral dissertation. It examines the theory of land reform's effect on agricultural production, and predicts the impact of land redistribution on Brazilian agricultural output. The predictions are based on statistical estimates from data for approximately one thousand farms. But the study contains no examination of the past results of land reform in Brazil, because practically no land redistribution has taken place to date.

I am greatly indebted to Professors Gustav Ranis, William N. Parker, R. Albert Berry, Donald Hester, and Clark Reynolds for their careful guidance as dissertation advisors. My deep appreciation goes to Professors Werner Baer, W. Arthur Lewis, Gordon Smith, and Janes Angelo de Souza for inspiration and insights during the development of this study. I thank Dr. Isaac Kerstenetzky and Dr. Julian Chacel of the Getulio Vargas Foundation for their help during my stay in Rio de Janeiro in 1966, and I thank the Ford Foundation for its support of my research through the Foreign Area Fellowship Program. Finally, I wish to express my gratitude to my wife Ruth Harwood Cline for her patience and encouragement during the preparation of this study, which is dedicated to her.

Princeton, New Jersey
November 1969

W. R. CLINE

Ford Foundation Visiting Professor
Institute of Economic and Social Planning (IPEA)
Brazil

CONTENTS

INTRODUCTION TO THE SERIES V

PREFACE VII

LIST OF TABLES XI

INTRODUCTION AND GUIDE TO THE STUDY XIII

Chapter 1

THE BACKGROUND FOR AN ANALYSIS OF BRAZILIAN LAND REFORM 1

    1.1. The agricultural sector in Brazil 1
    1.2. Law and action 4
        1.2.1. The *Estatuto da Terra* of 1964 4
        1.2.2. The course of land reform since 1964 7
    1.3. Previous studies on land reform 8

Chapter 2

LAND REFORM AND AGRICULTURAL PRODUCTION: THEORETICAL CONSIDERATIONS . . . 11

    2.1. Introduction 11
    2.2. Goals of land reform 13
        2.2.1. Equity: income redistribution and labor absorption 13
        2.2.2. Production: static efficiency 15
        2.2.3. Long run growth 16
    2.3. Relationship of efficiency to scale of inputs utilized ('production-efficiency') 19
    2.4. The relation of farm size to land use ('farm-efficiency') . . . 22
        2.4.1. Labor-market dualism 23
        2.4.2. Land held as portfolio asset 32
        2.4.3. Land market imperfections 36
        2.4.4. 'Own consumption' on small farms 36
        2.4.5. Monopsony 38
        2.4.6. Non-maximization by large farms 41

	2.4.7. The relation of land quality to farm size	43
	2.4.8. Implications of the alternative explanations of land use intensity	45
2.5.	Social efficiency	47
	2.5.1. Land reform's effect on factor combinations	47
	2.5.2. Farm size and social efficiency	48
2.6.	Relationship of tenure-form to efficiency	52
2.7.	The hypotheses and the empirical tests	53
2.8.	Conclusion	55

Chapter 3

THE RELATION OF PRODUCTION-EFFICIENCY TO SCALE OF INPUTS UTILIZED AND TO TENURE STATUS OF THE FARM OPERATOR 58

3.1.	Introduction	58
3.2.	Data used	59
3.3.	Test for returns to scale	62
3.4.	Test for effects of total farm size and ownership status	74
3.5.	Conclusion	78

Chapter 4

LAND USE INTENSITY, FARM SIZE AND TENURE 79

4.1.	Introduction	79
	4.1.1. Purpose and contents	79
	4.1.2. General	80
4.2.	Aggregate data	80
4.3.	Hypothesis tests	80
	4.3.1. Model IV.1	80
	4.3.2. Model IV.2	89
	4.3.3. Model IV.3	109
4.4.	Tests for discrimination among alternative causes of land use patterns	115
	4.4.1. Factor ratios	116
	4.4.2. Rate of decline of land use intensity	122
	4.4.3. Further scatter diagram analysis	125
	4.4.4. Concentration of land ownership	126
	4.4.5. Summary	127
4.5.	'Social efficiency' and farm size	128
4.6.	Conclusion	130

Chapter 5

PREDICTION OF THE IMPACT OF LAND REFORM ON BRAZILIAN AGRICULTURAL PRODUCTION 133

5.1.	Introduction	133

5.2. Assumptions. 135
5.3. Sample expansion 138
5.4. Land reform calculations 140
    5.4.1. 'Total reform'. 140
    5.4.2. 'Partial reform' 153
5.5. Costs 162
5.6. Alternative methods of analysis 163
5.7. Conclusion 164

Chapter 6

CONCLUSION 166

6.1. Alternative policy measures 166
    6.1.1. Measures to increase production. 166
    6.1.2. Measures to improve the use of land and labor 167
    6.1.3. Evaluation of alternative policies 170
    6.1.4. Policy choice as a function of diagnosis. 170
6.2. Political considerations 172
6.3. Summary of the study 173
    6.3.1. Theory 173
    6.3.2. Empirical results 175
    6.3.3. Prediction of the impact of land redistribution on agricultural production 178
6.4. Conclusion 180

Appendix A

COLONIZATION 182

Appendix B

NOTES ON THE SAMPLE DATA USED 187

B.1. Survey methods of the samples. 187
B.2. Size-distribution bias of the FGV sample 189
B.3. Weighting of sample data for land reform calculations . . . 190
B.4. Imputed wages 193

Appendix C

STATISTICAL APPENDIX 195

BIBLIOGRAPHY 201

INDEX 209

LIST OF TABLES

1. Percentage of persons occupied in agriculture by number of workers per farm (Brazil, 1960) 30
2. Land prices for Rio Grande do Sul rice farms, 1949–64, versus wholesale price series, Brazil. 34
3. 'Own consumption' on farms as a percentage of total production, by farm size group, Tapes county, Rio Grande do Sul. 37
4. Definitions of variables in sample data 60
5. Number and size distribution of farm observations in sample data of this study . 62
6. Percent of Brazilian agricultural production represented by product sectors of this study 63
7. Unconstrained production functions 64
8. Constrained production functions 68
9. Functions over the world 70
10. Constrained production functions with size-group and tenure dummy variables. Nine crop sectors, pooled model 76
11. Land use intensity as a function of farm size and tenure 84
12. Percent of usable farm area in crops, pasture, and 'effective pasture' (by farm size group) 86
13. Relationship of value added per hectare of farm area with farm size, tenure type, and land price 92
14. Value added per hectare of farm area (by farm size group) 95
15. Value added per 'constant quality' hectare of farm area 96
16. Ratio of value added to total land value: small farms and large farms 108
17. Ratio of large farm land use intensity to small farm land use intensity 109
18. Relationship of inputs to farm size 112
19. Expected trend in factor combinations as farm size rises, for various market situations 117
20. Factor ratios by farm size groups: sample survey data (100 cruzeiros/ha) . . . 118
21. Factor ratio trends as farm size rises 122
22. Adult equivalent workers per farm, by farm size group 123
23. Informal test for existence of labor-market dualism: two-step intensity of land use 124
24. Distribution of farm area by farm size group (universe, by product sector) . . 127
25. Pre-reform number of workers on farm of size equal to post-reform 'parcel' size ('high unemployment' parcel size) 145
26. Results of 'total' land reform based on family units (2.5 adult-equivalent workers). Percentage change of inputs and production 146
27. Net income per worker on land reform parcels, as a fraction of target income (regional minimum wage + 10%) 151

XII   LIST OF TABLES

28 Production change from land reform, by sector, as a percent of Brazilian agricultural production. 152
29 Partial reform. Expropriation of farms over 300 ha with above-average land quality. Reform parcel of family unit (2.5 adult-equivalent workers) 158
30 Direction and magnitude of production change resulting from policy A if cause of misallocation of resources in agriculture is cause B 171
31 Production and transport costs for some agricultural goods, Brazil. 'Frontier-colonization' areas versus traditional agricultural areas. 183
32 Percentage distribution of number and area of farms among various size groups. 1960 census versus Getulio Vargas Foundation survey sample. 190
33 Sample weighting factors for simulated universe sectors 193
34 Imputed wage, per year, FGV sample, adult equivalent worker 194
35 Percentage composition of land use by farm size group. 195
36 Percentage of inputs and production in each farm size group – simulated universe 197

INTRODUCTION AND GUIDE TO THE STUDY

This study considers some of the possible economic effects of a future redistribution of land from large land owners to small farmers and landless workers in Brazil. At the present time, legal provisions for land reform exist but virtually no land redistribution has occurred. The central question examined is how land redistribution would affect the use of resources, and therefore production, in agriculture. Several other economic issues are also important in analysis of land reform, but they are treated only indirectly in this study. These issues include income redistribution, the absorption of unemployed labor, the effect of land reform on the marketed agricultural surplus, and the amount and type of compensation to be paid to expropriated landowners.

The study begins with general background, proceeds to theory, then to empirical estimation, and finally to prediction of land reform's impact on agricultural production. The background chapter describes the growth of Brazilian agriculture in the 1950's and 1960's, the 1964 land reform law and its limited implementation to date, and the relation of this study to the existing literature on land reform.

Chapter 2 contains a theoretical analysis of the economic effects of land redistribution. Agricultural economies of scale and land use as related to farm size are the main concerns of this chapter. The goals of land reform are initially summarized as equity (income distribution and labor absorption), static efficiency, and long run growth. The relationships of savings and innovation to farm size are considered briefly.

The first major issue then considered is whether economies of large scale production exist in Brazilian agriculture, for inputs actually utilized (section 2.3). If increasing returns to scale exist, then from the standpoint of efficiency large cooperative or state farms would be preferable to the relatively small scale 'family farms' envisioned in the land reform law as the post-reform organizational unit.

The second major issue considered is the relationship of land utilization to farm size (section 2.4). Data from several less developed countries, especially in Latin America, indicate that small farms use their land more intensively – in terms of inputs and output per total farm area – than do large farms. Seven major influences are examined to explain this phenomenon. The low utilization of land by large farms, in the face of rural unemployment and underemployment on small farms, is the main reason to expect land redistribution to increase agricultural production.

The other issues treated in the chapter are the effect of land reform on factor combinations in agriculture; the relation of 'social' efficiency to farm size; and the effect of tenant operation, as opposed to owner operation, on production.

In chapter 3, sample survey data for some 1000 farms in seven Brazilian states are used to test the hypothesis that increasing returns to scale exist in agriculture. A Cobb–Douglas type production function is estimated for each of seventeen state-product sectors. Analysis of covariance is used to determine whether or not the degree of homogeneity differs significantly from unity. Then, a modified from of the Cobb–Douglas function is used to search for any departures from the overall degree of homogeneity for certain farm size groups. The modified function is also used to determine whether owners have higher production efficiency than non-owners.

Chapter 4 contains statistical tests of the hypothesis that 'land use intensity' declines as farm size rises. Three formal models are examined: the first relates the percent of 'usable' farm area cultivated or grazed at normal rates to farm size and tenure type; the second relates value added per farm area to farm size, tenure type, and land price (to account for land quality); and the third estimates a linear logarithmic relationship between each input and farm size. Then informal tests are conducted, based on factor ratio trends and on scatter diagrams of value added per area against farm size, to examine in more detail which of the proposed explanations for land use are most important. However, the most crucial distinction – land quality versus other influences as the cause of land use patterns – is tested formally in the first two models of the chapter. Informal examinations are also made of the viewpoints (a) that some large farms are 'efficient' while others are not; (b) that the inefficient large farm exists only in Brazil's Northeast, not in the South; and (c) that the inefficient large farm exists in cattle sectors, not in crop sectors. Finally, chapter 4 reconsiders the questions of returns to scale and land utilization from the viewpoint of 'social efficiency', although actual measurements are not made since 'shadow prices' of factors are unavailable.

Chapter 5 presents estimates of the impact of land redistribution on agricultural production. The production functions of chapter 3 and the input-farm size relationships of chapter 4 are used in these calculations. The 'family farm' is assumed as the post reform organizational unit. There are two sets of estimates; one set for a 'total reform' in which all farms are reorganized by reform, and another set for 'partial reform' in which farms under 300 ha, and farms with below average land price, are excluded from expropriation.

Finally, the appendices treat colonization and details concerning the data of the study. Appendix A contains an analysis, based on transport costs, of the feasibility of colonization in frontier areas as an alternative to land redistribution. Appendix B discusses the sampling technique of the survey data used in this study, and appendix C contains additional statistical tables.

In conclusion, it is important to reiterate that the study does not examine the effects of actual Brazilian land reform to date – since this reform has been very limited. Furthermore, in the predictions of land redistribution's production effect, no estimates are made of costs, of long run effects of post-reform savings behavior and adoption of new techniques, or of short run changes in output due to the 'disruption' of reform. These exclusions are due to lack of data and to limitations on the scope of this study.

CHAPTER 1

THE BACKGROUND FOR AN ANALYSIS OF BRAZILIAN LAND REFORM

1.1. The agricultural sector in Brazil

To set the stage for analysis of potential land reform, this chapter surveys the recent growth of Brazilian agriculture, the land reform law and its implementation, and the previous economic literature on land reform.

In the early 1960's, agriculture in Brazil accounted for 29% of net domestic product[1] and 50.5% of country's 24 million workers. It earned the bulk of Brazil's foreign exchange receipts. In the early 1960's, some 87% of export earnings came from agricultural goods: chiefly, coffee (53%), cotton (7%), cocoa (5%), and sugar (4%). Despite these exports, a substantial share of import expenditures were on one agricultural good, wheat, which accounted for 10% of total imports by value.

In comparison with some other Latin American countries, Brazil has enjoyed rapid agricultural growth. In the postwar period, agricultural production has grown on the order of 1.8% yearly in Chile[2] and 0.5% yearly in Argentina[3]. In Brazil, during the period 1949–53 to 1959–63, the real value of agricultural production grew at 5.3% annually; physical production grew at 4.7% annually.[4] Mexico, with an agricultural growth rate of 7.2% yearly (in 1945–49 to 1955–61),[5] was the only major Latin American country with agricultural growth faster than that of Brazil.

In an economy not dominated by imports and exports, sectoral growth

---

[1] Calculated from National Accounts. Fundação Getulio Vargas, Instituto Brasileiro de Economia, *Contas Nacionais* (Rio de Janeiro, 1966). Mimeographed.
[2] Comité Interamericano de Desarrollo Agrícola, *Chile: Tenencia de la Tierra y Desarrollo Socio-Económico del Sector Agrícola* (Santiago: Hispano Suiza, 1966), p. 22.
[3] Comité Interamericano de Desarrollo Agrícola, *Tenencia de la Tierra y Desarrollo Socio-Económico del Sector Agrícola: Argentina* (Washington, D.C.: Pan American Union, 1965), p. 11.
[4] Calculated from National Accounts. Fundação Getulio Vargas, *Contas Nacionais, op. cit.* 'Real value' refers to current value deflated by overall GNP deflator.
[5] United Nations, Economic Commission for Latin America, *The Economic Development of Latin America in the Postwar Period* (New York, 1964), p. 118.

rates should reflect domestic income elasticities of demand. Since foodstuffs generally have an elasticity of less than unity, and industrial goods, greater than unity, it is appropriate that agriculture grow more slowly than the rest of the economy. This difference in growth rates has occurred in Brazil: while agriculture has grown at some 5% yearly, the economy has grown (in real value terms) at 5.4% yearly, and the industrial sector, at 6.25% yearly (from 1949–53 to 1959–63).

In addition to the growth rate of over-all production, there are other criteria on which to judge the 'performance' of agriculture. One is the trend in the terms of trade between agriculture and industry; another, comparison between observed growth rates and 'desired' growth rates for individual products; a third, the price elasticity of agricultural supply; and a fourth, nutritional levels in the country.

The evidence is contradictory on terms of trade between agriculture and industry. The National Accounts income deflators show a shift in relative prices in favor of agriculture, for the 1950's. However, wholesale price indices show no secular trend favoring either agriculture or industry.[1] There is no conclusive case, therefore, that prices have moved in favor of agriculture or that agriculture has been a serious drag on the economy.

For an agricultural good produced primarily for the domestic market, one can speak of a 'desired growth rate' of demand, equal to the rate of population growth plus the income elasticity of demand for the good multiplied by the percentage increase in per capita income (assuming constant relative prices). A comparison[2] of this desired growth rate to the observed growth rate, for eleven major foodstuffs in Brazil during 1952–1962, shows that only beef and wheat production lagged seriously behind the desired growth rates. Furthermore, the lag in wheat does not represent a major problem since it is probably a product for which Brazil has a comparative disadvantage and which Brazil should import. Of course, if export opportunities exist the 'desired growth rate' represents a floor but not a ceiling target, since larger increments in production could be absorbed by the world market (except for

---

[1] The best discussion of the contradictory price information is by Gordon W. Smith, 'A Agricultura e o Plano Trienal', *Revista Brasileira de Economia*, 16 (Dezembro 1962), pp. 113–122.

[2] Based on income elasticities estimated by the Getulio Vargas Foundation, and on official production series. See William R. Cline, 'Economic Considerations for a Land Reform in Brazil', Ph. D. Thesis, Yale University, 1969, p. 241. These calculations excluded goods produced primarily for export, such as cotton, coffee, sugar, and cocoa.

goods such as coffee in which Brazil's world share is so large that rapid increases in its exports would depress world prices). Thus, the matching of 'desired' and 'observed' growth rates merely indicates that production has kept pace with domestic demand – an implication consistent with the absence of a clear shift in internal terms of trade towards agriculture.

Studies of agricultural supply elasticities in Brazil provide a third indication that agriculture's performance has not been bad. These studies[1] make empirical estimates of short run and long run elasticities which indicate that supply is relatively responsive to price. However, the studies use price variables which show essentially relative price among agricultural goods; thus, they indicate that farmers shift resources from one crop to another when relative prices change, but they tell nothing about the overall response of agriculture to general shifts in agricultural prices relative to prices in the rest of the economy.

Concerning nutrition, several studies[2] show low nutritional levels in the Northeast of Brazil. Since production responds to effective demand rather than 'need', low nutritional levels do not indicate poor agricultural performance. But they do imply that a large potential exists for increased demand for foodstuffs; this potential demand would become effective demand if the large low-income portion of the population were to obtain higher income. This point is especially important to remember when considering the possible effects of increased agricultural production due to land reform: the implication is that gains from production increases would not be seriously offset by declines in food prices, since the rural poor would use part of their increased income on increased food consumption.[3]

---

[1] See, for example, Antonio Delfim Netto, Affonso Celso Pastore, and Eduardo Pereira de Carvalho, *Agricultura e Desenvolvimento no Brasil*, Estudos ANPES no. 5 (São Paulo, 1966).

[2] See for example the reference to a 1957 study in the Northeast by the Food and Agriculture Organization, cited in: Inter-American Committee for Agricultural Development, *Land Tenure Conditions and Socio-Economic Development of the Agricultural Sector: Brazil* (Washington, D.C.: Pan-American Union, 1966), p. 32.

[3] Chenery's cross-country study of patterns of industrial growth finds that Brazil's industrial production is skewed toward a composition one would expect to find where income were distributed unequally. Namely, those industrial goods with high income elasticity of demand ('luxury goods') make up a larger portion of total production than would be expected on a basis of per-capita income. H. B. Chenery, 'Patterns of Industrial Growth', *American Economic Review*, 50 (September 1960), pp. 625–654. In line with Chenery's analysis, it would seem that more equitable distribution of income resulting from land redistribution would shift the composition of demand in Brazil toward goods such as foodstuffs (and cotton textiles, which require an agricultural input).

In sum, the available indicators suggest that agriculture has not performed badly in the recent past. Thus, any potential production gains from land reform are not as urgently needed as they would be if agriculture were stagnant. Nevertheless, from the production viewpoint, land reform would still be a desirable policy to the extent that it increased production of goods with price-elastic demand (including export goods), and to the extent that it reduced the cost of production of previous output levels. Finally, the country might wish to carry out land reform for equity purposes even if pre-reform production levels were such that the returns to land reform due to increased production were low.

1.2. Law and action[1]

1.2.1. The Estatuto da Terra of 1964

While the 1946 constitution referred to social use of land, and President Vargas in 1952 created a commission to study the land distribution question, only in the early 1960's under Goulart was there momentarily a political probability of land redistribution, and only after the 1964 military coup did congress pass a law providing for land expropriation and resale. This law *(Estatuto da Terra)*[2] governs agrarian reform in Brazil at the present time.

It is useful to examine briefly the 1964 land reform law. Three aspects of law are considered in turn: expropriation, tenancy regulations, and taxation.

The objectives of expropriation are to promote a socially just distribution of property, and to encourage rational land use (Article 18). Lands which are subject to expropriation are (principally): minifundia and latifundia (defined below); lands benefitted by large public works; and colonization lands which have not been used successfully. (Article 20). However, only in 'priority areas' – which are delineated by the Brazilian Institute of Agrarian Reform (IBRA) – are expropriations allowed[3] (Article 19). These areas must be populated areas with high land ownership concentration or with high in-

---

[1] A good survey of the development of land reform legislation in Brazil is given in: Ben-Hur Raposo, *Reforma Agrária Para o Brasil* (Rio de Janeiro: Ed. Fundo da Cultura, 1965).
[2] Estados Unidos do Brasil, *Estatuto da Terra: Lei No. 4504 de 30 de Novembro de 1964* (Rio de Janeiro: Departamento de Imprensa Nacional, 1965).
[3] To date, five zones have been declared 'priority areas': the coastal regions of Paraíba and Pernambuco; Brasilia; Rio de Janeiro state; Rio Grande do Sul; and Ceará. Other areas showed equally high 'priority' indices, and it was probably due to histories of political unrest in these regions that they were chosen.

cidence of renting and sharecropping. The designation 'priority area' lapses after three years, unless renewed.

Payment in expropriation is to be in government 'Agrarian Fund Bonds' bearing 6% interest, fully corrected for inflation, fully redeemable in twenty years and maturing in successive annual installments before that time[1] (Article 147 of the constitution, as amended). The price paid will consider the cadastral survey, the market value, and value declared for land tax purposes; IBRA is not obligated to pay more than the value declared for tax purposes (Article 19).

Expropriated lands are to be distributed by sale, in the form of 'family properties', of the 'model' size to be determined by region (Article 24). Preference to parcel buyers is given to: the former owner, if he will work the land; renters, sharecroppers, salaried workers or squatters, previously working the land; small owners in the region, whose lands are insufficient to maintain their families (Article 25). Full payment is to be made by parcel recipients, and each farmer has the right to credit – for land purchase – of one year's minimum salary, at 6% interest, on 20 year repayment (Article 81). Further purchase terms are left up to IBRA. Funds for expropriation were to come mainly from 3% of Brazilian tax revenue, earmarked for land reform; and 20% of funds in regional development agencies (SUDENE, SPVEA, CVSF, SUDOESTE) (article 28). However, constitutional changes in 1967 prohibited the tying of tax revenue to specific projects. Since then IBRA's funding has been from normal federal budgetary allocations, which have been very small.

The classification of farms as *'minifúndio'*, 'family property', *'latifúndio'*, or 'rural enterprise', involves technical considerations stipulated by the law and to be elaborated by IBRA. For each region and major activity (crop – permanent or temporary; livestock – small animal and large animal; garden farming; forestry) a 'model' area *(módulo)* is to be established by IBRA. This model is the size necessary to support an average-sized farm family at a level comparable to the regional minimum salary, with some margin for improvement. The *minifúndio* is any farm smaller than the *módulo*. The *latifúndio* is any farm larger than 600 times the *módulo*, or any farm larger than the *módulo* which does not use its land well so as to qualify as a 'rural enterprise'.

---

[1] Compensation in bonds represented a major breakthrough of the 1964 law. Previously the 1946 Constitution had required that immediate full monetary compensation be paid for any expropriated land.

To qualify as a 'rural enterprise', a farm must score well on four criteria: land utilization (50% of usable land must be in use[1]); economic efficiency (which considers whether bookkeeping is practiced, and what the level of non-land investment is); the social conditions (existence of tenancy, number of hired workers, existence of schooling for children of workers, condition of housing for workers); and the farm's agricultural yields (IBRA special Instruction No. 1)[2]. Data for calculation of these indices is to come from a nation-wide cadastral survey.

While minifundia and latifundia may be expropriated only in priority areas, minifundia may not be further split by inheritance in any part of the country (Article 65).

Expropriation and distribution of land are to be handled by IBRA, which also assists in establishment of cooperatives for parcel recipients *(Cooperativas Integral de Reforma Agrária)*.

The second concern of the law is tenancy conditions. The law states 3 year terms for tenancy contracts unless otherwise specified. A maximum rent of 15% of land value is stipulated (Article 95); share cropping is controlled with limits on share to the owner, from 10 to 50% depending on facilities provided by the owner; and compensation for improvements by tenants is required by the law.

The third dimension of the law is taxation. Farms smaller than 20 hectares are exempt from the land tax. All other farms pay a basic tax of 0.2% on land value. This rate is increased (by successive multiples up to 4.5) as the farm size (stated in multiples of the regional 'model') increases. The rate, furthermore, is increased (or reduced) depending on nearness to urban centers, on the degree of participation of the owners in the farm's activity, and on the economic efficiency of the farms. The maximum rate for which a farm may be liable reaches 2.7% of land value.

---

[1] To the author's knowledge, the law leaves 'land-use' very ill-defined. It is not clear, for example, whether land left in natural forest, without lumbering activity, is considered 'used'; whether fallow land is 'used' for crop rotation, etc.

[2] The rather arbitrary nature of these qualifications may be shown by a passage from the IBRA instruction: 'the grade obtained in accordance with paragraph II... will be subtracted, from the constant fifteen, and the result divided by the constant ten, obtaining the coefficient of economic efficiency.' While arbitrary, such grounds for classification of a farm as a 'rural enterprise' minimize the likelihood of corruption and favoritism in reform administration.

1.2.2. The course of land reform since 1964

Land reform based on the 1964 law is still very much in its infancy in Brazil. One large sugar plantation (20,000 hectares, with 2000 families) has been expropriated in Pernambuco, and IBRA has conducted studies of the farm and hopes to use it as a pilot project, for experience for future reform activities. Very limited expropriations of minifundia have also been made (some 100 families in the Agreste region of Pernambuco – Quatis country – and some cases of squatter eviction in Rio de Janeiro state).

The major action which IBRA has taken has been the comprehensive cadastral survey of January, 1966. The heads of Brazil's four million farms filled out questionnaires. These data were recorded and used to classify farms into the categories 'minifundia', 'family properties', 'latifundia', and 'rural enterprises', for tax purposes and for potential expropriation purposes.[1]

The other major land reform development, still in inception (if not yet moribund) is a plan – outside of the direct control of IBRA – to 'restructure' the sugar cane industry in the Northeast. This plan (the GERAN plan) has been drawn up by a joint commission of representatives from SUDENE (the Northeast development agency), IBRA, the Institute of Sugar and Alcohol, and the U.S. Aid mission. The plan envisions modernization of sugar production, which is substantially behind the South's modern techniques and higher yields. The plan would reduce land area in sugar cane, and mechanize many operations now done by hand. In return for loans for mechanization from the government (and from American aid), plantation owners would be expected to donate or sell substantial areas of land for use in a land reform project, to absorb in small family farms (15 hectares) the labor which would be displaced by mechanization (70,000 out of 170,000 sugar workers, for Pernambuco). By the end of 1966 only one out of Pernambuco's 28 major sugar plantations had undertaken modernization. To the author's knowledge, no further modernization projects had been executed by the middle of 1969.

In sum, despite the existence since 1964 of legislation providing for expropriation and redistribution of large farms, virtually no land redistri-

---

[1] Preliminary data from the survey were published in *A Estrutura Agrária Brasileira, Dados Preliminares, Volume I* (Rio de Janeiro: Instituto Brasileiro de Reforma Agrária, 1967). This publication reported that 76% of the farms registered were 'minifundia', which comprised only 14% of Brazilian farm area. The report did not give the breakdown of the remaining farms into 'family properties', 'latifundia', and 'rural enterprises'.

bution has occurred in Brazil to date. Therefore, this study investigates the possible economic effects of a future land reform in Brazil rather than the results of land redistribution which has actually occurred.[1]

1.3. Previous studies on land reform[2]

The literature on land reform is vast. Much of it describes the history of land reform in specific countries or regions.[3] However, relatively little of the literature spells out theoretically how land reform affects economic growth. Furthermore, while many econometric studies have investigated agricultural production functions, very few have investigated patterns of resource use in relation to farm size and tenure, and none, to my knowledge, have made projections of the output effects of land reform.

The major empirical study on agrarian structure in Brazil is a study done by the Inter-American Committee for Agricultural Development (CIDA).[4] The principal non-empirical writings on land reform include contributions

---

[1] Finally, colonization should be mentioned. The extent of colonization programs has been limited. Theoretically, the colonization of frontier areas would be an alternative to land redistribution, as a solution to the problem of access to land for impoverished rural workers. In practice, it would seem that the potential colonization areas in Brazil would be very costly to develop. Prohibitive transportation costs would require that colonization regions be based on subsistence farming rather than on production for sale to the urban centers. Furthermore, large outlays would be necessary for road construction, land clearance, and health extension facilities. See Appendix A for an analysis of transport costs for potential colonization areas.

[2] For a detailed review of the literature expressly on land reform for Brazil, as well as the literature on Brazilian agriculture generally, see W. R. Cline, 'Economic Considerations...', *op. cit.*, appendix B. Note furthermore that while it is beyond the scope of section 1.3 to review the general literature on agriculture in economic development, a comparison of land reform to more conventional means of activating agriculture is given in the Conclusion of the study, in section 6.1.

[3] For a picture of the wide range of literature on land reform in Latin America alone, see Richard P. Schaedel, 'Land Reform Studies', *Latin American Research Review*, 1 (Fall 1965), pp. 75–122.

[4] Inter-American Committee for Agricultural Development, *Land Tenure Conditions and Socio-Economic Development of the Agricultural Sector: Brazil* (Washington, D.C.: Pan American Union, 1966). Note that CIDA has published similar studies for Argentina, Chile, Colombia, Ecuador, Guatemala, and Peru. A synthesis of the findings of these studies has been given by Solon L. Barraclough and Arthur L. Domike, 'Agrarian Structure in Seven Latin American Countries', *Land Economics*, 42 (November 1966), pp. 391–424.

by Raup[1], and Bachman and Christensen[2]. The writings of Chayanov[3], Mellor[4], Sen[5], and Georgescu-Roegen[6] are important references on the theory of peasant behavior, and Schickele[7] has written on the effects of tenure form on production.[8]

In the empirical field, the CIDA study examines a sample of the 1960 Brazilian agricultural census, and finds three major phenomena. First, the latifundia–minifundia complex, or existence of a skewed distribution of land into very small and very large farms, is prevalent in most regions of Brazil. Second, the small farms as a group cultivate a higher percent of their land than do large farms as a group. Third, the small farms have a higher labor density per area than do large farms. The CIDA study then makes rough estimates of how much more labor agriculture could absorb if land presently in large farms were to be used with labor/land ratios found on intermediate ('family') size farms. However, these estimates have little meaning because they are unrealistic: the calculations show that 55 million workers could be employed in agriculture if large farms used 'family farm' labor/land ratios; but the total agricultural labor force was only 15 million workers in 1960. The present study, like the CIDA study, finds a pattern of low labor intensity and low land utilization on large farms in comparison with small farms.[9] However, the general purpose of this study is to determine the production

---

[1] Philip M. Raup, 'The Contribution of Land Reforms to Agricultural Development: An Analytical Framework', *Economic Development and Cultural Change*, 12 (October 1963), pp. 1–21.

[2] K. L. Bachman and R. P. Christensen, 'The Economics of Farm Size', in: H. M. Southworth and B. F. Johnston, eds., *Agricultural Development and Economic Growth* (Ithaca: Cornell University Press, 1967), pp. 234–257.

[3] A. V. Chayanov, *The Theory of Peasant Economy*, ed. by D. Thorner, B. Kerblay, and R. E. F. Smith (Homewood, Ill.: Richard B. Irwin, 1966).

[4] John W. Mellor, 'Toward a Theory of Agricultural Development', in Southworth and Johnston, *op. cit.*, pp. 21–60.

[5] A. K. Sen, 'Peasants and Dualism with or without Surplus Labor', *Journal of Political Economy*, 74 (October 1966), pp. 425–450.

[6] N. Georgescu-Roegen, 'Economic Theory and Agrarian Economics', *Oxford Economic Papers*, 12 (February 1960), pp. 1–40.

[7] Rainer Schickele, 'Obstacles to Agricultural Production', *Journal of Farm Economics*, 24 (May 1942), pp. 447–462.

[8] See chapter 2, section 2.4.1 for discussion of the analyses of Chayanov, Mellor, Sen, and Georgescu-Roegen. See section 2.6 for discussion of the analysis of Schickele.

[9] Other authors have discussed the same phenomena. On the degree of land utilization as related to farm size, see: Solomão Schattan, 'Estrutura Econômica da Lavoura Paulista', *Revista Brasiliense*, 26 (Nov.–Dec. 1959), pp. 21–34; Janes Angelo de Souza, 'A Dimensão Ótima da Propriedade Agrícola em São Paulo', *Revista Brasileira de*

effects of land redistribution, at both the theoretical and empirical levels.

In the non-empirical field, Raup has written on the role of land reform in economic development, and his study reflects much of the literature on the subject. Raup emphasizes the role of security of tenure in the investment decisions of tenants. Concerning economies of scale, Raup maintains that output-raising innovations, not labor-saving innovations, are essential for agriculture in less developed countries, and thus that large scale units are not necessary.[1] Bachman and Christensen[2] make the same point about small scale agriculture and suggest that optimal farm size varies with the stage of economic development, since labor becomes more expensive relative to capital as the economy develops, and smaller farms are more labor intensive than larger farms.

While the author agrees with many of the arguments made by Raup and by Bachman and Christensen, this study suggests several new ways in which land reform can affect production and therefore economic growth.

In the author's view, the major contribution of this study to the understanding of economic development in low income countries is the argument that where the distribution of land ownership is highly skewed, land redistribution from large farms to new 'family farms' would increase agricultural production and employment. The literature on land reform has not generally acknowledged potential production gains from land redistribution, as is shown by the following quotation from a recent textbook in economic development:

> Where plantation agriculture is practiced, a shift to peasant ownership would typically cause a sharp and permanent decline in production.[3]

The findings of this study contradict this judgment of Professor Hagen. The following chapters examine the reasons why land redistribution might increase agricultural output, make relevant hypothesis tests for Brazil, and estimate the impact land redistribution would have on Brazilian agricultural production.

Economia, 16 (Junho 1962), pp. 35–42; and M. D. Sund, *Land Tenure and Economic Performance of Agricultural Establishments in Northeast Brazil*, Ph. D. Thesis, University of Wisconsin, 1965. On the existence of excess labor on very small farms, see Norman Rask, *Tamanho da Propriedade e Renda Agrícola – Santa Cruz do Sul*, Universidade do Rio Grande do Sul, 1965, mimeographed.

[1] Raup, *op. cit.*, p. 7; p. 18.
[2] Bachman and Christensen, *op. cit.*, p. 240.
[3] E. E. Hagen, *The Economics of Development* (Homewood: Richard D. Irwin, 1968), p. 82.

CHAPTER 2

LAND REFORM AND AGRICULTURAL PRODUCTION: THEORETICAL CONSIDERATIONS

2.1. Introduction

The purpose of this chapter is to state the ways in which land reform may affect agricultural production. In subsequent chapters, estimates of production functions and input utilization models serve both to test hypotheses raised in this chapter, and to predict the impact of land reform on agricultural production.

A land reform which expropriates large farms and distributes the land to newly created small farms can affect production in the following ways. First, production will fall to the extent that large scale activities are more efficient than the same activities conducted on a small scale.[1] Thus, the existence of economies of scale in production will be an argument favoring creation of large scale post-reform units, on a cooperative or state farm basis.

Second, production will rise to the extent that new small farms make more intensive use of the land, in terms of inputs[2] and output per total farm area, than did previous large farms. This result would occur if the incentives to use

---

[1] Furthermore, if large farms have a different, more efficient production function than that of the small farms because large operators have superior knowledge about modern seed varieties, fertilizers, and pesticides, then replacement of large farms by small could reduce production efficiency unless the information regarding modern inputs were made available to the new small farmers. Note that this case is different from the case in which large farms use a different technique choice, along a given isoquant, from that of small farms, due to factor market disequilibria in which factor prices differ for large and small farms. In the case of superior production functions on large farms, due to superior knowledge or access to information, a forced empirical estimate of only one production function for all farm sizes – for a given crop – would show increasing returns to scale. This study estimates only one function for each product and these estimates would disguise any shifts to superior production functions as increasing returns to scale in a given production function.

[2] Including the 'land input', defined as area cultivated for crop farms and pasture area for cattle ranches. Note that throughout this study 'intensive land use' refers to the Ricardian sense of the term, rather than the more recent use of the 'factor intensity' concept. By current usage, 'land intensive methods' would refer to combinations of much land with little labor and capital. By 'intensive land use' this study means just the opposite.

land for production are higher for family farmers than for large landowners.[1]

Third, factor combinations within agriculture would improve. Before reform, the ratio of labor to cultivated area (for a crop farm) is much higher on small farms than on large farms. But a condition for Pareto optimality in factor allocation is that marginal products of factors be equal across firms. Thus, assuming homogeneous production functions, a condition for efficient factor allocation would be identical labor/cultivated area ratios across all farm sizes, for a given product. By reducing or eliminating factor market imperfections, land redistribution would equalize factor combinations. Thus, output would rise not only because of an increase in the percent of farm area used as a productive input (for example, cultivated area on crop farms). It would also rise because of increased uniformity across farms in the ratios of labor, cultivated land, and capital inputs.

Fourth, production would increase due to increased use of formerly unemployed labor.

Fifth, an increase in production might be caused by transfer of ownership to former renter or sharecropper operators. This production effect would be expected to be positive only if empirical evidence shows that at present 'owners' obtain higher production, *caeteris paribus*, than do tenants.

Finally, in addition to these five causes of a one-time shift in agricultural production, there would be the long run effects on production of any changes in savings behavior and in the rate of absorption of modern inputs, caused by transition to a family farm organizational basis.

This chapter examines these various ways in which land reform can affect agricultural production. The absorption of unemployed labor is considered in section 2.2.1, as one of the goals of land reform; section 2.3 treats the relation of production efficiency to the scale of inputs utilized; section 2.4 investigates the relation of land use intensity to farm size; section 2.5.1 considers the effect of land reform on factor combinations; section 2.6 discusses the relation of tenure type to production efficiency and land utilization; and section 2.2.3 analyzes the relationship of savings behavior and technological diffusion to farm size, and therefore the influence of the agrarian structure on long run growth.

---

[1] Part of the increase in inputs applied to land formerly in large farms is due to an equalization of input combinations, for inputs already used in agriculture (see below). Another part of increased inputs comes from purchases of capital, seeds, and fertilizer above the amounts previously used in agriculture.

2.2. Goals of land reform

2.2.1. Equity: income redistribution and labor absorption

While the subject of this study is the effect of land redistribution on agricultural production, it is necessary at the outset to clarify land reform's impact on social equity. Redistribution of wealth and income, and employment of formerly unemployed labor, are the two main effects relevant to social equity.

Redistribution of wealth occurs immediately if land is redistributed without fee to its recipients, or if tenants cease paying rent and become owners *gratis*. Even when owners of expropriated land are paid compensation, three types of redistribution of income or wealth may occur. First, there may be a shift of real income from the general public toward the purchasing small farmer, to the extent that tax revenues are used to pay expropriated owners but plot recipients repay over time at interest rates below market levels. Second, there is a shift of wealth from the owner to the plot recipient, equal to the difference between the price paid by the state for the landlord's property and the price which the state would have had to offer to induce the landlord to sell voluntarily. Such a difference could exist, even when the state pays the 'fair' value of the farm. The landowner might want to keep the land to obtain future monopoly profits, or to maintain his prestige. Third, access to land may make available to the plot recipient a stream of income over time greater than that which he otherwise could have obtained.[1] An increase in the plot recipient's income might be possible without any decrease in the income stream of the landlord: the landlord could invest his expropriation receipts elsewhere, and the new small farmer might bring into production

---

[1] For the landless worker before reform, the annual income would be the 'institutional wage' paid by capitalistic farms, multiplied by the probability of obtaining work on these farms. (This probability would be an inverse function of the size of the pool of unemployed.) After reform, this worker would have income equal to the average product of labor on the plot he receives, net of capital charges and intermediate input costs. This income would be a mixture of return to land and return to labor. The increase in the worker's income stream would be the difference between the present discounted value of his pre-reform income stream, on the one hand, and the present value of the stream of his net average product on his 'parcel', less the price he pays for the parcel, on the other hand. For the farmer who already owned a plot before reform, the change in income would be the difference between present value of his pre-reform stream of net average product of labor on his farm, on the one hand, and the present value of the stream of net average product of labor on the parcel received, less the price paid for the parcel, on the other.

land previously held idle. The share of rural laborer classes in national income would rise in relation to that of landlords, in this case.

While the principal policy objective of income redistribution would be the welfare target of equity, a second objective might be a change in the composition or level of demand in the economy. Some authors have argued that income redistribution is necessary for economies such as that of Brazil to avoid stagnation.[1] An analysis of this aspect of income redistribution is beyond the scope of this study.

In the Brazilian case, labor absorption is another objective of land reform. The manufacturing sector has grown rapidly in Brazil, but manufacturing employment has grown quite slowly. Nevertheless, rapid rural–urban migration has occurred. In the decade 1950–60, urban population grew at 5.4% per year while rural population grew at only 1.6% per year. Industrial employment grew at a rate of 2.5% yearly. The surplus of the migrating labor

---

[1] See Celso Furtado, 'Development and Stagnation in Latin America: A Structuralist Approach', *Studies in Comparative International Development*, 1 (1965), pp. 159–175. In the Furtado model, a secular decline in labor share, and thus increasing concentration of income, prevents expansion of the market, and therefore investment tapers off, for lack of prospective demand. The very process of development causes the fall in labor share. The economy moves from production of agricultural goods and simple import substitutes, with low capital intensity, to sophisticated import substitutes (e.g. capital goods) with high capital intensity. Wages are fixed at the subsistence level by a pool of unemployed, so that labor's share declines directly with the fall in labor intensity of production.

Such arguments run counter to the conventional argument that a more skewed income distribution accelerates growth, through its effect on savings. The Furtado argument implies that investment is a function not only of savings availability but also of prospective demand. Thus, some 'optimal income distribution' might exist, which would maximize *ex post* investment subject to these savings and *ex ante* investment functions.

It should be pointed out, however, that any strictly Keynesian demand deficiency would probably not exist in Brazil. A Keynesian demand deficiency requires the hoarding of money, and such hoarding is highly unlikely in an inflationary situation. Instead, the major effects of income distribution on growth would probably be these: first, persons with higher incomes might have a higher propensity to import than the poor; thus, redistribution of income might increase total demand for domestic goods. Second, the composition of production would be influenced by distribution of income; if mass-consumer goods had greater economies of scale than luxury goods, then redistribution of income could spur growth through a shift in production toward goods with economies of scale. However, in the absence of special circumstances such as these two, income redistribution would not be expected to stimulate economic growth. Total demand would not generally increase, but would shift in composition from high income goods to low income goods. Furthermore, demand composition would shift from investment goods to consumption goods, to the extent that the marginal propensity to consmue were higher for the recipients of the transfer than for the losers in the transfer. Such a shift would slow the growth rate.

has flowed into the urban services sector, mainly into low-productivity, marginal services. Urban slums have swollen with migrants. If agriculture absorbed more labor through a structural change,[1] the migration flow to the cities might be checked. Land reform could do this: the cultivation of land previously unused would absorb workers.

2.2.2. Production: static efficiency

A second goal of land reform is to increase agricultural production by improving the use of factors now available to agriculture. This study maintains that Brazilian agriculture produces at a point inside its production possibility frontier, and that land redistribution could move the production point out to the production possibility curve, increasing static efficiency and agricultural output. The bulk of this study is concerned with the effect land reform would have on static efficiency in Brazilian agriculture.

The major improvement in static efficiency which land reform could cause is the new employment of formerly unused land and labor. Much of Brazil's farmland is held idle or poorly used in large farms, while at the same time there is rural unemployment (especially in the Northeast). Section 2.4 discusses the reasons for poor land use by large landowners.

Another improvement in static efficiency would come from land reform's effect on factor combinations as outlined in the introduction to this chapter. This effect is discussed in section 2.5.1.

A constraint in the process of improving static efficiency through land reform is that increasing returns to scale may exist, for inputs actually utilized. If so, 'family farms' would be inefficient post-reform units. The likelihood that increasing returns to scale exist in Brazilian agriculture is examined in section 2.3.

Another aspect of static efficiency concerns the relation of agriculture to the rest of the economy: are the proper amounts of factors allocated to agriculture, and how would this allocation be changed by land reform? This study makes no analysis of whether land reform would shift employed factors out of other sectors of the economy into agriculture, to the point of

---

[1] One source has found that, *caeteris paribus*, migration to Recife has been smaller from rural counties where land distribution is evenly spread over numerous small farms, than from counties with large farms and high ownership concentration. Instituto Joaquim Nabuco de Pesquisas Sociais, *As Migracoes para o Recife*, Vol. 1 (Recife: Ministerio da Educação e Cultura, 1961), p. 85.

optimal allocation. However, the discussion of 'socially optimal' farm size in section 2.5.2 implicitly refers to choice of a post-reform farm unit which would cause the right amounts of factors (from the viewpoint of the whole economy) to be employed in agriculture. Furthermore, while the estimates of land reform's production effect (chapter 5) make no attempt to determine the optimal levels of capital to be employed in agriculture after reform, these estimates do include two alternatives: one in which the total amount of capital employed in agriculture after land reform is constrained to equal the pre-reform level, and one in which post-reform capital is allowed to vary and is determined by the capital use of pre-reform farms of the same size as the post-reform family units. Labor available (including rural unemployed) and land available to agriculture are assumed to remain unchanged after reform.

Finally, the treatment of static efficiency in this study abstracts from any short run 'disruption effect' of land reform, such as lowered investment by owners who fear expropriation, and the physical discontinuity of production on expropriated farms. Analysis of these changes is excluded partly because they would not be permanent changes in static efficiency, partly because data are lacking for analysis, and partly because one could expect the 'disruption' effect to be either positive or negative. It is usually assumed that the threat of land reform causes short run production declines due to uncertainty. However, the threat of reform may stimulate production if owners who meet efficiency criteria are exempted from expropriation.[1]

2.2.3. Long run growth

Before turning to analysis of land reform's effect on static efficiency, it is important to consider briefly land reform's effect on savings and innovation, and therefore its effect on long run agricultural growth.

It might be argued that a land redistribution from large landowners to new small farmers would decrease the rate of adoption of modern techniques in agriculture. There is reason to expect the large farmer to be more receptive to innovation than the small farmer: the large owner is further from the level

---

[1] Felipe Pazos has argued that this expectation effect was the cause of initial production increases in the Cuban land reform. Felipe Pazos, 'Comentarios a dos Artículos Sobre la Revolución Cubana', *Trimestre Economico*, 29 (Enero–Marzo 1962), pp. 1–13.

§2.2   GOALS OF LAND REFORM   17

of subsistence, and can afford the risk of a new technique.[1] He also has a higher educational level.

A further argument favoring the large farmer is that his higher level of income permits him a higher savings ratio and therefore he contributes more to long run capital accumulation than the small farmer. Finally, in the critical mission of supply of an agricultural surplus to the cities, the large-farmer may be superior: he produces for the city market and not for his own consumption.

There are two themes underlying these arguments: first, large farmers are more receptive to innovation; second (implicitly) income distribution should be skewed in order to boost savings, and prevalence of large farmers keeps agricultural income distribution skewed.

With regard to 'receptivity to innovation', there may be some validity to the idea that large farms are superior especially in the absence of government extension services. However, in certain regions the large owners may have a strictly traditionalist mentality and they may not take advantage of their wide margin for risk in the adoption of new techniques. Also, any greater use of modern techniques by large farms must be adjusted to account for their easier access to credit, in order to make an unbiased test of the superiority of large farms over small farms. Furthermore, given the large owner's incentive to use relatively little labor (to be discussed below), he is likely to use labor-saving machinery before the small farmer and have the appearance of greater receptivity to modern techniques. Finally, the innovations desirable in a context of under-unemployment (i.e., some form of 'labor surplus') are labor-intensive innovations, which are perfectly compatible with the small farms (fertilizer, improved seed, pesticides, are examples). The large farms will be tempted to 'innovate' in the direction of labor-saving machinery, which is socially inappropriate if labor has a low opportunity cost to the economy, although privately profitable.

The arguments which favor large farms on a basis of a higher savings ratio and greater percentage of production marketed, may make two mistakes. First, it is by no means clear that larger owners save a higher percent of their

---

[1] Nicholls and Miller-Paiva view the large farmer in Brazil as an important force favoring technical change, especially in the absence of improved government extension services. See William H. Nicholls and Ruy Miller Paiva, 'The Structure and Productivity of Brazilian Agriculture', *Journal of Farm Economics*, 47 (May 1965), p. 361.

income.[1] The large landlord in Latin America is frequently charged with conspicuous consumption. Second, it must be asked, what is the economy trying to maximize? Presumably the maximand is a welfare function over time. It is by no means clear that the gains for that time stream to be made through higher savings based on inequality of income, are greater than gains to be made from a slower growth rate with higher consumption of the lowest income groups at all times.[2] Even a model with high returns to saving could favor slower growth if the maximand weighted equality of income heavily enough (that is, if marginal utility of income were a rapidly declining function of income).

Despite the great importance of the question of land reform's effect on long run agricultural savings and innovation, this study contains no empirical analysis of the matter since relevant data are not available. Instead, the study examines land reform's impact on 'static efficiency' in terms of theory (in the

---

[1] Barraclough and Domike assert that consumption is a large percentage of income of large farmers in Chile. They cite a study by Sternberg in which a sample of 20 large farm operators of the Central Valley of Chile showed consumption of 84% of disposable income. Disposable income was 95% of total income. Marvin Sternberg, *Chilean Land Tenure and Land Reform* (Berkeley, California, University of California), Ph. D. Thesis, 1962. Cited in S. Barraclough and A. Domike, 'Agrarian Structure in Seven Latin American Countries', *Land Economics*, 42 (November 1966), p. 406.

[2] The issue of 'large farms for savings' versus 'land reform' is quite analogous to the debate between Galenson and Leibenstein on the one hand and Chenery, Sen, and others on the other hand, with regard to technique choice. See W. Galenson and H. Leibenstein, 'Investment Criteria, Productivity and Economic Development', *Quarterly Journal of Economics*, 69 (August 1955), pp. 343–370; H. B. Chenery, 'Comparative Advantage and Development Policy', *American Economic Review*, 51 (March 1961), pp. 18–51; A. K. Sen, 'Some Notes on the Choice of Capital Intensity in Development Planning', *Quarterly Journal of Economics*, 71 (November 1957), pp. 561–584. Galenson and Leibenstein favor capital intensive techniques because these supposedly minimize the wage bill and maximize reinvested profits. Chenery and others favor labor intensive techniques in a labor surplus context, since labor intensive techniques will maximize current production – unless they are strictly 'dominated' by the capital intensive techniques. In this controversy, the conclusion was that the time discount rate determined which policy to favor. However, the argument of the social welfare function over time, and the trade-off between increase in the function due to greater equity versus increase over time due to greater saving, was not even considered. The Galenson–Leibenstein approach would favor large farms, if it is true that the large farms have the highest 'reinvestment ratio'. The small farms, due to greater intensity of land use, would maximize present production. Thus, a decision based on the time discount rate would tell which farm type to favor. To this decision should be added the consideration suggested here – the differential impact of growth versus equity on the social welfare function.

rest of this chapter) and empirical prediction for Brazil (in the following chapters).

2.3. Relationship of efficiency to scale of inputs utilized ('production-efficiency')

The first aspect to be considered concerning land reform's impact on static efficiency is the relation of efficiency of production to the scale of the inputs utilized. This aspect is relevant to the choice of the post-reform unit: the policy question is whether 'family farms' can be created without a sacrifice of potential efficiency in production.

It is useful to distinguish between what may be called 'production-efficiency' and 'farm-efficiency', with efficiency defined as the relation of production to total factor cost. From the private standpoint, which is the concern of this section, factor cost is evaluated at the factor prices confronting the entrepreneur. 'Production-efficiency' refers to the ratio of product to factor cost, where only the factors employed in the activity are included. 'Farm-efficiency' refers to the ratio of product of the farm to factor cost, where all resources of the farm are included in cost. The difference is that only 'cultivated land' (for crop farms, or pasture area for cattle ranches) is included as a factor in 'production-efficiency' while 'total farm area' is included in 'farm-efficiency'. This distinction is necessary in order to avoid false conclusions about returns to scale in agriculture. Due to a tendency of large farms to use a low per cent of their land, one might find decreasing returns to scale if only 'farm-efficiency' were measured. But analysis of the optimum scale for the post-reform unit requires information about returns to scale on the economic operation as such, that is, production on the cultivated area for a crop farm, and on pasture area for a cattle farm.

There are three major reasons why 'production-efficiency' may be related with farm size.[1] First, there may be increasing returns to scale in production. A proportional increase of all factors by a multiple a may increase production by a multiple greater than a. Economies of scale may exist with both divisibility and indivisibility of factors. The need for a minimum farm area to employ fully a farm machine would represent an economy of scale due to

---

[1] Since the potential 'production' activity's size parallels the farm size in the sense of total area, it is meaningful to speak of 'farm size' even when the reference is more specifically related to the size of the 'production activity', as in the first point made here.

factor indivisibility.[1] However, the importance of machine indivisibility is greater for agriculture in the advanced economy than for agriculture in the less developed economy. The ratio of the price of labor to the price of capital rises as development progresses; at a lower stage of development, capital will be so expensive relative to labor that certain farm machinery will be unprofitable.[2] In this situation, there will be no 'minimum area' constraint from the standpoint of machine indivisibility.

A second reason for a relation between production efficiency and farm size is that entrepreneurial ability and the motivation of labor may be related to farm size. The small farmer who is both owner and principal worker on his farm has a more direct interest in the outcome of the farm than does the salaried worker on the farm of a large owner. This higher incentive would lead to higher 'production-efficiency' on small farms than on large. In contrast, the entrepreneurial skill of the large farmer may be superior to that of the small farmer due to the better education of the large farmer.

The familiarity of the farm director with the farm is another aspect of entrepreneurial skill as related to farm size. The owner of a vast area will have poorer knowledge of the exact response of the various soils on his farm to inputs than will the owner of a smaller area.[3] Similarly, hired temporary labor will have much less familiarity with the specific soils of the farm than will permanent family labor.

Still another facet of the relation of entrepreneurial efficiency to farm size is the high cost of supervision of large numbers of workers. The spatial dispersion of workers in agriculture makes their supervision more difficult than in industry.[4]

---

[1] However, machines may be used on small farms if rental services are available or if small farmers participate in machinery cooperatives.

[2] Assuming the machinery's effect is primarily to substitute for labor, rather than to raise output. A good example of a farm machine which is practically non-existent in less developed countries, including Brazil, but which becomes profitable as the relative price of labor rises with development, is the mechanical harvester.

[3] Brewster has argued that the need for 'on the spot decisions' in farming limits the size of the farm one man can manage effectively. J. M. Brewster, 'The Machine Process in Agriculture and Industry', *Journal of Farm Economics*, 32 (Feb. 1950), pp. 69–81.

[4] Erven Long emphasizes the cost of labor supervision. He notes that in the relation of efficiency to farm size, 'if only managerial responsibilities are affected, the outcome is the net result of two forces working in opposite directions: on one side the presumed advantage of centralized and hence improved management decision-making, on the other side the paired forces of cost of overhead supervision and the reduction of individual incentives'. Erven Long, 'The Economic Basis of Land Reform in Underdeveloped Economies', *Land Economics*, 37 (May 1961), p. 120.

A third reason for a relation between production efficiency and farm size is the existence of external economies, such as these associated with irrigation, disease control, and product processing. External economies may be made internal to the firm if the firm is large enough. Disease control requires cooperation among adjacent farmers or else one large farm: spraying one plot is ineffective unless the neighboring plot is also sprayed. Processing may require coordinated timing of delivery of the raw material to the plant.[1] Irrigation will in some cases require cooperation of farms supplied by the same water source, and the supply system could be internalized on a large farm.[2] However, major irrigation projects are so large that it is unrealistic to speak of large firms necessary for their undertaking. Here the government carries out the project and supplies irrigation services to farms of whatever size.

In summary, the relationship of the size of the economic operation to 'production-efficiency' depends on the existence of economies of scale (primarily due to machine indivisibility), on entrepreneurial ability and motivation of labor, and on externalities that can be made internal to large farms. It seems quite possible that economies of large scale organization could be achieved in some 'dimensions' (irrigation, pest control) while the owner-producer dimension remained small, if appropriate cooperative or governmental institutions were created.[3]

In chapter 3, Brazilian data are used to test the hypotheses about 'production-efficiency' as related to farm size. One test is made for returns to scale; another test examines entrepreneurial ability as related to farm size. No test is made of the hypothesis that external economies exist which can be internalized on large farms, nor is the hypothesis tested that economies of scale can be achieved in some dimensions while the ownership units remain small.

---

[1] In the case of sugar cane, cane must arrive at the mill soon after being cut, or it loses sucrose content. The supply to the mill must be staggered over a long period of time. Thus some coordination between mill and suppliers is necessary.

[2] However, 'tube well' irrigation is a straightforward case of 'economies of scale' due to factor indivisibility, rather than an example of externalities. That is, a minimum amount of crop area to be irrigated will be necessary to justify the fixed cost of drilling the well and installing pump equipment.

[3] This cleavage of 'scale' into different dimensions, and its benefits for small owners, were emphasized in a symposium on agricultural development at Massachusetts Institute of Technology. David Hapgood and Max F. Millikan, eds., *Policies for Promoting Agricultural Development. Report of a Conference on Productivity and Innovation in Agriculture in the Underdeveloped Countries* (Cambridge: M.I.T. Center for International Studies, 1965), p. 85.

2.4. The relation of farm size to land use ('farm-efficiency')

The second aspect of land reform's impact on static efficiency concerns the utilization of available land resources by land owners. In this section, reasons are given to explain why fuller use may be made of land on smaller farms than on large farms. The main theoretical bases on which one could expect land-use to be less intense on large farms than on small ones are: (1) 'labor-market dualism' within agriculture; (2) land-holding for 'portfolio asset' reasons; (3) land market imperfections; (4) production on small farms for their own consumption as well as for the market; (5) monopsony power over labor on large farms; (6) land-holding for prestige rather than profit maximization; and (7) poor land quality and poor facilities for transport to market on large farms. If large farms do have low land utilization, a land reform which transfers land from large owners to new small owners would presumably cause greater utilization of land and therefore increased production.

Data from many less developed countries indicate higher labor inputs and production per total farm area on small farms than on large; while output per worker appears to be higher on large farms. Studies[1] for Argentina, Brazil, Colombia, Chile, Ecuador, Guatemala, and Peru show these patterns of higher land use intensity on small farms than on large farms. Data from Indian Farm Budget studies show the same patterns for India.[2]

Before the specific arguments concerning land use are examined, it is useful to consider a general principle underlying them: the incentives of the farm's decision maker to use high levels of labor per farm area and to achieve high production per farm area decline as farm size rises. This decline is due to the fact that production decisions of the family farm director are partially based on 'pressure to produce' and pressure to use the given stock of family labor, whereas the decisions of the larger owner are based on pure profit maximization.

The conventional approach to low land use by large landholders in Latin

---

[1] Inter-American Committee for Agricultural Development (CIDA), *Land Tenure Conditions and Socio-Economic Development of the Agricultural Sector. Argentina; Brazil; Chile; Colombia; Ecuador; Guatemala; Peru* (Washington, D.C.: Pan American Union, 1965 and 1966). Some of these studies have production data which show these trends directly. All contain data on land use, and show a uniform tendency for small farms to cultivate a larger percent of their area than do large farms.

[2] As presented in Mortin Paglin, 'Surplus Agricultural Labor and Development: Facts and Theories', *American Economic Review*, 55 (September 1965), pp. 815–834.

America is to assume that these owners are not profit maximizers, that they hold land for political or social reasons. In this study, the emphasis is not that large land owners ignore profit maximization, but instead that profit maximization itself leads them to lower intensity of land use than that achieved by smaller farm units.

The arguments that follow may be viewed as instances of the divergent results from the profit incentive on larger farms as opposed to 'pressure' to use land and family labor on smaller farms. Profit maximization will lead to low land and labor use on large farms if the wage for hired labor exceeds the marginal product of labor on small farms for institutional reasons, or if the land price is lower for large farms than for small. Profits may be maximized by the large landowner through the holding of idle land, if crop price fluctuations and land price increases are such that the holding of idle land is more attractive than landholding *cum* production. But the smaller the farm and the greater the incidence of family labor, the lower the likelihood that profit maximization will lead to low utilization of land. Lower employment on the family farm means not lower labor costs but idle family labor along with lower total product.

In short, the pressure on the smaller, family-labor farm to use its available land and labor will generally lead to land use intensity that exceeds or equals that of the large farm which uses hired labor and maximizes profits.

While seven distinct causes of land use patterns are described below, the formal statistical tests of Brazilian data (in chapter 4) examine only the general hypothesis that 'land use intensity' declines as farm size increases. 'Land quality' is the only influence explicitly included in the statistical tests. However, data are informally examined (in section 4.4) to determine the relative importance of each of the influences discussed here.

2.4.1. *Labor-market dualism*

A case can be made for land redistribution if it can be shown that dualism exists within agriculture. Dualism refers to the phenomenon described by Lewis[1] and Ranis and Fei[2] in which a modern sector pays labor its marginal product, while a coexistent traditional sector pays an institutional wage

---

[1] W. Arthur Lewis, 'Economic Development with Unlimited Supplies of Labour', *The Manchester School of Economic and Social Studies*, 22 (May 1954), pp. 139–191.

[2] J. C. H. Fei and G. Ranis, *Development of the Labor Surplus Economy: Theory and Policy*. (Homewood, Ill.: Richard D. Irwin, 1964).

greater than the marginal product but equal to or less than the wage in the modern sector. In any such dualistic model, there is gain in production to be obtained from reallocation of resources, simply because a necessary condition for Pareto optimality is that the marginal product of each factor be equated among all sectors.

Dualism in agriculture is the coexistence of large farms organized on a capitalist basis, with 'family' farms in which the primary source of labor is the family's labor. In the former type, production is based on profit maximization, and one of the costs is the wage bill paid to labor. The family farm, however, does not produce exactly for 'profit maximization' nor does it deduct wages from its calculation of economic gain.

The nature of 'peasant maximization' or maximization of the family farm, has been discussed by Chayanov[1], Mellor[2], Sen[3], and Georgescu-Roegen[4]. All of these writers agree that the peasant farm produces to the point at which the family's marginal utility of production equals marginal disutility of effort. In Sen's model, which is the most completely specified, a family of B consuming members and A working members behaves as if utility were additive across individuals. Family welfare is

$$W = \sum_{i=1}^{B} U_i - \sum_{i=1}^{A} V_i$$

where U_i is the total utility from consumption of one member, and V_i is total disutility of labor from one working member. All members receive identical utility weights, so a condition of optimality is that work be distributed equally among workers and product be distributed equally among consumers. Thus,

$$L = Al \quad \text{and} \quad Q = Bq$$

where L = total labor, Q = total product, l = labor per worker, and

---

[1] A. V. Chayanov, *The Theory of Peasant Economy*, ed. by: D. Thorner, B. Kerblay, and R. E. F. Smith (Homewood, Ill.: Richard D. Irwin, 1966).

[2] John W. Mellor, 'Toward a Theory of Agricultural Development', in: H. M. Southworth and B. F. Johnston, eds., *Agricultural Development and Economic Growth* (Ithaca: Cornell University Press, 1967), pp. 21–60.

[3] A. K. Sen, 'Peasants and Dualism with or without Surplus Labor', *Journal of Political Economy*, 74 (October 1966), pp. 425–450.

[4] N. Georgescu-Roegen, 'Economic Theory and Agrarian Economics', *Oxford Economic Papers*, 12 (February 1960), pp. 1–40.

q = product per consumer. Welfare maximization occurs where $\partial W/\partial L = 0$ or

$$\frac{\partial \sum_{i=1}^{B} U_i}{\partial L} - \frac{\partial \sum_{i=1}^{A} V_i}{\partial L} = 0$$

which implies

$$\frac{\partial \sum_{i=1}^{B} U_i}{\partial Q} \frac{\partial Q}{\partial L} - \frac{\partial \sum_{i=1}^{A} V_i}{\partial L} = 0.$$

This gives the equilibrium condition,

$$Q'(L) = \frac{V'(L)}{U'(Q)}.$$

That is, marginal product of labor equals marginal disutility of labor divided by marginal utility of product. The difficulty of units usually involved in utility analysis is circumvented by the fact that $Q'(L)$ is in units of product per worker; $V'(L)$ is in 'utiles' per worker and $U'(Q)$ is in 'utiles' per product, such that the 'utiles' divide out and leave product per worker.

In the peasant equilibrium, therefore, the marginal product of labor is determined by the pressure on the family for consumption and the family's opportunity for production. This marginal product of labor need not equal that on the capitalist farm, which is set equal to the wage rate for salaried labor so that the capitalist owner can maximize profits. For example, in a period of severe agricultural price depression the capitalist owner might completely stop production, whereas the family farm could continue production in order to meet its product utility–labor disutility equilibrium.

Dualism[1] in agriculture causes factor misallocation because the marginal product of labor in the family farm's equilibrium is usually below the marginal product of labor on the capitalist farm. There are several reasons why this is so. First, it is likely that the family worker considers his income

---

[1] It should be emphasized that 'dualism' as used here does not refer to the cleavage between commercial agriculture and subsistence or non-market agriculture. Instead, the relevant dichotomy is between the capitalist farm and the 'family farm'. The former hires labor, the latter uses its own family labor. Both may produce for the market, but the first produces for profit net of wages, while the latter reaches its equilibrium by equating the family's marginal disutility of effort with marginal utility of product without regard to deduction of the family's labor at accounting wages.

to be the average product of labor on the family farm. If he is to respond to a wage outside the farm, it must be higher than his average product on the family farm. This fact means that the wage on capitalist farms will exceed or equal average product of labor on family farms. It follows that marginal product of labor on the family farm, which is below average product, is below the marginal product (wage) on the capitalist farm.

It is true that the family farm might hire out its labor, to the point where marginal product would be equated across capitalist and family farms. The rationale would be: a family member would work outside and contribute his earnings to the family in return for a share in total family income. Thus the total family income would be maximized at that point where gains from outside work just equaled loss from withdrawal of labor on the family farm: i.e., where marginal product were equal on capitalist and family farms.[1]

---

[1] A simple model shows the mechanics of out-hiring and, more generally, labor flow in the dualistic model. In the 'traditional' sector the family member receives average product as income, Q/N where Q = family production, N = number of family workers. The marginal product of the worker, however, is substantially below this average product income. Let the marginal product of one worker be a. Consider a modern sector in which marginal product of labor is b. Consider first the situation in which b is very high, and $b > Q/N$. Assume migration cost is zero. Then it is to the advantage of a family member, as well as the rest of the family, that the member migrate to the modern sector: he will earn b there, which exceeds his previous income. The remaining family members will now each receive $(Q-a)/(N-1)$, which is larger than the original share, Q/N, since $a < Q/N$. However, as more and more persons transfer from the traditional sector to the modern sector, modern sector marginal product of labor falls. Consider the point where b has fallen to $b = Q/N$. At this point, a family member is indifferent between remaining on the farm and migrating to the modern sector. The family remaining on the farm would prefer that the member leave, since their per-person income would rise, thus, to $(Q-a)/(N-1)$. In order to be induced to leave, the member would require a supplement to his income, out of family farm production. If such an arrangement is possible, it will pay the family to send the member to work in the modern sector at wage b, because when all earnings are pooled, family income from on-farm work plus out-hiring of one member is $(Q-a+b)$, and each family member, including the one hired out, receives $(Q-a+b)/N$ which exceeds the original Q/N. In such a process, migration to the modern sector continues until $b = a$. Then the marginal product is equated in the two sectors and 'dualism' ends.

However, if it is impossible for the family remaining on the farm to send a supplemental income to the member hired-out, then b will fall only to the point $b = Q/N$. Thus, modern sector marginal product is higher than traditional: $b > a$. Two reasons might cause such a situation. First, it might be physically impossible for the family remaining on the farm to send supplementary income to the member hired out, because of infrequency of visits of the hired-out member, or because family income would be in kind rather than monetary. Secondly, the family workers remaining on the farm might act irrationally: they might refuse to send an income supplement on grounds that they do not see how the hired-out member would be contributing to family production.

§2.4   FARM-EFFICIENCY   27

However, this process of allocation could fail to occur for the following reasons. First, it might be impossible for the family to send income supplements to the worker transferred. Second there might be a preference for work on the family farm over work on someone else's farm.[1] Third, in a labor surplus situation the transfer of labor to the point of equalization of marginal product of labor between capitalist and family farms would cause the wage to fall close to zero. The populace would not permit this decline due to an institutional notion of a 'just' wage. Fourth, a legal minimum wage for salaried workers might exist at a level above labor's marginal product in agriculture.

Fifth, in a risk minimization sense, it might be to the worker's advantage to stay on the family farm rather than work elsewhere for a wage. This advantage would be greatest if there were expectation of inflation. On the family farm, the family is guaranteed income equal to the valuation of its product at the 'reserve price', at which the family chooses to consume the whole produce. In addition to this minimum income, the family stands to gain windfall income from any real price rise which induces it to sell some of its product.

It is noteworthy that the Lewis, Ranis–Fei models do not specify why transfer of labor would not occur spontaneously until marginal product of labor, net of migration costs, were equated across the modern and traditional sectors. There is implicit in these models some assumption such as this one, non-pooling of modern sector earnings with the traditional sector family income.

[1] One might object that any pure preference of workers for work on their own farms should be included in the 'welfare function' and that thus there would exist no social inefficiency even though labor were more concentrated on family farms and had lower marginal product there than on capitalist farms. Such a view-point would be valid if one were choosing between the alternatives of 'doing nothing' and forcing excess labor off of family farms to work for wages on capitalist farms. However, if a third policy choice is considered, 'land reform' in which more land is made available to workers presently on family farms, then it can be said that the alternative of 'doing nothing' is socially inefficient. This is so, because in the land reform alternative, production would increase due to equalization of labor–land ratios throughout agriculture (assuming homogeneous production functions), while there would be no decline in the number of workers who worked on their own farms, and thus no fall in the welfare function due to decrease in 'own-farm' labor. Indeed, if the land reform expropriated large farms and turned previous salaried workers into owners, the 'own-farm preference' component of the welfare function would increase. Of course, it cannot be stated that such land reform would be more efficient than 'doing nothing', if the large owners were not compensated so as to feel no worse off than before, or, alternatively, if large owners were injured by reform and one were unwilling to make value judgments in weighing the welfare of the landlords against that of the small farmers and landless workers.

Consider the family farm facing prices such that the family is indifferent between consuming and selling its product, i.e., the product is at its 'reserve price'. Suppose now that the product price rises while prices of goods the family would like to buy remain constant. In this case the family will market some or all of its produce, and receive a windfall gain above its guaranteed minimum income. Suppose, again at the initial point of indifference between own consumption and marketing, a family member were to leave the farm for outside work. From the viewpoint of the family as a whole, with no expected price changes, this departure would be advantageous so long as the outside salary exceeded the value of the decline in on-farm production which would occur. Once price movements were considered, however, a much higher outside salary might be necessary to induce the departure. If it were expected that food prices would rise and other prices lag behind, then the family would keep the member to produce on the farm for two reasons. First, his marginal product on the farm would be expected to rise due to the expected food price rise, assuming the farm produces food. Second, any lag of the outside salary behind food prices would cause a decline in the real salary available outside.

A necessary assumption to this argument is that wage adjustments in the labor market lag behind price adjustments in the product market. The argument seems to have had some empirical application in the case of Brazil.[1] To summarize, it may be a rational risk minimization policy for workers to remain on the family farm even though their marginal product at the moment is lower than the wage and the marginal product of labor on large capitalist farms.

In sum, dualism in agriculture implies factor misallocation. Excessive labor is crowded onto small family farms, too little labor is used on large capitalist farms. The marginal product of labor is higher on large capitalist farms; the marginal product of land is higher on small family farms. Land redistribution would increase total production by equating marginal products (both of land and labor) throughout agriculture.[2]

---

[1] Exactly such a process of real wage deterioration was occurring in the Pernambuco sugar zone in the late 1950's. See Caio Prado, Jr., 'Nova Contribuição à Análise do Problema Agrária no Brasil', *Revista Brasiliense*, 43 (Setembro–Outubro 1962), pp. 12–51.

[2] An Edgeworth box diagram may be used to show the misallocation of resources under 'dualism'. Small, family farms are one sector, with origin at A, and large farms are the other sector, with origin at B. Isoquants from both origins refer to levels of agricultural production. Agriculture is not on the contract curve, but at the inefficient point P. Large

farms behave as if the ratio of the price of labor to the price of land were given by slope Px; family farms, as if this ratio were slope Py. The exact shape of the contract curve is not important.

It may be noted here that an observed decline in the percent of land used as farm size increases (examined in chapter 4) may be due to the lower marginal productivity of labor on small farms (due to 'dualism'). Alternatively, this decline may be due to the fact that large farms hold land idle for reasons of speculation or non-economic motivation (as discussed in the present chapter, below). The former explanation may be presented

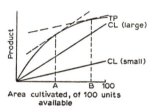

graphically. First, assume that cultivated land requires a fixed coefficient of labor. Assume, further, that all land is of varying quality, but the qualities are randomly distributed with regard to farm size. Thus, as any farm increases the percent of its area under cultivation, it brings into use less and less fertile land (each farm has its own Ricardian margin). The small farms cultivate a larger percent of their land because the real cost of labor to them is lower than that to the large farms, and it pays the small farms to bring into cultivation land of poorer quality. In the diagram below, total production (TP) rises more and more slowly as more hectares of a total 100 available are cultivated (land quality declines as the marginal land is used, so output per hectare declines). It is assumed that the rate of decline of land quality within the farm is identical for all farms regardless of size. The real labor cost (CL) rises directly with the number of hectares cultivated (due to the fixed labor coefficient assumption). For the small farm, this cost is lower than for the large, although the physical labor input is identical.

The area cultivated will be that which equates marginal product with marginal cultivation costs, i.e. the slope of TP = the slope of CL. (For the small farms, this point is B, for the large, it is point A.) Thus, dualism causes the percent of farm area cultivated to fall as farm size increases.

Note that this conclusion does not depend on the fixed proportion of labor to cultivated land, assumed only for convenience. Suppose large farms use less labor per hectare cultivated than small, lowering their cost curve CL. Their output curve will also be lowered, by $x\%$, where $x\% = c(z\%)$ where $z\%$ is the percent decline in labor applied per hectare and c is the elasticity of output with respect to labor. The point at which marginal product equals marginal labor cost will still be below B, unless the elasticity of output with respect to labor is negligible and furthermore the large farms are able to lower physical labor per

How important, in Brazil, is the factor misallocation caused by 'dualism'? A first indication may be found in the percentage of total labor working on 'family' farms, as opposed to the percent working as hired labor. One would expect no labor misallocation in either of two extreme cases: all labor in 'family' farms, or all labor in 'capitalist', large farms on a salaried basis. Roughly, one would expect greater misallocation, the more equal these two forms are in percentage use of the labor force. That is, it is the coexistence of family farms with large capitalist farms that causes labor misallocation. Table 1 shows the breakdown of agricultural labor force by number of

TABLE 1

Percentage of persons occupied in agriculture by number of workers per farm (Brazil, 1960)

<5	5–10	10–20	20–50	50–100	>100
35.6%	32.4%	15.9%	8.5%	3.3%	4.2%

Source: Instituto Brasileiro de Geografia e Estatística, Serviço Nacional de Recenseamento, *Censo Agrícola de 1960, Brasil. VII Recenseamento Geral do Brasil. Série Nacional, Volume II–1. Parte* (Rio de Janeiro, 1967), p. 29.

workers per farm. Roughly one-third of Brazilian farm workers in 1960 were on farms of fewer than five workers. This percentage represents a sizeable 'family' sector of farms, coexistent with a large sector of farms based on hired labor.[1] As another indication of substantial incidence of 'family' farms,

---

hectare to the point where their labor cost per hectare is as low as that of small farms. Finally, note that the inclusion of capital in this analysis would not change the conclusion so long as capital were not cheaper for large farms than for small.

[1] The distribution of labor by number of workers on the farm does not in itself establish 'misallocation of resources'. The point here is merely that a situation which may cause labor market dualism – the coexistence of family labor farms with capitalistic large farms – does exist. To prove misallocation of labor requires a further step showing that family farms do indeed have higher labor density per farm area than large, capitalistic farms.

It may fairly be asked, would existence of both 'family' and 'hired-labor' farms in any country be sufficient grounds for land redistribution? It is highly interesting that in the United States in 1957, 'family workers' accounted for 75% of the farm labor force – a higher percent than in Brazil. See United States Department of Commerce, *Historical Statistics of the United States: Colonial Times to 1957* (Washington, D.C., 1960), p. 285. Yet it would be difficult to argue that the existence of both 'family farms' and 'large, capitalistic farms' requires land redistribution in the U.S., away from large farms into new small farms. (Indeed, the American 'farm problem' is usually viewed as a need to eliminate farms which are too 'small and poor'. The implicit assumption in this view is that alternative employ-the 1960 census shows that of Brazil's 3,337,769 farms, the number that hired no labor was 2,338,229. Finally, the 1960 Brazilian agricultural census showed that of a total labor force of 15.6 million persons in agriculture, 9.8 million or 63% were of the category 'farm head and non-remunerated family members'.[1]

The second and more direct indication of factor misallocation due to dualism is found in the sample data used in this study. The 'dualism' theory would predict a greater intensity of labor per farm area on small farms than on large. The sample data confirm this prediction. Table 20, in chapter 4, shows factor ratios by farm size. In sixteen of the seventeen product-state sectors investigated in this study, the intensity of labor per total farm land area is greatly higher for the small farm size groups than for the large. Among these sectors, the average ratio of labor density per farm area for farms under 10 hectares, to labor density for farms over 1000 hectares, is 21.5 to 1. However, influences other than dualism – such as speculative holding of

---

ment is available for the small farmers who would be pushed out of agriculture to solve the 'farm problem'.) The differences between the advanced country and the less developed country, in this regard, are the following. First, in the advanced country, the farm labor force is a small percent of the total labor force. Furthermore, wages for hired labor – urban or rural – are substantially above a 'subsistence minimum'. The result is that family workers may migrate from the family farms to industry or to wage labor on large farms, without causing a decline in the market wage to below the subsistence level, or, alternatively, without creating a large pool of unemployed in the face of a wage fixed at an institutional floor. In contrast, the family farm is the primary location of 'surplus labor' in the less developed country, and if this labor were suddenly to move toward outside jobs, there would either be a decline in the wage to below the institutionally acceptable level, or large open unemployment. In short, from the standpoint of total employment opportunities, land redistribution could be much more important for the less developed country with skewed land ownership, than for the advanced country. By implication, the scope for increased output due to the fuller use of available labor, through land reform, is smaller in the advanced country than in the less developed country. Second, many of the 'family farms' of the advanced country are undoubtedly large and mechanized, and could not be characterized as 'small farms with excess labor' in contrast to 'large farms with little labor'. Third, since capital is cheaper relative to labor in the advanced economy than in the less developed economy, agricultural economies of scale may be important – the use of tractors and mechanical harvesters may require large farm areas – so that redistribution of land would be inefficient if it created small units.

A stronger case could be made that, for the less developed countries as a group, the existence of both family labor farms and hired labor farms is *prima facie* evidence that factor allocation may be improved by land redistribution, and that the improvement can be greater, the more highly skewed the distribution of land-ownership.

[1] Instituto Brasileiro de Geografia e Estatística, Conselho Nacional de Estatística, *Anuario Estatístico do Brasil: 1967* (Rio de Janeiro, 1967), p. 94.

land, or non-maximization of profit – could also cause a fall in labor per total farm area. Therefore, the influence of dualism is more convincingly illustrated by the fact that labor per cultivated area falls, as farm size increases, and labor per unit of capital also declines. In the ten crop sectors, labor density per cultivated area is an average of 3.7 times as great for farms under 10 hectares as for farms over 1000 hectares. The ratio of labor to capital, furthermore, is 4.02 times as great for the former as for the latter.

It is possible to derive the difference in implicit factor prices from the different factor ratios, between small and large farms. Suppose the elasticity of substitution between factors is one, as the Cobb–Douglas-type production function assumes. Then if small farms use a ratio of labor to cultivated land $x\%$ larger than this ratio for large farms, the ratio of the price of cultivated land to the price of labor must be $x\%$ greater for small farms than for large. Therefore, these figures imply that the effective price ratio of cultivated land to labor is 270% greater for farms under 10 hectares than for farms over 1000 hectares, and the effective price ratio of capital to labor is 300% greater for the small farms than for the largest farms.

In summary, the argument for land reform based on labor market dualism appears to be of substantial importance in Brazil. However, it is difficult to determine whether labor-market dualism or one of several other influences is the chief cause of observed factor misallocation in land and labor use patterns. Several causes would be consistent with the observed data.

2.4.2. Land held as portfolio asset

A second major reason why large farms may make little use of their land is that land is held as a portfolio asset rather than a productive input. Inflation aggravates this tendency by eliminating currency as a viable portfolio asset. However, inflation alone does not explain low land use, since low use of land by large land holders is encountered in countries with inflation (Brazil, Chile, Argentina) as well as countries without inflation (Peru, Guatemala, pre-revolutionary Cuba).

The general reason why land may be held unused as a portfolio asset is that as such it is a relatively attractive asset, both with regard to risk and return. Brazilian land tax has been almost negligible.[1] A severe tax on unused

---

[1] In 1961, of total Brazilian revenue, only 0.27% came from land tax. Instituto Brasileiro de Geografia e Estatistica, Conselho Nacional de Economia, *Anuario Estatístico do Brasil: 1963* (Rio de Janeiro, 1963), p. 413. All land tax has traditionally gone to the county,

land, or even on land generally, would discourage the holding of idle land. Furthermore, until the 1964 Land Reform Law, there was no threat of expropriation of land held idle. Thus, there has been little dis-incentive to the holding of idle land.

There are two considerations in the argument that land is held idle as a portfolio asset. First is the point that land is attractive relative to other assets. Second is the point that land held idle may be preferred to land used for production. In Brazil, the main alternatives to land as an asset have not been attractive. Money has not been viable because of inflation.[1] The stock market is poorly developed. Control of many companies by families, difficulty of obtaining information on the firms, and great fluctuations in stock values, inhibit investment in stocks.[2]

The primary form of short term paper in Brazil, *Letras de Câmbio*, has yielded negative real returns, although these assets have attracted some funds merely because other alternatives for investors were even worse.[3] Urban buildings are another alternative asset. But urban construction investment has not been lucrative due to rent ceilings in the face of inflation. Also the market for construction has been limited by the poor availability of home loans – caused in turn by interest rate ceilings specified by the usury law.[4]

Land would thus seem to have been an attractive alternative portfolio asset. Land prices have kept up with inflation, on a basis of the limited in-

---

where the influence of local landlords was great and thus land taxes were held down. Even in comparison with other underdeveloped countries, Brazil's land tax is low: the percentage of total revenue coming from land tax, in 1950, was 9% in India, 5% in Mexico and Pakistan, 4% in Chile and Cuba. Haskell P. Wald, *Taxation of Agricultural Land in Underdeveloped Economies: a Survey and Guide to Policy* (Cambridge: Harvard University Press, 1959), p. 62.

[1] From 1912 to 1939 prices increased an average of 14% per year. Wholesale prices rose an annual average of 14.8% during 1950–53, rose 30.3% in 1954 alone, rose an average of 14.2% annually, 1955–58, an average 35.6% in 1959–61, and rose 53.2, 73.5, 91.6 and 50.7% in 1962, 1963, 1964 and 1965, respectively. From price series in *Conjuntura Econômica*, various issues.

[2] According to the Government's Planning Agency, EPEA, 'stocks ... do not exert great attraction over the investors, who prefer to apply their reserves in the acquisition of rural lands, urban real estate, and the accumulation of inventories'. Escritório de Pesquisa Econômica Aplicada (EPEA), *Situação Monetária, Creditícia e do Mercado de Capitais: Diagnóstico Preliminar* (Rio de Janeiro: Ministério de Planejamento e Coordenaçao Econômica, 1966), p. 40.

[3] *Ibid.*, p. 38.

[4] Mário Henrique Simonsen, *A Experiência Inflacionária no Brasil* (Rio De Janeiro: instituto de Pesquisas e Estudos Sociais, 1964), p. 68.

TABLE 2

Land prices for Rio Grande do Sul rice farms, 1949-64, versus wholesale price series, Brazil

Crop year	A Rice-land price per hectare (cruzeiros)	B A as index, 1949-50 = 100	C Wholesale price index, Brazil (1949 = 100)	D Land price relative to wholesale prices (B/C)
1949-50	1,500	100	100	100
1950-51	2,000	133	103	129
1951-52	2,500	167	127	131
1952-53	3,000	200	140	143
1953-54	3,000	200	161	124
1954-55	5,000	333	210	159
1955-56	5,000	333	237	141
1956-57	5,000	333	282	118
1957-58	10,000	667	318	210
1958-59	n.a.	n.a.	356	n.a.
1959-60	19,800	1,320	492	268
1960-61	30,000	2,000	644	311
1961-62	35,000	2,333	890	262
1962-63	40,000	2,667	1,365	195
1963-64	100,000	6,667	2,368	282
1964-65	150,000	10,000	4,537	220

Source: 'A': Instituto Rio Grandense do Arroz, *Anuario Estatístico do Arroz* (Pôrto Alegre), yearly issues 1950-66. Total land value divided by area. 'C': Index 44 of *Conjuntura Econômica*, converted to 1949 base.

formation available. Table 2 shows the price of rice land in Rio Grande do Sul, and compares the land prices to the wholesale price index. These land prices advanced ahead of general price levels, from 1950 to 1965.[1]

Other limited information[2] also suggests that Brazilian land prices have

---

[1] If the series were deflated by the cost of living index for Pôrto Alegre, capital of Rio Grande do Sul, the increase in real land value would be even greater.

[2] Alberto Franco, *Nature and Conditions Associated with the Existence of Latifundia in Southern Brazil* (Rio de Janeiro: Inter-American Center of Agrarian Reform, 1965), pp. 78-79. Franco cites land prices for milk-producing areas in São Paulo: land price rose from 3352 cruzeiros per hectare in 1951 to 12,544 cruzeiros in 1957, or from an index of 100 to 374. The cost of living in São Paulo, capital city rose from an index of 100 in 1951 to 307 in 1957 (*Conjuntura Econômica* Regional Index 4, São Paulo). Franco also cites a study by R. N. G. Soares, which shows that average value of farmland in São Paulo increased from 349 cruzeiros in 1940 to 1973 cruzeiros in 1950, based on census data. This

kept pace with inflation, and that land thus has been a viable 'store of value' asset. However, even if land is an important portfolio asset, why would it be held idle?

One reason for idle land holding would be the attitude of the owner who keeps land as a store-of-value asset: he may be uninterested in the actual operation of a farm. For example, his primary activities may be in the city. Also it is likely that the risks associated with land use in production are greater than the risk of holding land idle, because of crop price fluctuations and labor difficulties. For rice in Rio Grande do Sul, the time series of land prices, given above, shows faster growth and smaller fluctuation around its trend line than does the corresponding time series for the price of rice. In a linear regression of the logarithm of price on time, land price shows an annual growth rate of 29.5% from 1949 to 1964, while rice prices grew at 24.1%. The average absolute percentage deviation of estimated from predicted price was 24.3% for land price and 31.8% for the price of rice.[1] Thus, assuming risk to be a function of price fluctuation, the risk for holding idle land was lower than the risk of producing rice on the land. Finally, landholders are discouraged from renting or sharecropping their land by requirements of the 1946 Constitution that the owner compensate tenants for improvements and that the tenant may not be evicted after a ten year period. Therefore, a land owner uninterested in agricultural production himself is discouraged from turning his land over to sharecroppers or renters.

In summary, it is quite likely that some large landowners in Brazil hold idle land as a portfolio asset. It is important to note that while land redistribution would be one corrective measure, other measures could also reduce holding of idle land for portfolio motives. Taxation of idle land would be one measure. Reduction of inflation and improvement in the stock market and in government bond reliability would be other, more indirect, measures.

---

meant an increase from an index of 100 to an index of 565. General prices in Brazil rose in this decade from an index of 100 to a level of 250 (that is, 14% per year, 1940–47; 3.4% in 1948, 4.5% in 1949, and 9.2% in 1950. EPEA, *Situação Monetária...*, *op. cit.*, p. 45).
[1] Land prices: shown in table 2. Rice prices: from *Anuario Estatístico* various years. The regression model was:

$$\log P_t = A + b(t)$$

where P_t is price in year t; t, from 1 (for 1949) to 16 (for 1964).
Results: (a) land price: $b = 0.295$ (0.017), $R^2 = 0.9611$; (b) rice price: $b = 0.241$ (0.021), $R^2 = 0.9031$.

2.4.3. Land market imperfections

The earlier discussion of 'dualism' suggests that the marginal value of land to small farms is very high, and that it is low for large farms. Land sales by the large owners to the small do not occur to the point where marginal product of land is equal for the two groups, because several imperfections hinder this process. First, long term credit is not available for small or landless farmers to purchase land.[1] Second, the 'small plot' market is different from the market for large farms. The large holder is reluctant to sell parcels of his land and break up his farm's continuity; thus, the price per hectare is higher for small plots than for large land areas, for identical quality land.[2]

Land rental is a second feature of the land market. Land rental should permit allocation of land to small farmers to the point where labor/land ratios are equated among farms. This allocation does not occur, in part because land is not a mobile factor. If labor is landless and is mobile, then this fact is not a problem. But when the laborer in question is already located on a small farm which he owns, then unless the new land available for rental happens to be adjacent or near to his property, rental of the new land will not be a feasible option for the laborer. A second reason why rental of land does not function well in Brazil is that owners who rent land are obliged by the Constitution to compensate renters for improvements, and renters may not be evicted after they have remained on a farm for a ten year period.

2.4.4. 'Own consumption' on small farms

Another reason why farm land is more intensively used on small farms than on large farms is that the market is more certain for the small farm's output. The reason is that the small farm produces partly for commercial sale and

---

[1] Inter-American Committee for Agricultural Development, *Land Tenure Conditions and Socio-Economic Development of the Agricultural Sector: Brazil, op. cit.*, p. 108. However, the reference does not give data to support this assertion.

[2] The Brazilian Institute of Agrarian Reform in 1966 expropriated a large plantation in Pernambuco. The basis for compensation was the price recently charged for small land parcels by a nearby private company, reduced to less than one half the price per hectare, since: 'Small property prices in the area are usually greater than twice the price for large areas from which they are dismembered' (my translation). Instituto Brasileiro de Reforma Agrária, *Ante Projeto do Plano de Reforma Agrária da Área Prioritária de Emergência do Nordeste* (Rio de Janeiro, 1966) mimeographed, p. 14.

TABLE 3

'Own consumption' on farms as a percentage of total production, by farm size group, Tapes county, Rio Grande do Sul

Size group hectares	Percent of production consumed on the farm		
	Crops	Animal	Total
<25	28.6%	79.0%	38.5%
25–50	22.0	67.5	34.6
50–100	13.3	71.0	24.7
100–500	9.4	26.8	15.4
500–1000	0.9	6.9	2.2
1000–2500	1.1	4.4	2.0
2500–5000	0.1	3.0	0.7
>5000	0.1	1.8	0.3
All farms	9.4	34.6	15.3

Source: Instituto Gaucho de Reforma Agrária, *Socio-Economic Survey of Tapes* (Pôrto Alegre, 1966), typewritten.

partly for its own consumption.[1] Therefore the small farmer is less affected by the risk of market price fluctuation than is the large farmer.

The relatively high incidence of 'own consumption' on small farms is clear in the one set of data available to the author. The percent of output consumed on the farm, for each farm size class, is shown in table 3 for one county in Brazil's South.

The crop mix provides another indication of the greater incidence of 'own consumption' on small farms than on large farms. In Brazil's Northeast, large crop farms tend to specialize in 'industrial' crops such as sugar cane and cotton. Their production is mainly for export to other regions and abroad. The smaller farms produce foodstuffs.[2]

As an explanation of land use patterns, 'own consumption on small farms' is probably much less important than the three influences described before – labor-market dualism, speculative land holding, and land-market imperfection. It is doubtful that the agricultural market is generally so depressed

---

[1] Note that so long as at least some portion of the farm's output is marketed, the existence of 'own consumption' on the farm does not mean that the farm is 'backward', as one would assume for farms wholly cut off from the market.

[2] For example, the 1960 agricultural census shows that of the total area of farms specialized in corn in Pernambuco, 45.8% was in farms of less than 20 hectares. Of the total area of farms specialized in sugar cane, 1.7% was in farms of less than 20 hectares, and 41% was in farms larger than 10,000 hectares.

that subsistence production is much more attractive than commercial production. Still, the 'own consumption' pattern is important to keep in mind when considering the impact of land redistribution. The 'income effect' of land redistribution would cause higher demand for food in the agricultural population, and most of this increased demand would probably be met by 'own consumption' on the new family farms. Therefore, one probable effect of land redistribution would be to increase the percent of output consumed on the farms. Whether the marketable surplus would rise or fall after land redistribution would depend on whether the increase in production were greater or less than the increase in farmers' 'own consumption'.

2.4.5. Monopsony

Another influence which may cause low utilization of land by large farms is their monopsony power over labor.[1] By monopolizing all land in a given region, large farms can deny labor the opportunity of alternative work, and thus can hold down wages. In the monopsony case, large farms will have low land use in two senses. First, land use intensity in the sense of labor and output per farm area will be lower on large farms with monopsony power than on small farms. Second, land will have low utilization in comparison to that which would occur if there were no monopsony in the labor market.

The second of these points is derived from standard monopsony theory. Monopsony output and employment are lower than the competitive levels because in competition labor is hired to the point where its marginal product equals its marginal cost, or its wage. The monopsonist hires labor to the point where its marginal product equals its marginal cost, which is greater than the wage. For the monopsonist, if wage is a function of labor hired, $w = f(N)$ where w = wage, N = labor, the marginal cost of labor equals $w + f'(N) \cdot N$. Thus, not as much labor is hired under monopsony as under pure competition.

The other point above is that if there is a small, competitive group of farms alongside a monopsonist, the former group will have higher output and labor input per farm area than will the monopsonist, assuming capitalistic (and not

---

[1] Note that Solis and Barraza have stated a preliminary model for pre-revolutionary Mexico, in which they conclude that agricultural production was kept below a competitive level due to monopoly of large farms in regional product markets and monopsony of the same farms in labor markets. L. Barraza and L. Solis, 'Notes on Land Reform', (n.p., n.d.), mimeographed.

'family' or 'dualistic') behavior by both the competitors and the monopsonist. This phenomenon occurs because the monopsonist sets the wage by achieving his equilibrium, and then the small competitive farms attempt to hire labor at that wage until the marginal product of labor on their land equals the set wage. This action by the handful of competitive farms will raise the wage somewhat, and thereby partially shrink the profits of the monopsonist. In the final equilibrium, the group of competitive farmers will have hired labor to the point where its marginal product equals the wage, while the monopsonist will have marginal product of labor equal to marginal labor cost but higher than the wage. Thus labor and therefore output per farm area will be higher on the small farms than on that of the monopsonist.

These points may be shown graphically (fig. 1).

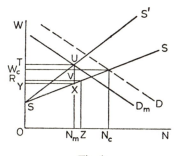

Fig. 1

In fig. 1, w = wage, N = labor, curve SS is the labor supply curve; curve $S'S'$, the marginal cost of labor curve.[1] $D_m D_m$ is the curve of labor's marginal product, for the monopsonist. DD is the same curve for the whole sector, including the small competitive farmers. If the whole sector were organized on a competitive basis, the labor market equilibrium would be at (W_c, N_c). Instead, the monopsonist reaches his equilibrium at N_m, at which level of employment the wage would be OY. The competitive small farmers try to hire labor at OY, pushing the wage up to OR before they arrive at their equilibrium, where marginal product of labor on their farms equals OR, and

---

[1] Note: if labor supply is $N = -a + bW$ such that, for the monopsonist, $W = (N+a)/b$, then total labor cost is $(N^2 + Na)/b$ and marginal labor cost is $a/b + 2N/b$. The marginal cost curve thus has twice the slope of the labor supply curve.

they hire the amount $OZ - ON_m$ of labor. The monopsonist is forced to pay wage OR also, thus reducing his monopsony profit from area $TUXY$ to area $TUVR$.

In sum, monopsony would cause smaller farms to use land more intensively than large farms assuming that large farms have monopsony power while small farms do not. More important than this observed 'distortion' would be the unobserved distortion, the amount by which competition would increase production and employment. It is useful to note that there is no incentive in the monopsony case for the large owner to correct the factor misallocation. He is not tempted to rent or sell his land, because by using it in production, he maximizes monopsonist profits.[1]

In examining the conditions under which monopsony influence will exist, a distinction may be made between a short-run monopsony situation and a long-run monopsony or oligopsony situation.

Short run labor immobility and a lack of choice among employers are sufficient conditions for 'short-run monopsony'. Labor immobility is a prerequisite; otherwise, the large land holder could not deny labor alternatives to his farm. Migration is not costless, and workers could work for a monopsonist at low wages rather than migrate, due to the high short run cost of migration.[2] Without migration, the range of alternative work

---

[1] Note that the monopsonist *cum* small competitive farmers equilibrium may be found algebraically. If the monopsonist has land L_m, and the competitors altogether have L_c; the production function is $Q = f(L,N)$, and the labor supply curve is $N = g(W)$, then there are three unknowns: N_c, N_m, and W, which are, respectively labor on small farms, labor on the monopsonist farm, and wage; and

(1) $$\frac{\partial Q_c}{\partial N_c} = W$$

(2) $$\frac{\partial Q_m}{\partial N_m} = W + \frac{\partial W}{\partial N_m}(N_m)$$

(3) $$N_c + N_m = g(W)$$

where subscript c refers to competitive farms and m refers to the monopsonist. If an equilibrium wage exists (which depends on the parameters of the labor supply curve, the production function, and the land endowments of the two farm groups) the competitive farmers will have more intensive use of land – higher labor per farm land and therefore higher output per farm area, since they will reduce marginal product of labor to a level below that of the monopsonist, as shown by eq. (1) versus eq. (2).

[2] This short run consideration would be especially influential in the worker's decision if he had a high time discount rate, as is likely at low levels of income.

locations for a worker is limited to land to which he can walk from his home each day. Thus, while the city worker with urban transit available and spatially concentrated employment opportunities would have many possible alternative employers, the agricultural worker living near a ten thousand hectare farm may have only one prospective employer. Another dimension of labor immobility may exist: debt peonage, or indebtedness of the worker to the 'company store' may be used on the large farm to keep the worker immobile.[1]

A long-run oligopsony situation would be one in which the whole feasible area over which labor might migrate were controlled by large owners who acted in concert. The existence of producers' associations for important cash crops in Brazil (sugar cane, cocoa, coffee, rice) makes 'action in concert by large owners' much more of a reality than one might expect *a priori*.

In sum, the principal conditions for existence of 'oligopsony power' would be limits on labor mobility and/or control of a large percent of a sector's land by a limited number of large landowners.[2]

2.4.6. *Non-maximization by large farms*

A common assertion about large landlords in Latin America is that they are not economic maximizers[3] but, instead, hold land for power or prestige. The 'structuralist' school cites this phenomenon as a cause of inelastic agricultural supply, rising food prices, wages, and thus of 'structural' inflation.

Wolf and Mintz[4] as well as Flores[5] have distinguished between the *hacienda* (or *latifúndio*) on the one hand, and the 'plantation' on the other,

---

[1] The author does not have data on the extent of debt peonage in Brazil.
[2] One could define oligopsony power to exist when an arbitrary number of owners, say 100, could by their joint action change the regional wage by an arbitrary percentage, say 5%. If employment potential were assumed proportional to land area, and if the elasticity of labor supply with respect to wage were known, then it could be determined for a given region whether or not oligopsony power existed. The answer would depend on whether or not the largest 100 farms in the region owned $(5\%)(E)$ of the land, where E is the elasticity of labor supply with respect to wage.
[3] The non-maximization of the large *latifundista* is different from the 'non-maximization of profits' by the family farm. The former refers to the holding of land for prestige, for example, without concern for production. The latter refers to a type of profit maximization in which labor costs are not deducted from profit, since labor is family labor.
[4] Eric Wolf and Sidney Mintz, 'Haciendas and Plantations in Middle America and the Antilles', *Social and Economic Studies*, 37 (September 1957), pp. 380–412.
[5] Edmundo Flores, *Tratado de Economia Agrícola* (México: Fondo de Cultura, 1962).

as two types of large farm. The former seems more an organization for social control than a unit with the goal of profit maximization. The latter tends to be more capitalized, specializes in cash crops for export, pays salaries rather than more feudal remuneration (such as subsistence plots given in return for labor), and disciplines by firing workers rather than punishing them.

Two situations seem to cause the formation of the non-maximizing *latifúndio*. One is the existence of an indigenous population to be controlled. (This point would suggest greatest incidence of the nonmaximizing *latifúndio* in pre-revolutionary Mexico, in Peru, Guatemala, and other areas with large Indian populations.) Another is a situation in which the landholder enjoys political power, not directly related to his production from the land.

Some studies indicate the existence of 'non-economic' motives for landholding in certain regions of Brazil. Greenfield and Vasconcelos maintain that in Minas Gerais, sharecroppers give their political support to the landlord's candidate in return for certain paternalistic benefits: the landlord supposedly provides for the education of the workers' children and gives aid to the workers in time of sickness.[1] One could infer that landowners consider their farms to be primarily a means to political power and only secondarily economic units. For the Northeast of Brazil, the region which would be the most likely sphere of non-economic or 'feudalistic' motivation of landlords, Vilaça and Albuquerque show how landlords in the past have dominated the area politically.[2]

The author is skeptical of the assertion that large owners do not maximize profits. This study relies more heavily on the assumption that large owners maximize profits, but in the very process of maximization the influences of dualism, non-availability of assets alternative to land, relatively low land

---

[1] Sidney Greenfield and Edgard de Vasconcelos Barros, 'Rural Labor and Economic Development in Brazil', *Inter-American Economic Affairs*, 19 (summer 1965), p. 75.

[2] Marcos Vinicius Vilaça and Roberto C. de Albuquerque, *Coronel, Coroneis* (Rio de Janeiro: Editôra Tempo Brasileiro, 1965). The following passage is illustrative:
'The saving thus generated in the three entrepreneurial sectors of economic activity of the farm ... that accumulated with the growth of livestock, and that generated by the commercialization of crops and animal production, these last two more monetary ... goes in large part to the purchase of land with which the *coronel* expands his dominance and strengthens the basis of his power and prestige. It is the most secure way he sees for investment, almost the only way which he has traditionally expanded. More than its profitability, a non-economic good attracts him: the social value linked to the dominion over extensive properties, inherent in the very system which prevails' (p. 26).

prices for large buyers, and other economic influences cause a low use of land by large-holders, relative to the use by smaller farms.

2.4.7. The relation of land quality to farm size

In formulating land reform policy, it is of critical importance to know whether land held idle in large farms is of good quality. If such land is of poor quality, it would be incorrect to expect production to increase through expanded land use after reform.

Accurate information on the relation of land quality to farm size is virtually non-existent for Brazil. Analysis of the question is necessarily indirect. The author's acquaintance with Brazilian agriculture permits some statements regarding Northeastern sugar areas and rice areas in Rio Grande do Sul. These are both important regions, especially since they are two of the five 'priority' regions selected for land reform by present Brazilian legislation. In both areas the large farms have perhaps the best land. In the Northeast the large sugar plantations in the coastal, humid zone monopolize the best lands.[1]

In Pernambuco the small farms are concentrated in the *Agreste* – the transitional zone between the humid coastal zone and the arid interior *(Sertão)*. These *Agreste* lands are of lower quality than the coastal zone lands where large plantations prevail. In the interior *Sertão*, large farms again dominate. These are cotton or cattle farms. In this region both small and large farms have poor climatic conditions; the availability of irrigation water is the major determinant of land 'quality'.[2]

In the major rice areas of Rio Grande do Sul, the largest farms tend to be in the newly opened, fertile lands of the 'frontier zone' (bordering Argentina), as opposed to the older, more exhausted area of the 'central depression' and

---

[1] See for example T. Lynn Smith, *Brazil: People and Institutions* (Baton Rouge: Louisiana State University Press, 1963), p. 350, for description of the amassing of good sugar lands by plantations.

[2] A very small amount of land in the *Sertão* is irrigated; much of the public work in dams has gone into building of reservoirs, which tend to be used by large cattle ranchers for water for their livestock rather than for irrigation for food crops. This phenomenon is criticized by Albert O. Hirschman, *Journeys toward Progress: Studies of Economic Policy Making in Latin America* (New York: Twentieth Century Fund, 1963), p. 44; and by Antonio Callado, *As Indústrias da Sêca e os 'Galileus' de Pernambuco: Aspecto da Luta Pela Reforma Agrária no Brasil* (Rio de Janeiro: Ed. Civilização Brasileira, 1960), p. 12.

the 'coastal zone'.¹ This would imply larger farms in the rice area have if anything higher than average land quality.

With regard to other areas of Rio Grande do Sul, the region of very small farms – the 'colonial zone' where European immigrants settled at the end of the 19th century, and where inheritance has fragmented farms – the land tends to be hilly, of lower than average quality.

For coffee in São Paulo, the Food and Agriculture Organization Survey in 1958 found that farms on the *Terra Roxa* soil – probably the best of the four soil types on which coffee is important in São Paulo – tend to be above average size.²

The only available study on land quality as related to farm size is by Alberto Franco. Unfortunately this study investigates only two counties – one in Rio Grande do Sul (Alegrete) and one in São Paulo (Ibitiruna). Franco chooses two counties dominated by *latifúndios*, principally large cattle ranches. The soil in the two counties has low fertility and water retention; rainfall is low or fluctuates greatly; in Ibitiruna the land is hilly and thus satisfactory for grazing but not for mechanized crop production. Access to market in the two counties is not particularly more difficult than for any other region in the two states.³

One would hesitate to generalize from Franco's finding that the two counties characterized by 'latifundia' have low land quality.

The agricultural census provides indirect evidence of the relation of land quality to farm size. The breakdown of land use by farm size includes one category for unproductive land, defined as: '... those areas not usable for crops or pasture and those occupied with roads, constructions, reservoirs, etc.' For the seven states with which the sample data of this study are concerned, the category of 'unproductive land' is a relatively constant proportion of total area. The only exception is a high percentage of 'unproductive' land in the smallest size group – farms less than 5 hectares. This rise would probably be due to the higher percent of area in buildings and roads that would be found on a very small plot.

Therefore, the hypothesis that land quality is poorer on large farms than

---

[1] Based on discussion with technician at the Rio Grande do Sul Rice Institute, June 1966.
[2] United Nations, Food and Agriculture Organization, *Coffee in Latin America: Productivity Problems and Future Prospects. Vol. 2. Brazil. State of Sao Paulo, Parts 1 and 2* (Mexico, 1960), p. 24.
[3] See Alberto Franco, *op. cit.*

on small would be rejected on a basis of census data for 'unproductive land'. Table 35 in appendix C shows percentage land use, by farm size group, from Census data. A second category which could possibly be interpreted as 'poor quality land' is area in forest. Natural forest area increases as a percent of total area, as farm size increases. However, this pattern means that small farms clear a larger portion of their land for intensive use, and there is no reason to believe that forest land is of below average quality.

Finally, although land price probably overstates the quality of land on small farms and understates quality on large farms, it is used as a variable to represent quality in a hypothesis test of chapter 4. The test is described in detail in chapter 4. The result is that a significant fall in land use intensity does occur as farm size rises, even after the influence of land quality has been removed. Land quality is accounted for by the inclusion of land price as an independent variable in the estimated relationship between land use intensity and farm size.

2.4.8. *Implications of the alternative explanations of land use intensity*

Seven reasons have been suggested in sections 2.4.1 through 2.4.7 to explain why land use intensity declines as farm size rises. It is important to examine whether the explanations have identical implications for land reform.[1] If poor land quality on large farms is the reason for their low land utilization, little increase in production can be expected from land reform. However, the other six influences discussed above would imply that unused land in large farms could be brought into production. The dissimilarities among these six influences may be examined with regard to two considerations: quality of land unused, and availability of capital and labor for land reform.

The six influences on land use intensity suggested here may be divided into two major groups. In the first group there are four influences which cause large landowners to use their land less intensively for agricultural production than do small landowners; these influences are: (1) labor-market dualism; (2) land market imperfection; (3) production for 'own consumption' on small farms; and (4) monopsony of large farms over labor. In the second group there are two influences which could conceivably cause large landowners to use their land for virtually no agricultural production; these influences are:

---

[1] In section 6.1, the different implications of the arguments for policies other than land reform are examined.

(1) landholding for speculative or portfolio asset purposes; and (2) non-economic behavior. Even acting under one of these last two influences, a farm owner might well conduct some economic activity on his farm. The land inheritor whose primary interests are in the city could keep his land for lack of a better alternative asset for which to exchange it, and could permit the families which traditionally lived on the farm to continue living and working there, while a new purchaser of land holding it as a portfolio asset would engage no one to produce on it. In any case, if land is held totally idle it will be for the speculative or prestige-holding motive rather than because of one of the other four influences mentioned.

Concerning land quality, unused land will be of better quality[1] if it is concentrated in farms that are almost completely unused, than if it is scattered among many large farms that already use a high percent of their land for production. The reason is that unused land on a farm is probably of poorer quality than land in use on the farm. Therefore, the four arguments in the first group above imply that unused land on large farms will be of below average quality for these farms, although it will be of better quality than land used at the margin on small farms. The other two arguments imply that the whole area of the large farm might be unused and therefore the quality of the unused land is average. In sum, the land reform planner could expect a greater increase in production after land reform if unused land were concentrated in large farms with almost no land use (due to speculative holding or non-economic behavior) than if the unused land were distributed among many large farms which already use a substantial percent of their area (although this percent is lower than that on small farms, due to labor market dualism, land market imperfection, 'own consumption', or monopsony).

Concerning the availability of capital and labor for land reform, the influences of 'labor-market dualism', land market imperfection, and 'own consumption on small farms' all imply an excess of labor and capital applied per land area on small farms. This 'excess' of labor and capital would be available during land reform for transfer to land previously held in large farms. 'Monopsony', however, would probably occur in sectors where small

---

[1] For given over-all land quality as represented by the average land price for the farm. Note that this discussion assumes equal rates of decline in land quality within the farm, for all farms.

farms had very little weight, so their contribution of 'excess' labor and capital to land reform would be of little importance.

Despite these differences in quality of unused land and in the availability of labor and capital during land reform, the six influences discussed here have generally similar implications for land reform. This similarity is useful for the analysis which follows, since the relative importance of each of the six forces is not rigorously determined.

2.5. Social efficiency

2.5.1. Land reform's effect on factor combinations

It was suggested in the previous section that land reform would improve static efficiency in agricultural production by transferring land held idle or little used from large owners to new small owners. It was also suggested earlier that the scale of post-reform units would not be a constraint in land redistribution, because increasing returns to scale are unlikely in the Brazilian context. It is useful to extend the analysis of land reform's effect on static efficiency, and ask: (a) whether land reform would affect factor combinations; and (b) whether there is an 'optimal farm size' judged in terms of output per 'social' factor cost.

While low utilization of land by large farms is the principal distortion caused by market imperfections and behavioral rigidities described in the preceding section, some of these influences also cause distortions in factor combinations even for those factors used. Labor market dualism causes large farms to employ less labor relative to capital and cultivated land than do small farms. Land market imperfection causes large farms to use less labor per cultivated land area than do small farms. Monopsony will also cause lower ratios of labor to capital and cultivated land on large monopsonistic farms than on competitive farms.

The decline in labor applied relative to cultivated land and capital, as farm size increases, indicates divergence between 'social' factor costs and private factor costs. Private costs change as farm size rises, while there is only one set of social opportunity costs for the productive factors. The idea of a 'socially optimal farm size' is examined below. However, it is important to note first that one likely effect of land reform would be an equalization across farms of the combinations of labor, cultivated land, and capital.

A complete reorganization of agriculture which establishes a uniform farm size for each product will eliminate the factor combination divergences associated with divergent farm sizes. Even if agriculture is only partially reformed, leaving some large farms alongside family farms created by the reform, input combinations will tend to equalize, particularly for the set of previous small farms and new family units. Workers crowded onto small farms will be attracted to new land reform units because the barrier to their re-allocation will now be broken: they will now have access to more land on an ownership basis, whereas before land reform they could only work the land held by large farms as salaried employees. General improvements in factor markets during land reform will also tend to equalize factor combinations, as small farmers obtain credit to purchase land, capital equipment, seeds, and fertilizers.

The equalization of combinations of factors already used in agriculture is one way in which land reform would increase static efficiency and production.[1] This effect is partly additional to the effect of increased land use, but not completely independent of it. Some of the excess labor and capital on very small farms would shift, after land reform, into employment on land previously used in cultivation on large farms; this change would represent equalization in combinations of factors already used. Some of the labor and capital on very small farms would shift into use in cultivation of land formerly held idle; this shift would represent increased land use.

2.5.2. *Farm size and social efficiency*

'Production-efficiency' in the sense of output per cost of inputs actually utilized, was discussed in section 2.3. The influences causing 'farm efficiency' or the 'intensity of total land use' to fall as farm size rises, were discussed in section 2.4. In this section, these two efficiency concepts are extended to account for divergence between private and social costs.

The main concern of this section is: what is the optimal farm size, on a basis of 'social cost' analysis? Ideally this question could be answered by the use of 'shadow prices' for the cost of factors. The market imperfections and behavioral rigidities discussed in section 2.4, show why private factor costs differ among farms. In addition, there is reason to believe that private labor costs to capitalists generally exceed the 'shadow price of labor' in the under-

---

[1] This statement and the entire discussion of this section require the assumption that the production functions are homogeneous.

developed economy. This divergence exists because the 'institutional wage' which entrepreneurs must pay hired labor – both in industry and in capitalistic agriculture – exceeds the marginal product of labor in the traditional sectors such as family farm agriculture and urban services.[1] Second, labor unions and social legislation hold wages above levels which would clear the labor markets. Furthermore, while the wage probably exceeds the shadow price, or opportunity cost, of labor, imperfection in the capital market may cause the price of capital to be below its social opportunity cost. This divergence occurs, for example, if large firms have access to official credit at low interest rates, which may be lowered and even become negative because of inflation.[2]

The appropriate 'shadow price' of a factor, for social cost accounting, is the opportunity cost or marginal product of the factor in the economy at large.[3] When the factor has different marginal products in different sectors of the economy, the correct planning price for the factor is its lowest marginal product among the major sectors, as long as the factor will be withdrawn from the sector in which its marginal product is lowest.

The ideal evaluation of 'production efficiency', from a social cost standpoint, would be a comparison of output value against total cost of inputs utilized, where inputs would be valued at shadow prices. The land input – cultivated land for crop farms, or pasture land for cattle ranches – would be included in factor cost, with the land input evaluated at the shadow price per hectare of farm land.[4] 'Social farm efficiency' would be evaluated in a

---

[1] As generally supposed in the 'surplus labor' models of W. Arthur Lewis and J. C. H. Fei and G. Ranis.

[2] However, low interest rates for large borrowers do not represent a distortion of price from social cost if the reason for the low rate is an economy of scale in lending – such as the existence of a fixed administrative cost per loan independent of loan size.

[3] It should be recognized that this rule refers to the price to be used for factor allocation in production. Since the use of these prices may also have income distribution implications, however, it may be necessary to make compensatory payments to avoid income redistribution while achieving efficiency of factor allocation. For example, a shadow price of labor below its 'market' wage will encourage the planning of labor intensive projects and will redistribute income toward laborers if the 'market' wage is paid to them.

[4] The shadow price of a hectare of land of given quality, in a specific sector, would be the amount by which sectoral output would fall if one hectare of total farm area were removed from production and the factors formerly employed on the hectare were transferred to their best alternative use in the sector.

similar way, except that total farm area would be included for land cost, evaluated again at the shadow price per hectare of land.

The actual application of social cost analysis is not feasible for this study, because valid economy-wide 'shadow prices' for factors are not available. However, some comments can be made about such an analysis.

First, the measurement of 'social production efficiency' would permit a qualification to the 'returns to scale' analysis of production efficiency. For example, constant returns to scale would imply private 'production efficiency' is identical for all farm sizes. However, if a consistent shift occurs in the combination of factors utilized, as farm size rises, 'social production efficiency' can change with farm size even though returns to scale are constant.[1] Suppose the shadow price of labor were below its market price and the shadow price of capital were above the market price, and suppose that less and less labor were used in relation to capital and cultivated land, as farm size rose. Then 'social production efficiency' would tend to decline as farm size rose, despite constant returns to scale in the production function. It should be noted that 'social production efficiency' would serve to qualify 'returns to scale' in present agriculture, but would be of little relevance for land reform planning. The purpose of analyzing returns to scale is to determine whether or not large scale state farms are necessary for efficient production after land reform; yet if post-reform farms were state operated, the factor combinations could be determined by fiat and would not necessarily equal those used on pre-reform farms of similar scale.

---

[1] That the return to scale information does not show effects of shifts in factor combinations may be shown as follows. Consider a Cobb–Douglas production function, $Q = aL^b N^c$ where Q = output, L = land cultivated, and N = labor. In value terms the function would be:

$$QP_q = a*(LP_L)^{b*}(NP_n)^{c*}$$

where the P's refer to respective prices. If identical accounting prices are used to examine all farms, then the P's are constant and may be factored out, such that

$$Q = \tilde{a}* L^{b*} N^{c*}$$

where
$$b* = b, \quad c* = c, \quad \text{and} \quad \tilde{a}* = a*P_L^b P_n^c / P_q.$$

Now suppose that at one set of prices, $P_{L1}/P_{n1} = r_1$, and that at another set, $P_{L2}/P_{n2} = r_2$, $r_2 > r_1$. The degree of returns to scale, $b+c$, would remain unchanged by whatever set of prices were used. Suppose a consistent shift occurred away from N toward L as scale increased. Then a cost per unit analysis based on the second price set would favor smaller scale operations than would analysis based on the first price set, if returns to scale were constant.

Second, 'social farm efficiency' would be more relevant than 'social production efficiency' both for estimating the relative social efficiency of various farm sizes at present, and for planning land reform. The reason is that 'social farm efficiency' includes the total farm area in the cost, whereas 'social production efficiency' includes only land cultivated (for crop farms, and only pasture for cattle farms).

Third, 'social farm efficiency' could appropriately be used to determine each product's present 'optimal farm size', that size at which output per social cost is the greatest. Since smaller farms tend to use much labor and little capital (as discussed in section 2.4.1), since the 'shadow price' of labor is likely to be low, and since smaller farms tend to use a higher percent of their land than large farms (as discussed in section 2.4), one would expect to find the optimal farm size in the range of small farms. However, the optimal size would be above the very smallest size, since the smallest size farms would probably use too much labor, even considering labor's low shadow price.

Fourth, the post reform unit would not necessarily have to be the same size as the pre-reform 'socially optimal' farm size, to achieve social efficiency. If post-reform units were state-operated, their factor combinations could be determined directly and would not necessarily be identical to factor combinations on pre-reform farms of identical size.

Even if post-reform units were private farms, the relevance of the pre-reform optimal farm size would depend on whether present relationships of factor combinations to farm size are caused by (1) remediable market imperfections, or by (2) technology and/or (3) behavior which would not change after reform. If the declining labor/land ratio (as farm size rises) is caused by market imperfections which could be remedied in the reform,[1] then the post-reform unit would not have to be the same size as the pre-reform optimal farm size, to achieve efficient factor allocation. However, if technology were the cause of factor combination patterns,[2] then the post-reform farm unit would have to be of the pre-reform optimal size for social

---

[1] Such as a lack of long term credit for land purchase.
[2] For example, if labor intensive techniques were used on small farms because machines could not be fully utilized, or if machine techniques were used on large farms because large labor teams could not be controlled effectively.

efficiency.¹ Similarly, if 'special behavior' of the farm operator were responsible for observed differences in factor combinations, market improvements would not remedy misallocation of factors, and the post-reform unit would have to be the size of the pre-reform optimal farm for efficient factor allocation.

It is the author's view that there exist both market imperfections (chiefly in the land market and possibly the capital market) and behavioral rigidities (chiefly preference for work on the family farm, and landholding for speculation), so that market improvements alone would not bring about optimal factor allocation. Thus, the post-reform farm size would have to be in the range of the pre-reform 'optimal size' (based on shadow price analysis), for social efficiency after land reform. It is also the author's impression that this optimal farm size would be relatively small, due to the likelihood of a low shadow price of labor and to the intensive use of labor on smaller farms.

2.6. Relationship of tenure-form to efficiency

The various tenure forms (owner–operator, renter, share-cropper, squatter, administrator–operator farms) can have different effects on production. There are three primary arguments with regard to tenancy. First, non-ownership can reduce the farmer's incentive to work. Second, insecure tenancy arrangements can reduce the operator's willingness to make long term investments, and short tenure contracts will increase the operator's willingness to exploit the soil without regard to long-run conservation. Third, sharecropping may cause sub-optimal application of inputs, if the arrangement is that the sharecropper pays all of the input expense but receives only a share of production. The sharecropper will apply inputs only to the point where his share of the marginal product equals the input cost, rather than to the optimal point where marginal product of the factor equals its price.²

While these arguments suggest that tenant farmers will achieve less

---

[1] That is, the relation of factor combinations to farm size could not be changed by market improvements, so that in order to obtain the optimal factor combination, the specific pre-reform optimal farm size would have to be chosen as the post-reform farm unit.

[2] See Rainer Schickele, 'Obstacles to Agricultural Production', *Journal of Farm Economics*, 24 (May 1942), pp. 447–462.

production than owner–operators in similar circumstances, there is the possibility that rental payments are so burdensome that the tenant will be compelled to exert greater effort than the owner with similar amounts of land and family labor available (the negative income effect of tenancy on leisure will cause higher production to be achieved by the tenant than by the owner).

The influence of tenure-type on 'production-efficiency' is tested statistically in section 3.4. In chapter 4, two statistical models test the hypothesis that land is used more intensively on owner-operated farms than on tenant-operated farms.

2.7. The hypotheses and the empirical tests

Several reasons why land reform can affect agricultural production have been suggested in this chapter. At this point, it is useful to enumerate these considerations in two groups: first, those hypotheses which are statistically tested, for Brazil, in the following chapters; and second, those hypotheses which are suggested but not tested empirically, for lack of data.

The issues raised in this chapter which are subsequently tested are the following questions. First, do there exist returns to scale in agricultural production? This question is examined empirically, product by product, for Brazil.[1] Second, is entrepreneurial ability related to farm size?[2] Third, do farms directed by administrators, renters, sharecroppers, or squatters have lower output per inputs used, or, secondly, lower intensity of land use, than farms run by owners?[3] Fourth, does the intensity of land use – in terms of percent of farm area 'used', or, alternatively, the intensity of inputs and output per farm area – decline as farm size rises?[4] Fifth, is any, or all, of the variation in land use intensity explained by differences in land quality and access to the market?[5] Finally, two sets of estimates are made of the changes in production, employment, and input use that would occur after

---

[1] Tested in section 3.3.
[2] Section 3.4.
[3] Section 3.4; chapter 4, models IV.1, IV.2.
[4] Chapter 4, models IV.1, IV.2, IV.3.
[5] Chapter 4, model IV.2.

land reform for specific state-product sectors in Brazil.[1] These estimates are based on production function estimates and estimated relationships of land-use to farm size.

The following issues raised in this chapter are not empirically tested.

First, no test is made of 'social efficiency' as related to farm size. This concept involves the use of economy-wide opportunity costs of factors, which are not available.

Second, no formal statistical tests are made to determine the relative weights of the several alternative reasons suggested for declining land-use intensity as farm size rises. It is not determined to what degree the land-use pattern is caused by 'labor market dualism', as opposed to speculative land-holding, or land market imperfection, or the 'own consumption market' for small farms, or monopsony elements, or non-economic behavior by large owners. Only the 'land quality' influence on land use is examined with formal statistical tests. However, the other influences just listed are examined on an informal basis.[2]

Third, no formal empirical test is made of the hypothesis that there exist two discrete types of large farms, the large efficient 'plantation' and the large inefficient 'latifundium', although this hypothesis is informally examined.[3]

Fourth, there is no empirical examination of the effects of land reform on the adoption of modern methods and on agricultural savings. The relevant data are not available.

Fifth, with regard to production functions, the assumption of homogeneity is not tested, since such a test is impossible. Furthermore, no test is made to determine whether or not large farms have completely different production functions from small farms. One identical production function is estimated for all farm sizes for a given state-product sector. Any difference in efficiency caused by different production functions for large versus small farms would only show up, as spurious information, in the estimated returns to scale for the single production function estimated.

Sixth, no test is made of the suggested possibility that there may exist for small farms externalities which could be internalized on a large farm. Instead,

---

[1] Section 5.4.
[2] Section 4.4.
[3] Section 4.3.2.

this effect would show up as spurious increasing returns to scale in the production function estimated.[1]

Seventh, there is no empirical test of the argument that cooperative organization could permit achievement of economies of scale in some dimensions while production would still be organized in small units in other dimensions.

Eighth, the sensitivity of agricultural output to policies other than land reform is not examined empirically.

Finally, in the estimates of the production effects of land reform, no estimates are made on the cost side, for lack of cost information.

2.8. Conclusion

The major theoretical considerations concerning the impact of land redistribution on agricultural output are:

1. The principal determinants of the effect of land reform on production are: (a) the existence or non-existence of increasing returns to scale for inputs actually used in agriculture; (b) the relationship of land utilization to farm size; (c) the amount of unemployed labor which would be absorbed in land reform; and (d) the relationships of the savings ratio and of willingness to adopt technical change, to farm size.

2. If increasing returns to scale exist in agriculture, land re-distribution from large farms to small will create inefficient units, and land reform should create large cooperative or state farms. Machine indivisibility is the chief reason why economies of scale may exist. Since the relevance of machinery is limited for the less developed country with cheap labor, returns to scale are likely to be constant until capital becomes cheaper relative to labor. If returns to scale are constant, post-reform farms may be small without loss of efficiency.

3. The intensity of land use in terms of output and inputs per farm area is higher on small farms than on large, in Brazil. The argument for land re-distribution, on production grounds, is that unused land on large farms

---

[1] For example, if spraying of crops on a small farm is ineffective because neighboring farms do not spray, and if the problem does not exist on a large farm where the owner sprays the whole relevant area, the estimated production function would show increasing returns to scale – the large farm would have higher output than the small, for the given inputs. But these returns would be spurious in a technical sense, because the technical production function refers to *caeteris paribus* conditions for all scales of production.

may be combined with unemployed and underemployed labor in agriculture, to increase production. There are several reasons why large farms have relatively low land use. The conventional reason given by advocates of land reform in Brazil is that some large landowners are 'traditionalistic' or 'non-economic' in behavior; this type of owner is sometimes called the *latifundista*. While the author acknowledges that non-economic behavior may partly cause the relatively low use of land by large farms, other reasons are suggested which are probably more important. They are:

(a) 'Labor market dualism' exists, in that the effective price of labor is lower for smaller farms with family labor than for large farms with hired labor. The family worker leaves for outside work when the outside wage exceeds his average product on the family farm. Therefore the wage (and the marginal product of labor) on large, hired-labor farms, exceeds or equals the average product of labor on family farms, and therefore exceeds the marginal product of labor on family farms. Thus, more labor per farm area is used on the small farm, and a higher percent of land is cultivated on the small farm as more marginal land is brought into use.

(b) Land is held as a portfolio asset rather than used for production, by some large owners. Land prices for Rio Grande do Sul rice farms show faster growth than general prices, and faster growth as well as smaller fluctuation than rice prices. Therefore, the holding of idle land is an attractive activity and involves less risk than landholding *cum* production. The absence of good alternative assets explains why land may be held as a portfolio asset.

(c) The land market seems to be imperfect: credit is not available for land purchase for small land buyers; and the price per hectare of a given quality is lower when the area is purchased in large blocks than when it is purchased in small parcels.

(d) Part of production is consumed on small farms; very little production is consumed on large farms. Therefore, smaller farms have a more stable 'market' for their output than do large farms.

(e) Very large farms may exercise monopsony power over local labor and therefore keep output per farm area below the level it would reach under pure competition, as well as below levels attained by smaller, competitive farms in the sector.

(f) Land quality and access to market may be poorer on large farms than on small, although census data for 'unusable land' by farm size do not show such a pattern.

§2.8   CONCLUSION   57

The author finds it difficult to state *a priori* which of these influences are the most important. For land reform purposes, however, the most crucial distinction is between land quality and other influences, since poor land quality on large farms would mean that no production gain could be expected if large farms were distributed to new small owners.

4. If economy-wide 'shadow prices' were available, output could be compared with factor cost evaluated at shadow prices and a 'socially optimal' farm size could be found. This analysis is not done in this study, because 'shadow prices' are not available. An optimal farm size could exist even with constant returns to scale for inputs utilized, both because the percent of land utilized declines as farm size rises, and because factor combinations shift from labor toward land and capital as farm size rises. The 'socially optimal farm size' would have to be chosen as the post-reform size if the factor combinations and 'land use' on that farm size could only be obtained on a farm of that size, for 'engineering' and/or behavioral reasons. If the socially appropriate factor combinations could be achieved by market improvement alone, or by fiat on state farms, the post-reform unit would not have to be the pre-reform 'optimal size' to achieve social efficiency. Note that, given labor's low shadow price in the less developed economy, and given the high labor intensity of smaller farms, the socially optimal farm size would probably be found in the small size range of farms.

5. With regard to land tenure, owner operators should be more efficient in production than tenant-operators, because: (a) they have greater certainty about future control of the farm than do tenants and are therefore more willing to make long term investments; and, (b) in the case of share-cropping, perverse incentives cause the sharecropper to obtain lower output than would an owner-operator, since the sharecropper equates the marginal cost of an input with his share of the marginal product, rather than with the full marginal product.

6. Large landowners may have higher savings rates than small farmers; if so, land redistribution can hurt long run capital formation. However, data are not available to test this point for Brazil.

In chapters 3 and 4, some of the theoretical arguments of this chapter are tested empirically, as enumerated above. In chapter 5, production functions and input-use patterns are used to predict land redistribution's effect on Brazilian agricultural production.

CHAPTER 3

THE RELATION OF PRODUCTION-EFFICIENCY TO SCALE OF INPUTS UTILIZED AND TO TENURE STATUS OF THE FARM OPERATOR

3.1. Introduction

This chapter considers two main hypotheses about 'production efficiency' raised in the preceding chapter. The first hypothesis states that, a farm with a large scale of cultivated acreage and other inputs is a more efficient unit than a small farm. If this is verified, then on grounds of technical efficiency, a land reform oriented toward the family farm is inefficient. If new farms are created by a land reform, they should be organized into large units, through producer cooperatives or other devices. On the other hand, if there are constant returns to scale, then one scale of operation is as satisfactory as another, and the family farm may be promoted without fear of inefficiency.

The second hypothesis examined here states that tenant farms have lower total factor productivity than owner-operated farms. If this is true then a public policy opposing tenancy is justifiable on grounds of efficiency as well as equity.

These hypotheses are tested by fitting production functions of the Cobb–Douglas type to Brazilian data. First, functions are estimated for major products in a number of Brazilian states – a total of eighteen 'state-product' sectors, with about 1000 farm observations from sample surveys. The purpose of these estimates is to examine returns to scale, for inputs actually used ('production-efficiency'). Second, a constrained linear homogeneous production function with dummy variables for the farm size group and for tenure type (owner versus non-owner) is estimated for a pool of nine crop sectors. The purpose of this model is to determine whether entrepreneurial ability associated with farm ownership and with a given size class of farm results in greater output than the utilized inputs alone would explain.

In the analysis of this study, the use of the Cobb–Douglas production function does not involve the major problem of that function in some applications. Nerlove[1] has pointed out that in a situation of perfect markets and profit maximization, estimation of the Cobb–Douglas function would be impossible, because all firms would have identical factor ratios. Thus, the inputs would be exactly collinear, and estimates of factor elasticities would be based wholly on error terms rather than on intended variation of factor ratios.

The problem of exact collinearity of inputs is not serious in the present study. Factor markets are so imperfect that large differences in factor ratios exist. Thus, although the use of the Cobb–Douglas production function has been questioned in the literature, its use is justifiable in this study. Furthermore, its easily interpreted degree of homogeneity makes it ideal for analysis of returns to scale.

In the analysis of this chapter, acreage cultivated, for crop sectors, or pasture land, for cattle, is the measure of the land input. But a farm efficient in these terms may be using a small part of its available land and may be inefficient from the viewpoint of the economy as a whole. The analysis of 'farm-efficiency' (or intensity of land use) in relation to the size and tenure type of the farm is made in chapter 4.

The analysis here is based on current conditions, since the data reflect current techniques; widespread adoption of new techniques might change the size–efficiency relationships. It should be noted too that the analysis of the relation of size and tenure to efficiency is conducted on an individual product basis. In agriculture, as in industry, one would expect the optimal scale of production to vary from product to product.

3.2. Data used

The data used in this chapter, and in the two following come from three

---

[1] Marc Nerlove, *Estimation and Identification of Cobb–Douglas Production Functions* (Chicago: Rand McNally, 1965). Another problem noted by Nerlove is simultaneity caused by correlation of the error term with factor inputs. If a firm has an 'error term' from the general production function, and if the deviation is due to managerial ability, and if the firm knows about its deviation, and if the firm has a target output then the firm will hire different amounts of inputs from those implied by the production function, to compensate for the 'error term'. Thus the error term will be correlated with inputs and the parameter estimates will be biased. The behavioral assumptions underlying this simultaneity problem would not seem particularly relevant to Brazilian agriculture, where, at least for the family farms, the task is to produce the maximum possible given relatively rigidly fixed amounts of land and labor.

TABLE 4

Definitions of variables in sample data

Source	Variable Name	Description	Units
FGV	L	Land input: Area cultivated, crop sectors; area in pasture, cattle sectors. Pasture plus area cultivated for one cattle/general-crops sector	Hectares
	N	Labor: Value of labor utilized in crop year. Family labor imputed at regional wage for similar labor	100 cruzeiros of crop year*
	K	Capital: Value of buildings, machinery, vehicles, and work animals, on day of visit of surveyor to farm	100 cruzeiros of survey year*
	S	Seeds, fertilizer, insecticides: annual expenditure	100 cruzeiros of crop year*
	A	Animal capital: Value of stock of non-work animals on day of visit of surveyor to farm	100 cruzeiros of survey year*
	V	Vaccines and feed: annual expenditure	100 cruzeiros of crop year*
	Q	Production: Total value of production on farm in crop year including production consumed on the farm	100 cruzeiros of crop year*
	X	Total farm area	Hectares
	XV	Total farm land value on day of visit of surveyor to farm	100 cruzeiros of survey year*
IAA**	L	Land cultivated in sugar cane	Hectares
	N	Number of man-days worked in crop year. Includes direct field labor and indirect administrative labor	Man-days
	K	Index of animal-days and machine-hours used in in crop year. Price ratio in the 1964 study used for weighting	Animal-day equivalent
	S	Index of seeds, fertilizer, and insecticides used in crop year. Relative prices of fertilizer and insecticides used to determine seed-equivalent for index	Metric tons sugar cane-equivalent
	Q	Production in crop year	Metric tons sugar cane
	X	Total farm area	Hectares
	P	Average land price per hectare of farm land	100 cruzeiros of 1963-64
IRGA***	L	Land cultivated in rice	Hectares
	N	Labor applied in crop year. Permanent worker weight = 1. Temporary worker weight = 0.125	Man-years
	K	Index of oxen, tractors, combines on farm. Based on 1964 price relationship: ox = 1, tractor = 60, combine = 100	Oxen equivalents

Table 4 continued

Source	Variable Name	Description	Units
	S	Value of seeds and fertilizer for crop year	1000 cruzeiros of 1964
	Q	Rice production in crop year	50 kg sacks unshelled rice

* 'Crop year': 1962 for sectors in Ceará, E. Santo, Pernambuco, Rio Grande do Sul; 1963 for sectors in São Paulo and Minas Gerais. 'Survey year': date of survey. 1963: Ceará, E. Santo, Pernambuco, R. G. Sul; 1964, February: São Paulo, Minas Gerais.
** *Fornecedor* or 'supplier' data: for crop year 1963-64. *Usina* or 'mill' data: for crop year 1964-65.
*** Crop year: 1963-64.

sources: two sample surveys by the Getulio Vargas Foundation, and a stratified random sample of 200 rice farms drawn by the author from the yearly census of 5000 rice farms in Rio Grande do Sul, done by the Instituto Riograndense de Arroz (IRGA). The first survey (FGV) by the Getulio Vargas Foundation was a sample of 2500 farms in seven states of Brazil, conducted in 1963. The second survey (IAA) by this foundation was a sample of sugar cane farms, carried out in combination with the Institute of Sugar and Alcohol. The survey was carried out in two parts. First, a sample of roughly 100 'suppliers' in each of five states was conducted in 1963–64. Second, about 30 sugar 'mill' farms were sampled in each of the same states in 1964–65. The latter sample included about half of the universe for sugar 'mill' farms. A description of sampling techniques used in collecting these data is given in appendix B.

The variables used in subsequent analysis are described in table 4. Table 5 shows the size distribution and total number of observations in each product sector[1] of the sample data. In table 6, the value of production of the 'universe'

---

[1] The 'product sector' presents no difficulty in the sugar survey and the rice data: in each case, the input data are only for those inputs used in sugar (rice) and the output is exclusively sugar (rice) in physical units. For the FGV data, however, output is for total value of the farm's production. Thus, a farm qualifies for inclusion in a 'product' sector if it derives more than 50% of its output value from the product in question (for some sectors the average percentage is substantially higher). Then the farm is treated as if its only product were the principal one; all inputs and all output value are assigned to the product of the sector. Due to this screening on a basis of product specialization, the data taken from the FGV survey include only some 630 farms of the total 2500 surveyed. Treatment of the whole body of data was beyond the scope of this study.

TABLE 5

Number and size distribution of farm observations in sample data of this study

Sector	Total	Sizegroup (ha total farm area)					
		<10	10–30	30–100	100–300	300–1000	>1000
		Number of farms					
FGV							
Ceará cotton	68	10	18	24	12	2	2
Pernambuco cotton	39	8	12	11	5	2	1
E. Santo coffee	64	1	16	37	9	1	0
S. Paulo coffee	64	1	16	24	11	6	6
Pernambuco sugar	31	0	1	3	8	16	3
S. Paulo cereals	77	7	23	32	9	5	1
R. G. Sul rice	30	4	4	7	7	5	3
Minas Gerais corn	29	6	5	9	6	3	0
S. Paulo cattle/gen.	37	1	3	10	18	4	1
Ceará cattle	50	2	10	13	19	5	1
E. Santo cattle	28	0	3	12	10	2	1
M. Gerais cattle	44	0	8	13	12	9	2
R. G. Sul cattle	33	4	1	6	11	7	4
S. Paulo cattle	35	1	2	13	6	5	8
IAA							
Alagoas sugar	87	0	1	10	19	34	23
Pernambuco sugar	82	3	4	4	18	30	23
S. Paulo sugar	123	5	8	12	14	39	45
IRGA*							
R. G. Sul rice	117	9	30	44	29	5	0

* IRGA data do not have farm size available. Composition here is by area of cultivated land.

of each product sector is shown as a percentage of total Brazilian agricultural production, for the year 1962. It may be seen in table 6 that the product-sectors for which this study has data represent roughly one-third of the value of all Brazilian agricultural production.

3.3. Test for returns to scale

To test for the existence of increasing or decreasing returns to scale, as discussed above in section 2.4, unconstrained Cobb–Douglas production

§3.3   TEST FOR RETURNS TO SCALE   63

TABLE 6

Percent of Brazilian agricultural production represented by product sectors of this study

Sector	Estimated production 1962 billion cruz.	Percent of Brazilian agricultural total prod.
Ceará cotton	14.1	1.06
Pernambuco cotton	5.9	0.44
E. Santo coffee	4.3	0.32
S. Paulo coffee	33.7	2.53
Pernambuco sugar cane	11.8	0.89
S. Paulo cereals (rice, corn, beans)	72.1	5.41
R. G. Sul rice	26.5	1.99
M. G. corn	27.1	2.03
Alagoas sugar cane	4.8	0.36
S. Paulo sugar cane	29.2	2.19
Ceará, cattle*	7.1	0.53
E. Santo cattle*	3.4	0.25
M. Gerais cattle*	77.7	5.82
R. G. Sul cattle*	27.2	2.04
S. Paulo cattle*	56.9	4.27
Total, sample sectors	401.8	30.13
Brazil, total		
14 major crops	947	
7 extractive products	57	
milk	194	
animal sales**	134	
Total, Brazilian agriculture	1332	

Source: Calculated from Instituto Brasileiro de Geografia e Estatística, Conselho Nacional de Economia, *Anuario Estatístico do Brasil*. 1963 (Rio de Janeiro, 1963).

* Cattle production: Milk production plus 71% of value of finished beef production. 1960 industrial census shows 71% of Food Industry production as intermediate costs. Assumed this percent represents sales of cattle for meat production, as percent of beef slaughter production value. Note: part of São Paulo beef production distributed to Rio Grande do Sul and Minas Gerais, based on size of cattle herds of the three states, since São Paulo slaughter houses process cattle from Minas Gerais and Rio Grande do Sul as well as São Paulo.
** 71% of value of animal slaughter production.

TABLE 7

Unconstrained production functions*

Sector	Intercept	Elasticities				Sum of Elast.	R. sq.	Sum of sq. resid.
		Land	Labor	Capital	SFI			
Ceará cotton	3.7399	0.4619 (0.074)	0.0326 (0.072)	0.2817 (0.061)	0.1594 (0.064)	0.9356	0.8003	18.67
Pernambuco cotton	3.5138	0.4801 (0.101)	0.1962 (0.124)	0.0495 (0.097)	0.3559 (0.089)	1.0817	0.7960	8.14
E. Santo coffee	2.8449	0.4976 (0.107)	0.2711 (0.084)	0.1419 (0.068)	0.1257 (0.062)	1.0363	0.6741	19.51
S. Paulo coffee	3.6468	0.6976 (0.122)	0.3195 (0.110)	0.0114 (0.104)	0.1680 (0.086)	1.1965	0.8712	22.69
Per. sugar FGV	5.0229	0.5770 (0.172)	0.1864 (0.151)	0.0557 (0.166)	0.0725 (0.052)	0.8916	0.8662	4.07
S. Paulo cereals	3.8090	0.2611 (0.115)	0.1927 (0.081)	0.1902 (0.094)	0.2134 (0.077)	0.8574	0.6576	32.05
R. G. rice FGV	3.9313	0.7613 (0.240)	−0.0036 (0.196)	0.4150 (0.171)	−0.0945 (0.144)	1.0800	0.9163	6.79
M. G. corn	2.5714	−0.1173 (0.248)	0.1614 (0.200)	0.3756 (0.246)	0.2952 (0.172)	0.7149	0.3524	18.66
S. Paulo cattle/gen.	2.2703	−0.1093 (0.154)	0.1095 (0.138)	0.3142 (0.162)	0.4688 (0.104)	0.7832	0.7644	7.16

§3.3 TEST FOR RETURNS TO SCALE

	Intercept					Sum of elast.	R. sq.	Sum of sq. resid.
Alagoas sugar	2.8819	0.9257 (0.092)	0.0813 (0.057)	0.0127 (0.054)	−0.0032 (0.038)	1.0166	0.9893	2.92
Per. sugar IAA	1.8145	0.5730 (0.093)	0.2641 (0.110)	0.1120 (0.051)	0.0545 (0.037)	1.0018	0.9836	4.81
S. Paulo sugar	1.4638	0.4599 (0.094)	0.6224 (0.074)	−0.0726 (0.070)	−0.0057 (0.060)	1.0040	0.9780	10.347
R. G. Rice IRGA	3.957	0.7065 (0.118)	0.0690 (0.060)	0.0688 (0.052)	0.1350 (0.073)	0.9794	0.9193	12.07

	Intercept	Pasture	Labor	Capital	Animal capital	Feed and vaccines	Sum of elast.	R. sq.	Sum of sq. resid.
Ceará cattle	1.9415	0.0415 (0.074)	0.2749 (0.080)	0.2069 (0.101)	0.0832 (0.113)	0.2778 (0.080)	0.8843	0.6764	14.59
E. Santo cattle	2.4189	0.2971 (0.119)	0.1226 (0.194)	0.1835 (0.135)	0.1562 (0.154)	0.1931 (0.108)	0.9525	0.7644	6.05
M. G. cattle	4.0284	−0.0252 (0.134)	0.2590 (0.159)	0.1720 (0.135)	0.0836 (0.129)	0.1357 (0.097)	0.6251	0.4373	23.12
R. G. Sul cattle	1.3911	−0.0688 (0.108)	−0.0135 (0.169)	0.1080 (0.152)	0.3702 (0.151)	0.4893 (0.079)	0.8852	0.8379	9.49
S. Paulo cattle	1.3431	0.3084 (0.161)	0.4398 (0.224)	−0.1427 (0.104)	0.2540 (0.211)	0.2948 (0.111)	1.1543	0.8250	14.19

* In this table and all subsequent tables showing regression results, figures in parentheses are standard errors.

functions are estimated, and the sum of elasticities is examined for each sector. The function is

$$Q = e^{\alpha} L^{\beta} N^{\gamma} K^{\delta} S^{\varepsilon}$$

or,[1]

$$\log Q = \alpha + \beta(\log L) + \gamma(\log N) + \delta(\log K) + \varepsilon(\log S)$$

where L, N, K, S, and Q are land input, labor, capital, seeds and fertilizer,

---

[1] Throughout this study 'log' refers to the natural logarithm.

With regard to the production function, it should be noted that the function estimated is not invalidated by the fact that some variables are expressed in value terms and some in physical terms. Use of value units instead of physical units merely changes the intercept, α. For example in the FGV sectors the production function is estimated with land input in physical terms and other variables in value terms. Suppose a function were desired wholly in physical terms. Instead of

$$Q = e^{\alpha} L^{\beta} N^{\gamma} K^{\delta} S^{\varepsilon}$$

it would be desired to find

$$q = e^{\tilde{\alpha}} L^{\tilde{\beta}} n^{\tilde{\gamma}} k^{\tilde{\delta}} s^{\tilde{\varepsilon}}$$

where, for the purpose of this exposition, the small letter denotes physical units of the corresponding term in value units. Then the coefficients $\tilde{\beta}, \tilde{\gamma}, \tilde{\delta}, \tilde{\varepsilon}$ would be identical to $\beta, \gamma, \delta, \varepsilon$. Only α would differ from $\tilde{\alpha}$. This would be true if identical prices faced all farms, such that $N = p_n n$, $K = p_k k$, $S = p_s s$, and $Q = p_q q$ where the subscripted p is the price per unit of the relevant variable.

Then

$$p_q q = e^{\alpha} L^{\beta} (p_n n)^{\gamma} (p_k k)^{\delta} (p_s s)^{\varepsilon}$$

and

$$q = e^{\alpha} p_n^{\gamma} p_k^{\delta} p_s^{\varepsilon} p_q^{-1} L^{\beta} n^{\gamma} k^{\delta} s^{\varepsilon}$$

But this would be the production function in physical terms. Therefore,

$$\tilde{\alpha} = \alpha + \gamma(\log p_n) + \delta(\log p_k) + \varepsilon(\log p_s) - \log p_q$$

and $\tilde{\beta} = \beta$, $\tilde{\gamma} = \gamma$, $\tilde{\delta} = \delta$, and $\tilde{\varepsilon} = \varepsilon$ which was to be shown. Note that in the estimates here, the land input is in physical units and presents no problem. Labor is in value units. Since the labor value is imputed at regional wage levels for family labor, the accounting price of labor is the same across farms, and the production function has a valid labor elasticity as just described.

By similar reasoning the elasticity of capital is not affected by the use of capital stock as the input instead of capital services, if it is assumed that capital services are a fixed percentage of capital stock. Finally the same reasoning makes it permissible to use capital data which were obtained for a period subsequent to data for other variables, in the FGV survey, even though serious inflation had occurred in the interim. That is, deflation of the capital data would affect the intercept but not the capital elasticity.

§3.3 TEST FOR RETURNS TO SCALE

and production, as described in table 4. For cattle sectors, the production function is

$$Q = e^{\alpha} L^{\beta} N^{\gamma} K^{\delta} A^{\varepsilon} V^{\eta}$$

where A is animal capital, V is vaccines and feed, L is pasture, and the other variables are as before.

The results[1] of the test are shown in table 7. All sectors show close to constant returns to scale. In eight of the 18 sectors, the sum of elasticities is slightly greater than one. In the rest, the sum of elasticities is slightly below one.

The hypothesis that the elasticity sums are significantly different from one is examined next. Cobb–Douglas production functions are estimated with the sum of elasticities constrained to equal one. The function becomes:

$$Q = e^{\alpha} L^{\beta} N^{\gamma} K^{\delta} S^{\varepsilon}$$

where

thus,

$$\beta + \gamma + \delta + \varepsilon = 1;$$

$$\log Q = \alpha + (1 - \gamma - \delta - \varepsilon)(\log L) + \gamma(\log N) + \delta(\log K) + \varepsilon(\log S).$$

Thus,

$$\log Q - \log L = \alpha + \gamma(\log N - \log L) + \delta(\log K - \log L) + \varepsilon(\log S - \log L).$$

It is the final equation that is estimated. The land elasticity, β, is derived as

$$\hat{\beta} = 1 - \hat{\gamma} - \hat{\delta} - \hat{\varepsilon}.$$

Analysis of covariance[2] is then used to determine whether the unconstrained model, which adds one parameter, significantly increases explanation over

---

[1] For purposes of estimation, it is assumed that error terms have a log-normal distribution.
[2] Throughout the statistical sections, 'analysis of covariance' refers to the standard test by that name. To test whether an additional w parameters increase total explanation sufficiently to be significantly different from zero, the ratio

$$\frac{SS_A - SS_B}{w} \bigg/ \frac{SS_B}{n - w - z}$$

is calculated where SS refers to the sum of squared residuals ('unexplained variation'), A refers to the model with fewer parameters, B to the model with w more parameters than model A, z is the number of parameters in model A, and n is the number of observations. The ratio has an F distribution with $(w, n - w - z)$ degrees of freedom in the numerator and denominator, respectively. If the ratio calculated is greater than the appropriate critical value, the additional w parameters contribute 'significantly' to explanation.

TABLE 8
Constrained production functions

Sector	Intercept	Elasticities Land	Labor	Capital	SFI	Sum of sq. resid.	F_1	F_2
Ceará cotton	3.3241	0.4797	0.0664 (0.062)	0.2931 (0.060)	0.1608 (0.064)	18.94	0.923	3.98
Pernambuco cotton	3.9394	0.4564	0.1568 (0.114)	0.0468 (0.096)	0.3400 (0.086)	8.31	0.693	4.09
E. Santo coffee	3.0181	0.4774	0.2565 (0.074)	0.1420 (0.068)	0.1241 (0.061)	19.56	0.146	3.99
S. Paulo coffee	4.9323	0.5605	0.1652 (0.089)	−0.0042 (0.107)	0.2785 (0.073)	24.61	5.002	3.99
Per. sugar FGV	4.2266	0.6611	0.1745 (0.153)	0.1203 (0.161)	0.0441 (0.049)	4.35	1.827	4.16
S. Paulo cereals	2.9520	0.3333	0.2660 (0.069)	0.2039 (0.095)	0.1968 (0.077)	33.26	2.718	3.96
R. G. rice FGV	4.2851	0.7107	−0.1093 (0.152)	0.4656 (0.160)	−0.0670 (0.139)	7.00	0.747	4.17
M. G. corn	0.2012	−0.0850	0.3068 (0.150)	0.5098 (0.213)	0.2684 (0.171)	19.59	1.19	4.18
S. Paulo cattle/gen.	0.8007	−0.0227	0.3018 (0.105)	0.2617 (0.167)	0.4592 (0.109)	8.90	4.13	4.11

§3.3 TEST FOR RETURNS TO SCALE 69

			Labor	Capital	Animal capital	Feed and vaccines	Sum of sq. resid.	F_1	F_2
Alagoas sugar	2.8438	0.8573	0.0899 (0.057)	0.0456 (0.043)	0.0072 (0.037)		2.96	1.067	3.96
Per. sugar IAA	1.8184	0.5709	0.2622 (0.110)	0.1120 (0.049)	0.0549 (0.036)		4.81	0.005	3.96
S. Paulo sugar	1.4784	0.4504	0.6233 (0.074)	−0.0735 (0.070)	−0.0002 (0.056)		10.353	0.007	3.92
R. G. rice IRGA	3.9497	0.7231	0.0813 (0.057)	0.0722 (0.051)	0.1235 (0.070)		12.12	0.398	3.93

		Pasture	Labor	Capital	Animal capital	Feed and vaccines	Sum of sq. resid.	F_1	F_2
Ceará cattle	0.9428	0.0361	0.3269 (0.067)	0.2095 (0.102)	0.1310 (0.106)	0.2965 (0.079)	15.05	1.414	4.03
E. Santo cattle	2.0327	0.3014	0.1638 (0.141)	0.1809 (0.132)	0.1612 (0.150)	0.1927 (0.106)	6.08	0.103	4.20
M. G. cattle	0.6424	0.0054	0.4636 (0.159)	0.3196 (0.139)	0.0805 (0.142)	0.1309 (0.107)	29.79	11.26	4.06
R. G. Sul cattle	0.4688	−0.0822	0.1059 (0.138)	0.0761 (0.150)	0.3880 (0.151)	0.5122 (0.077)	9.98	1.48	4.14
S. Paulo cattle	2.5691	0.2894	0.2430 (0.142)	−0.1097 (0.100)	0.2933 (0.209)	0.2840 (0.112)	14.82	1.33	4.12

TABLE 9

Functions over the world

Location of sample	Product	Elasticity of production			Sum of elasticities
		Land services	Labor services	Other services	
United States, northern Iowa	Corn	0.91	0.08	0.16	1.15
Japan, Honshu	Sweet potatoes	0.85	0.29	0.00	1.14
United States, southern Iowa	Corn	0.79	0.09	0.39	1.27
Japan, Hokkaido	Rice	0.75	0.18	0.07	1.00
India, Andhra Pradesh	Irrigated farms	0.57	0.14	−0.08	0.63
Japan, Honshu	Rice	0.56	0.29	0.15	1.00
United States, Montana	Wheat	0.50	0.04	0.58	1.12
India, Uttar Pradesh	Wheat	0.50	−0.26	0.69	0.93
Norway, southeast	Cereals	0.47	0.04	0.28	0.79
Taiwan, Tainan	Cereals	0.44	0.33	0.31	1.08
New Zealand, Canterbury	Sheep	0.42	0.15	0.54	1.11
United States, Alabama	Crops	0.39	0.32	0.46	1.17
South Australia	Dairy	0.39	0.25	0.54	1.19
Canada, Alberta	Wheat, beef	0.39	0.20	0.34	0.93
India, Uttar Pradesh	Sugar cane	0.37	0.69	0.03	1.09
Taiwan, Tainan	Sugar cane	0.36	0.25	0.34	0.95
Sweden	Mixed farms	0.35	0.05	0.57	0.97

§3.3 TEST FOR RETURNS TO SCALE

Location	Type			
India, Andhra Pradesh	Dry farms	0.31	0.04	0.07	0.42
Japan, Honshu	Tea	0.29	0.30	0.46	1.05
United States, Iowa–Illinois	Crop-share	0.29	0.25	0.48	1.02
Australia, New South Wales	Dairy	0.28	0.22	0.42	0.92
South Africa, Kalihari	Cattle fattening	0.28	0.13	0.55	0.96
India, Uttar Pradesh	Wheat, sugar cane	0.23	0.43	0.35	1.01
Norway, southeast	Fodder	0.23	0.32	0.57	1.12
United States, Iowa–Illinois	Livestock-share	0.23	0.18	0.53	0.95
Canada, Alberta	Cattle ranches	0.20	0.37	0.39	0.97
South Africa, Kalihari	Cow-calf ranches	0.19	0.19	0.52	0.90
India, Andhra Pradesh	Mixed farms	0.14	0.26	0.13	0.53
Austria	Mixed farming	0.13	0.26	0.61	1.00
Australia, New South Wales	Sheep	0.10	0.59	0.55	1.24
United States, Iowa–Illinois	Owners	0.09	0.17	0.73	0.99
Israel	Mixed farms	0.03	0.25	0.80	1.08
Norway, southeast	Beef cattle		0.42	0.79	1.21
United Kingdom, England	Dairy		0.29	0.83	1.12
Western Australia	Dairy		0.23	0.76	0.99
United States, Alabama	Livestock		0.23	0.74	0.97
Norway, southeast	Dairy		0.18	0.80	0.98
United States, southern Iowa	Hogs, cattle		0.12	0.98	1.10
United States, Montana	Cattle		0.08	0.94	1.02
United States, northern Iowa	Hogs, cattle		0.08	0.91	0.99
Sweden	Dairy		−0.05	1.23	1.18

Source: E. O. Heady and John L. Dillon, *Agricultural Production Functions* (Ames, Iowa: Iowa State University Press, 1961), p. 630.

that of the constrained model. That is, the coefficients estimated in the constrained model are used to predict the logarithm of output. Predicted 'log output' is substracted from observed 'log output', this vector of deviations is then squared, and the squared deviations are then summed. The sum of squared residuals is compared with the corresponding sum of squared residuals for the unconstrained model.

Table 8 shows the results of the 'constrained' production functions. In table 8, the column 'F_1' is the F value determined in the analysis of covariance of the constrained model in comparison with the unconstrained model. 'F_2' is the critical F value necessary to accept the hypothesis that the sum $\beta+\gamma+\delta+\varepsilon$ differs significantly from one at the 5% level. Only three sectors show a sum of elasticities significantly different from one.[1] São Paulo coffee shows increasing returns to scale, while São Paulo cattle/general and Minas Gerais cattle show decreasing returns to scale.[2]

The general result of the production function estimates, thus, is that returns to scale are constant. It should be mentioned that in seven of the eighteen sectors, one or more coefficients are negative. However, no negative coefficient is significant at the 5% level. A negative coefficient would be rejected on *a priori* grounds. For the purpose of evaluating 'returns to scale', a negative coefficient is not troublesome; it is included algebraically in the elasticity sum. However, in subsequent use of the production functions, in chapter 5, negative coefficients present a problem in that they cause a negative response of production to inputs. This problem is discussed in chapter 5.

It is informative to compare these production functions estimated for Brazil against functions estimated for other countries. Table 9 taken from Heady and Dillon, summarizes estimates for various products and countries.

Concerning returns to scale the striking information in Table 9 is the con-

---

[1] It would not be highly likely that for three out of eighteen sectors the hypothesis that returns to scale are constant would be rejected incorrectly, at the 5% level. The probability of this occurrence would be

$$\frac{18!}{15!\,3!}(0.95)^{15}(0.05)^3 = 0.047.$$

[2] It is important to note that higher land quality on larger farms may account for the increasing returns to scale estimated for São Paulo coffee. This fact may be seen in a comparison of table 14 with table 15 (chapter 4). A comparison of these two tables also shows that decreasing returns to scale in São Paulo cattle/general and in Minas Gerais cattle may be due to declining land quality as farm size rises.

sistent finding of constant returns to scale, that is, the elasticities consistently sum to one. This finding coincides with the results presented here for Brazilian agriculture.

A second comparison of the findings here with those shown by Heady and Dillon may be made for production elasticities of individual factors. For the land factor, it may be seen that in both the production functions here and those shown by Heady and Dillon, land has a low production elasticity in cattle production. Several of the world functions for livestock do not even include land as a factor, supposedly because production is on a feed-lot basis, and land is not a relevant factor. In the case of Brazil, as in the case of several other countries, there is probably a shift from intensive grazing to extensive grazing as the pasture area increases. Such a shift would explain the low or negative land elasticities.

For crops, the land elasticities reported by Heady and Dillon lie in a range similar to the elasticities estimated here for Brazil.

The labor elasticities we have estimated are also similar to those reported by Heady and Dillon: the large majority of functions estimated in both cases show a labor elasticity of 0.3 or less. Capital, excluding livestock, shows low elasticities in our functions. The Heady and Dillon functions show rather higher capital elasticities. Capital is included in 'other services' in table 9, but is shown separately in some instances in Heady and Dillon.[1] In most cases where capital has a high elasticity, in the present study, it is animal capital assets. This fact may be seen in the functions for cattle production. However, the functions estimated here show relatively high elasticities for technical inputs (fertilizer, seeds, insecticides, animal feeds, and vaccines) and these inputs are apparently included in 'capital services' in the Heady and Dillon functions. Thus, when the capital elasticity is added to the 'technical inputs' elasticity, the functions of this study show results similar to those given by Heady and Dillon.

However, the most important point is that the returns to scale seem to be constant in most agricultural production functions estimated for other countries. This finding is consistent with the results of this study for Brazil.

---

[1] For example, 'capital services' have the following elasticities: Canada, mixed farms: 0.34; Australia, agriculture: 0.61; Sweden diversified farms: machinery services: 0.11, building services: 0.05; Norway: dairy farms, crops: machinery services: 0.18, other capital services: 0.39; India: Uttar Pradesh farms: 0.18; sugar cane: 0.30; irrigated wheat: 0.53; Andhra Pradesh: dry farms: 0.07.

It may be noted also that in table 9, functions for the United States show slightly increasing returns, while functions for India show decreasing returns to scale. The average degree of homogeneity for the six United States crop sectors listed in table 9 is 1.12, while the average degree of homogeneity for the six Indian crop sectors listed is only 0.77. This distinction between the U.S. and India is consistent with the notion expressed in chapter 2, that increasing returns to scale are more likely to occur in the advanced economy than in the less developed country, because of the relative cheapness of capital and therefore the importance of machine indivisibilities in agriculture in the advanced economy.

3.4. Test for effects of total farm size and ownership status

The results of the test in section 3.3 are that returns to scale are constant. However, there are questions which the simple Cobb–Douglas function may not answer. First, are there ranges of scale over which returns are not constant, even though the overall returns are constant?[1] Second, does entrepreneurial skill vary in any consistent way, such that certain types of farms achieve greater output than that explained by the production function?

The test in this section attempts to examine these two questions. Farm size, in the sense of total area, and tenure type, are incorporated into the production function. Farm size represents two considerations: 'range of scale' and 'entrepreneurial type'.[2] To be sure, farm size is not a direct measure of production scale. It is shown in the next chapter that as farm size increases, the scale of production relative to farm size declines. Nevertheless, there is a close and positive relationship between farm size and scale, whether scale is measured by product or by inputs. With regard to scale, the test investigates for a departure in intermediate farm sizes from overall constant returns to scale. Any strictly increasing or strictly decreasing effect of farm size would not be expected, since this finding would contradict the constant returns already established.

Farm size represents entrepreneurial type. The small farmer is an entrepreneur as well as the main worker on the farm. The large farmer hires his help. One could expect the small farmer to produce more efficiently, in

---

[1] Nerlove found that in the electricity industry, returns to scale were increasing but at varying rates over different scale ranges. Nerlove, *op. cit.* chapter 6.
[2] See section 2.3 for the relevant theoretical discussion for this model.

§3.4   TEST FOR EFFECTS OF FARM SIZE AND OWNERSHIP STATUS

terms of output for given inputs, than the large farmer, because the 'worker' on the small farm has a more direct interest in the outcome of the farm. On the other hand, one might expect the large farmer to be the better entrepreneur because of better education. Finally, to the extent that the large farmer holds land for reasons other than production, one would expect him to be inefficient in the production activity which he does undertake just as he is inefficient in maintaining a small production activity relative to available land.

In sum, 'farm size' as a variable represents entrepreneurial skill, or interest and range of scale.[1] Tenure type also represents entrepreneurial motivation; one would expect the owner to be superior to the renter or sharecropper since the renter has less incentive to make long term investments and the sharecropper has incorrect 'signals' in that he equates only his share of marginal product with the marginal cost of inputs.[2]

The model is as follows:

$$\log Q = \alpha + \beta(\log L) + \gamma(\log N) + \delta(\log K) + \varepsilon(\log S) + \\ + Z_1 X_1 + Z_2 X_2 + Z_3 X_3 + Z_4 X_4 + Z_5 X_5 + tT.$$

The first five right-hand terms are the same as in the functions already fitted; the sixth through the tenth are size dummy variables. ($X_1 = 1$ for size < 10 ha, $= 0$ otherwise; with size groups $X_1 < 10$ ha; X_2: 10–30 ha; X_3: 30–100 ha; X_4: 100–300 ha; X_5: 300–1000 ha; excluded: > 1000 ha). The final term is a tenure dummy variable: $T = 1$ for owner, $= 0$ for non-owner.

Since the previous test established constant returns to scale, this model is estimated[3] with the constraint of constant returns to scale: $\beta + \gamma + \delta + \varepsilon = 1$. Thus, model 2 is estimated as:

$$\log Q - \log L = \alpha + \gamma(\log N - \log L) + \delta(\log K - \log L) + \varepsilon(\log S - \log L) + \\ + Z_1 X_1 + Z_2 X_2 + Z_3 X_3 + Z_4 X_4 + Z_5 X_5 + tT$$

---

[1] It should be noted that in the case of strictly rising 'size' coefficients, a difficulty of interpretation would occur. The simple interpretation would be that larger farmers are superior entrepreneurs. However, such a result could also represent the fact that a lower percentage cultivation of land on larger farms permits the use of higher quality land.

[2] In contrast, it is possible that the tenant is under greater pressure to produce than the owner, if the tenant has high rental payments to meet, and that the tenant therefore makes a greater effort and achieves higher production efficiency than the owner.

[3] An earlier version with this model unconstrained found the 'size' dummy variables showed strictly increasing efficiency as size rose but the sum of factor elasticities was depressed. Thus, it was unclear whether the size dummy variables represented increasing efficiency with farm size, or merely represented the influence of rising inputs due to misspecification of the model.

and the original equation is found by assuming that

$$\hat{\beta} = 1 - \hat{\gamma} - \hat{\delta} - \hat{\varepsilon}$$

This function is fitted to nine crop sectors jointly. That is, the function is estimated only once and is applied to the set of all observations from the nine sectors. There is no *a priori* reason to expect that the entrepreneurial effects of farm size and tenure should differ among sectors. If any difference existed

TABLE 10

Constrained production functions with size-group and tenure dummy variables. Nine crop sectors, pooled model

Sector	Intercept	Land	Labor	Capital	S and F
Ceará cotton (base)	3.4009	0.4756	0.0692 (0.055)	0.2938 (0.052)	0.1614 (0.056)
Per. cotton	+0.63 = 4.03 (0.65)	0.4512	+0.09 = 0.163 (0.12)	−0.25 = 0.040 (0.11)	+0.18 = 0.346 (0.10)
E. Santo coffee	−0.27 = 3.14 (0.50)	0.4802	+0.19 = 0.258 (0.08)	−0.15 = 0.141 (0.08)	−0.04 = 0.121 (0.08)
S. Paulo coffee	+1.63 = 5.03 (0.58)	0.5593	+0.11 = 0.182 (0.09)	−0.30 = 0.009 (0.10)	+0.099 = 0.61 (0.08)
Alagoas sugar	−0.38 = 3.02 (0.69)	0.9311	+0.02 = 0.086 (0.15)	−0.30 = 0.011 (0.12)	−0.17 = 0.006 (0.11)
Per. sugar IAA	−1.57 = 1.83 (0.91)	0.5799	+0.21 = 0.281 (0.22)	−0.21 = 0.087 (0.11)	−0.11 = 0.053 (0.09)
S. Paulo sugar	−2.34 = 1.06 (0.57)	0.4056	+0.64 = 0.709 (0.13)	−0.27 = 0.021 (0.11)	−0.29 = 0.136 (0.09)
Per. sugar FGV	+0.75 = 4.15 (1.24)	0.6492	+0.09 = 0.160 (0.19)	−0.14 = 0.155 (0.20)	−0.13 = 0.035 (0.08)
S. Paulo cereals	−0.36 = 3.04 (0.54)	0.3308	+0.20 = 0.271 (0.07)	−0.93 = 0.201 (0.09)	+0.36 = 0.197 (0.08)

Dummy variables						R^2
<10 ha	10–30	30–100	100–300	300–1000	Owner	
−0.08574 (0.103)	−0.1317 (0.086)	−0.1343 (0.78)	−0.08354 (0.74)	−0.01333 (0.052)	0.01486 (0.052)	0.9056

§3.4   TEST FOR EFFECTS OF FARM SIZE AND OWNERSHIP STATUS

among products, one would expect the divergence to be between cattle ranches and crop farms, since the cattle ranches are more likely to be owned by non-maximizing landlords than are crop farms.[1]

Different intercepts and factor elasticities were applied to the nine different sectors by using the first sector as a base and then using additive dummy variables for intercept and elasticities, for each sector. The 'size' and tenure variables were applied across all nine sectors jointly. Different intercepts among sectors were necessary because of differing units among the sectors as detailed in the data description above. The results are shown in table 10. The size-group dummy variables are not significant at the 5% level, nor is the tenure variable. The conclusions would be, therefore:

1. There are no intermediate scale ranges for which production deviates from that implied by constant returns to scale.
2. Entrepreneurial skill, in terms of production obtained from inputs actually used, does not appear to vary with farm size. No additional output unexplained by the factor inputs occurs either on small farms, intermediate, or large farms.
3. Owners do not appear more 'efficient' than non-owners.
4. Factor elasticities, with the exception of capital, vary significantly among sectors.[2]

The results of the simple functions of section 3.3 are therefore accepted as the basis for further analysis of the effect of land reform on production.[3]

---

[1] That is, crop production requires investments in labor and seeds whereas extensive cattle grazing is an activity that is more self-generating, and involves less labor and entrepreneurial attention than crop production.

[2] This conclusion is based on analysis of covariance conducted on results of the earlier version of the model of this section, in which the elasticities were not constrained to sum to 1. The test for difference among sectoral intercepts showed $F = 3.10$ with the critical F at the 5% level $F^* = 1.95$. For land: $F = 2.22$, $F^* = 1.95$. Labor: $F = 3.83$, $F^* = 1.95$. Capital: $F = 1.83$, $F^* = 1.95$. Seeds, fertilizer, and insecticides: $F = 3.49$, $F^* = 1.95$.

[3] In an earlier version, analysis was conducted for a possible simultaneous equations problem. Farm size and inputs are used here as exogenous variables. In chapter 4, however, it is shown that the intensity of input use with regard to farm size declines as farm size rises. In the model of this section $Q = f$ (inputs, size, tenure) $+ U$ while in chapter 4, inputs $= g$ (size, tenure) $+ V$. The problem is the probable correlation of residuals U and V, and therefore the interdependence of inputs and size in the model of this section. Residuals U and V are expected to be correlated because a farmer who uses higher inputs than would be expected for his farm size, would be an abnormally good entrepreneur and would probably have higher production per inputs used than the normal production function would predict. To account for this simultaneity, the land input in the model here was

For simulation of production change, in chapter 5, the constrained Cobb–Douglas functions are used, except for the three sectors which show the sum of elasticities varying significantly from 1.

3.5. Conclusion

The conclusions of this chapter are:

1. Returns to scale are generally constant in Brazilian agriculture. Analysis of covariance shows that the degree of homogeneity of Cobb–Douglas type production functions is not significantly different from unity (at the 5% level) for fifteen out of eighteen state-product sectors. Only one sector (São Paulo coffee) shows increasing returns to scale, and two cattle sectors show decreasing returns. Even these three exceptions may be due to changing land quality as farm size rises. The policy implication of constant returns to scale is that the unit created by land reform could be the 'family farm' without loss of efficiency.

2. Tenure type does not seem to affect 'production efficiency', since a dummy variable for 'owners' versus 'non-owner operators', included in a revised production function, is not statistically significant. Furthermore, no statistically significant departure from constant returns to scale occurs for any specific farm size class. This fact indicates that, in terms of output obtained from inputs utilized, entrepreneurial ability does not differ across farm size classes.

---

replaced by 'estimated land' from the regression of land input on farm size, tenure, and land price.

In the final version of the model used in 3.4, no attempt has been made to account for the simultaneity described since the model has no greater explanatory power than the simple Cobb–Douglas functions and thus is not to be used in the simulation estimates of chapter 5.

CHAPTER 4

LAND USE INTENSITY, FARM SIZE AND TENURE

4.1. Introduction

4.1.1. Purpose and contents

The purpose of this chapter is to test hypotheses about land utilization. Four sets of tests are made. First, there are tests of the general hypothesis raised in chapter 2, that available land is used more intensively on small farms than on large, and that land quality alone does not explain the difference in land use. Three formal statistical models are used for this test. First, the percent of potentially productive farm area cultivated or grazed at normal density is regressed against the logarithm of farm size. Second, value added (output minus seeds and fertilizer expenses) per farm area is regressed against the logarithm of farm size, and against land price (to account for land quality). Third, the logarithm of the input is regressed against the logarithm of farm size, for each of the four inputs (land cultivated, labor, capital, seeds and fertilizer expenses). These regressions show whether or not inputs increase more slowly than farm size, as hypothesized. In the first two tests, a dummy variable is included for tenure to test the hypothesis that owners use their land more intensively than tenant operators.

Second, this chapter informally tests the views often stated in Brazil that (a) large farms classed as plantations are 'efficient' in land use, while large farms classed as *latifúndios* are not; (b) poor use of land by large farms is only a problem in Brazil's Northeast; (c) poor use of land by large farms is only a problem in cattle ranches, not in crop farms.

Third, this chapter includes informal tests to determine which of the alternative explanations of land use patterns are most important: 'labor market dualism', 'speculative land-holding', 'land market imperfection', 'own consumption on small farms', 'monopsony behavior by large farmers', or 'non-economic behavior by large landowners'.

Fourth, this chapter examines factor ratio trends for implications about the relation of 'social efficiency' to farm size.

4.1.2. General

The previous chapter examined 'production-efficiency' in relation to farm size and tenure. Production was compared against inputs utilized and returns to scale were analysed. The land input was not total farm area, but cultivated area for crop farms and pasture land for cattle ranches. This chapter analyses the relationship of the utilization of available land resources to farm size and tenure. This utilization may be called 'farm-efficiency' since it refers to the contribution of the farm as a whole to the economy, as compared with the farm's available land resources.

The topic of chapter 3 is relevant for land reform because the government should know the optimal size of new economic operations to be installed. This relates to the important question of whether small scale family units are inefficient. The topic of the present chapter is relevant to land reform because the existence of unused land in large farms means that land reform could bring idle land into use by fragmentation and redistribution of these farms. A one-time gain could be made for the economy through reallocation of labor crowded on small farms and of landless, underemployed labor, onto land held idle (or used non-intensively) in large farms.

4.2. Aggregate data

Before the tests of sample data are presented, an informal examination of census data is useful. A general decline in the percent of farm area under cultivation occurs as farm size rises, as is shown in table 35, appendix C. Conversely, the percent of area in natural pasture rises. If cultivated land, planted pasture, and planted forest, are considered 'high intensity' land use, and natural pasture is considered 'medium intensity', and fallow and forest land considered 'low intensity', then table 35 shows that intensity of land use declines as farm size increases. The one apparent anomaly in this tendency is the larger percent of 'fallow' land found on small farms. The reason is probably that crop rotation requires some fallow land, such that a higher percent of area in crops will require a higher percent in fallow as well.

4.3. Hypothesis tests

4.3.1. Model IV.1

In the first formal test of sample data, the ratio of area 'used' to potentially productive farm area is related to farm size and tenure. The area 'used' con-

§4.3   HYPOTHESIS TESTS   81

sists of cultivated land plus pasture grazed at normal rates. The farm area in the denominator of the ratio excludes 'unproductive area' declared by the farmer interviewed. Since only 'productive' area is considered, land quality is at least partially standardized in the test.

The analysis is done on an individual product-sector basis, which has two advantages over analysis of all farms taken together. First, the 'product mix' is held constant so that an apparent difference in intensity of land use between farms is not due to different proportions of crop and cattle production, i.e. of cultivated land and pasture. In contrast, it is impossible to tell from aggregate census data whether the decline in the percent of land cultivated, as farm size rises, indicates declining 'land use intensity' or merely a shift from crop production to cattle production.

A second advantage of analysis by individual product sectors is that it minimizes the distortion in the 'land use' index itself. This index implicitly equates cultivated area with 'pasture area grazed at normal rates', since both are considered to be area 'used'. This equivalence is questionable, since the 'intensity' of land use is probably higher for 'cultivated area' than for 'pasture grazed at normal rates'. But since the composition of output by product is held more or less constant within the 'product sector', there should be no dramatic shift from cultivated area to pasture as farm size rises[1], in contrast to the prevalence of this shift in aggregate data. Therefore, the error introduced into the land use intensity index by equation of cultivated area with normally grazed area should not seriously distort comparison of land use of large versus small farms, within a product sector.

The first model examines the following index of land use:

$$U = \frac{C + \text{Min}\left[P, \frac{\text{A.U.}}{a}\right]}{S - N}$$

where

Min = 'the minimum of'
C = cultivated area (ha);
P = area declared in pasture (ha);

---

[1] However, some shift does occur from cultivated area to pasture area even within product sectors (see below, table 12).

A.U.= animal units[1] on the farm;
a = average animal units per hectare pasture land, for the sector (each farm weighted equally despite size);
S = total farm size, hectares;
N = non-productive area.

Therefore, *U* is the percent of potentially productive land which is used in cultivation or in grazing at normal rates. The second expression in the numerator is used to account for the fact that some farms may declare large areas in pasture but graze very little of the pasture area: in such a case the farm is given credit for pasture 'use' on a basis of how many head of livestock the pasture maintains.

This index of 'use' is related (by regression) to farm size and to tenure (owner versus non-owner). The 'use' index is arbitrary but nevertheless meaningful. It excludes land in forest or land lying fallow; yet this is appropriate since the index is not intended to mean that only *U* percent of the farm's land is 'used' but that land cultivated or grazed at average grazing rates is more intensively used than land lying idle or in forests.[2]

The present model does not discriminate among the seven causes of declining intensity of land-use as farm size rises, described in section 2.4. Only 'land quality' is indirectly separated from the other influences, since the denominator of the index *U* represents farm area net of unusable land. The other six influences – labor market dualism, speculative landholding, land market imperfections, monopsony, the own-consumption market, and non-economic behavior – are not distinguished in this test. The general hypothesis is tested that some or all of these influences work together to cause a fall in the intensity of land use as farm size rises.

---

[1] Equivalents for forage requirements. Adult cows, bulls = 1.1; calf = 0.6; sheep = 0.2; lamb = 0.1; goat = 0.17; kid = 0.14; horse or mule = 1.1. Based on 'animal units' given in Donald L. Huss, *A Glossary of Terms Used in Range Management* (Portland; American Society of Range Management, 1964).

[2] In none of our sectors is lumbering the principal activity, so there is no great danger of excluding forest where it should be included as an economic operation. To be sure, uncut forests are a capital asset and their growth constitutes economic activity but again our analysis makes the assumption that such activity is less intensive use of land than is cultivation or grazing.

§4.3   HYPOTHESIS TESTS   83

The regression forms[1] used for model IV.1 were the following:

(1) $U = A + b(\log S) + c(\log S)^2 + d(D)$
(2) $U = A + b(\log S) + c(\log S)^2$
(3) $U = A + b(\log S) \qquad\qquad + d(D)$
(4) $U = A + b(\log S)$
(5) $U = A + b(S)$

where S = farm size (ha), and D = a dummy variable = 1 for owner, = 0 for non-owner. The 'best run', based on multiple R-square, F ratio, and coefficient significance, is selected for each sector.

The exact forms for regression are chosen because they permit a gradual fall in percent of farm area used as farm size rises. The logarithm of size is used since it permits a decline in the rate at which percent of area utilized falls as absolute farm size rises. The second degree of 'log size' permits an even faster deceleration of this fall.

Some of the causes of declining land use intensity would perhaps give a different specification from these forms. The 'labor-market dualism' and 'own consumption market' causes would give a two-step pattern of land use intensity – one high level for 'family farms', a decrease, and then one low but constant level for all 'hired-labor' or 'capitalist' farms. Other influences – speculative land holding, land market imperfection – would cause a gradual fall in percentage land use, for which the specification here would be appropriate.

---

[1]
$$U = \frac{C + \mathrm{Min}\left[P, \dfrac{A.U.}{a}\right]}{S-N}$$

as defined above. 'n.a.' means 'not applicable' for the best regression run. The a coefficients, average number of animal units per hectare of pasture (each farm weighted equally, one or two extremes eliminated in each sector) were: Espírito Santo = 1.111; Minas Gerais = 0.8681; Pernambuco: cotton (arid zone) = 0.577, sugar cane (humid zone) = 2.66; Rio Grande do Sul = 1.145; São Paulo = 1.296. For Ceará the a was based not on pasture land but on all land other than that cultivated or non-productive. This is because livestock are often loosed in 'caatinga', a type of brush forage, not strictly 'pasture'. The result is that for roughly half of Ceará observations the U index is 1.0; that is, 100% of the area is under cultivation or else grazing at normal rates. For Ceará, $a = 0.5497$.

The data for hypotheses tested in model IV.1 are from the Getulio Vargas Foundation sample survey of 1963. Only this source, of the three data sources used in chapter 3, had detailed land-use information and data on livestock maintained of the farm.

TABLE 11

Land use intensity as a function of farm size and tenure

Sector	Nr. of observ's.	Best run	U mean	A	b	c	d	R^2
Ceará cattle	58	4)	0.8273	1.292	−0.105 (0.020)	n.a.	n.a.	0.3200
Ceará cotton	74	3)	0.8527	0.8905	−0.473 (0.0159)	n.a.	0.1642 (0.060)	0.2250
Espírito Santo coffee	78	1)	0.537	1.485	−0.31781 (0.1372)	0.02954 (0.0161)	−0.1908 (0.133)	0.1227
Espírito Santo cattle	37	5)	0.674	0.739	−0.000382 (0.00017)	n.a.	n.a.	0.1195
Minas Gerais corn	36	4)	0.615	1.1307	−0.14306 (0.022)	n.a.	n.a.	0.5510
Minas Gerais cattle	75	4)	0.612	1.119	−0.1100 (0.020)	n.a.	n.a.	0.3004
Pernambuco cotton	44	1)	0.529	1.112	−0.37251 (0.096)	0.03162 (0.013)	0.27749 (0.108)	0.4851
Pernambuco sugar cane	32	3)	0.627	1.103	−0.09210 (0.025)	n.a.	0.11891 (0.069)	0.3878
Rio Grande do Sul rice	28	4)	0.729	1.012	−0.06824 (0.021)	n.a.	n.a.	0.3158
Rio Grande do Sul cattle	35	4)	0.573	0.857	−0.06146 (0.021	n.a.	n.a.	0.2038
São Paulo coffee	65	4)	0.739	1.034	−0.06626 (0.017)	n.a.	n.a.	0.1909
São Paulo cereals	84	4)	0.685	1.129	−0.11535 (0.024)	n.a.	n.a.	0.2242
São Paulo cattle and cattle/general	80	3)	0.647	1.140	−0.08309 (0.016)	n.a.	−0.10360 (0.062)	0.2591

Since at this point the empirical test refers to the general hypothesis that some influences cause a falling percent of land used as farm size rises, the forms specified above are adequate. More detailed examination for different patterns in falling land use intensity, corresponding to different hypothesized causes, is given below in section 4.4.

The results of model IV.1 tests (shown in table 11) are that land-use intensity declines as farm size increases. Every sector tested shows a negative coefficient for the logarithm of farm size (b) which is significant at the 5% level. The results with regard to tenure are inconclusive, since only five sectors out of twelve have significant tenure coefficients, and of these, two are positive and three negative.

Since the coefficients of farm size are significant and negative, the hypothesis that land use intensity falls as farm size rises is accepted. The six influences mentioned above, do seem to be operative, although from this test the relative importance of each influence cannot be determined. Land quality probably does not cause the decline in land use intensity, since the decline occurs even though the farm area examined excludes 'unusable' land.

The data for model IV.1 may be examined in the form of average values for farm size groups. Table 12 shows the components of the land utilization index of model IV.1, by farm size group. C is cultivated area as a percent of farm area less unusable land; P is declared pasture area as a percent of farm area less unusable land. U is unusable area as a percent of total farm size. EP is 'effective pasture' as a percent of farm area less unusable land, where 'effective pasture' is the minimum of declared pasture and livestock units divided by the average livestock/pasture ratio, as discussed above.

There are four important patterns shown in table 12. First, and most important, the percent of farm area 'used', corresponding to the index U of model IV.1, falls as farm size rises, in all sectors. This percent is shown in the row $C+EP$.

Second, although separation of the data into product sectors does tend to keep constant the mix between cultivated and pasture area, there is nevertheless a shift in each sector from crop area to declared pasture area as farm size rises. The shift toward 'effective pasture' is less pronounced, since larger farms have smaller 'effective pasture' than declared pasture. To the extent that a shift from cultivated area to effective pasture does occur, the U index of model IV.1 is thrown into question. For that index to be meaningful, it is necessary either that no shift from cultivated area to effective pasture occur

Table 12

Percent of usable farm area in crops, pasture, and 'effective pasture' (by farm size group)

Sector*	\multicolumn{6}{c}{Size group**}					
	I	II	III	IV	V	VI
Cea. cotton						
C	76.6	54.9	33.6	44.5	25.7	20.0
P	15.5	16.8	24.2	22.8	0.0	11.5
EP	23.4	45.1	66.4	52.2	40.9	21.3
U	0.5	7.3	8.6	2.7	0.2	25.2
C+EP	100.0	100.0	100.0	96.7	66.7	41.3
Pern. cotton						
C	78.0	38.2	35.1	6.7	18.5	0.0
P	0.0	14.6	29.6	36.3	46.8	0.0
EP	0.0	14.6	29.6	15.6	24.9	0.0
U	9.1	5.0	7.7	4.7	3.0	0.0
C+EP	78.0	52.8	64.7	22.3	43.4	0.0
E. S. coffee						
C	64.4	44.4	39.1	34.2	27.2	0.0
P	10.4	22.1	26.0	23.1	67.1	0.0
EP	10.4	11.9	19.0	18.6	21.0	0.0
U	7.4	9.4	5.3	6.7	2.1	0.0
C+EP	74.8	56.3	58.1	52.9	48.1	0.0
S. P. coffee						
C	76.2	59.9	56.4	35.7	64.1	22.3
P	16.5	33.5	33.3	41.4	20.2	42.3
EP	16.3	26.3	15.7	36.2	16.2	23.7
U	1.7	3.6	0.9	1.7	2.5	5.7
C+EP	92.5	86.2	72.1	71.9	80.3	46.0
Pern. sugar FGV						
C	100.0	93.1	71.4	60.0	53.0	35.2
P	0.0	2.2	11.1	8.8	9.5	15.2
EP	0.0	2.2	5.5	8.8	4.6	6.6
U	2.0	9.1	19.5	8.5	5.8	7.8
C+EP	100.0	95.2	77.0	68.8	57.6	41.8
S. P. cereals						
C	72.2	60.7	50.9	26.8	36.8	20.5
P	17.9	22.7	30.9	42.6	17.7	53.4
EP	17.9	22.7	18.2	19.1	10.1	26.8
U	14.2	5.5	2.1	5.8	3.6	0.2
C+EP	90.1	83.4	69.0	46.0	46.9	47.3

§4.3 HYPOTHESIS TESTS 87

Table 12, continued

Sector*	\multicolumn{6}{c}{Size group**}					
	I	II	III	IV	V	VI
R. G. rice						
C	63.7	55.0	25.1	27.6	13.4	13.1
P	30.5	29.3	55.7	48.3	56.0	70.0
EP	30.5	29.3	52.1	37.7	46.0	57.1
U	2.1	1.0	1.8	0.8	1.2	2.4
C+EP	94.2	84.3	77.2	65.3	59.4	70.2
M. G. corn						
C	74.1	40.4	29.2	14.8	4.3	0.0
P	19.6	50.0	52.6	69.8	43.1	0.0
EP	19.6	50.0	42.8	25.1	10.1	0.0
U	0.0	1.6	2.6	2.7	4.6	0.0
C+EP	93.7	90.4	72.0	39.9	14.4	0.0
S. P. cattle gen.						
C	67.5	31.3	32.7	28.7	10.7	10.6
P	22.7	60.6	60.2	63.8	74.5	65.7
EP	22.7	60.6	36.5	49.2	31.0	9.7
U	2.8	2.4	1.6	1.2	1.3	0.0
C+EP	90.2	91.4	69.2	77.9	41.7	20.3
Cea. cattle						
C	50.3	29.7	34.9	11.2	14.7	5.8
P	0.3	34.4	27.4	53.6	48.5	34.7
EP	49.7	70.3	65.1	83.9	50.3	35.7
U	6.6	10.5	7.3	3.2	0.0	1.2
C+EP	100.0	100.0	100.0	95.1	65.0	41.5
E. S. cattle						
C	0.0	59.6	12.9	17.0	5.7	0.0
P	0.0	38.2	74.0	62.5	59.0	0.0
EP	0.0	38.2	66.0	57.6	30.5	0.0
U	0.0	2.1	4.3	3.6	0.5	0.0
C+EP	0.0	97.8	78.9	74.5	36.3	0.0
M. G. cattle						
C	100.0	16.9	20.7	9.7	5.1	0.8
P	0.0	78.7	63.5	71.4	55.4	79.1
EP	0.0	78.7	63.5	43.4	28.3	13.8
U	0.0	0.2	1.0	1.0	2.8	7.5
C+EP	100.0	95.6	84.2	53.2	33.4	14.6

Table 12, continued

Sector*	Size group**					
	I	II	III	IV	V	VI
R. G. cattle						
C	52.9	9.6	0.9	9.2	1.2	0.3
P	37.8	70.1	93.3	83.0	89.2	58.8
EP	37.8	60.1	82.1	48.7	45.5	20.9
U	0.6	5.8	1.0	4.3	0.6	1.1
C+EP	90.7	69.7	83.0	57.9	46.7	21.2
S. P. cattle						
C	7.3	9.7	16.1	8.3	8.4	8.4
P	66.4	79.0	69.8	69.3	57.6	77.3
EP	66.4	79.0	66.2	69.3	23.6	40.9
U	5.0	4.0	13.1	4.1	10.7	2.4
C+EP	73.7	88.7	82.2	77.6	32.0	49.3

* C = cultivated area, % of area less unusable land; P = pasture area, % of area less unusable land; EP = effective pasture %, = Min (P, animal units/average animal units per pasture area), % of area less unusable land; U = unusable area as % of farm size.

**

Sector	Size group (ha)					
	I	II	III	IV	V	VI
Cea. cot.	<10	10–30	30–100	100–300	300–1000	>1000
Per. cot.	<10	10–30	30–100	100–300	>300	n.a.
E. S. coffee	<16	16–30	30–100	100–250	>250	n.a.
S. P. coffee	<20	20–50	50–100	100–300	300–1000	>1000
Per. sug. FGV	<10	10–40	40–200	200–300	300–1000	>1000
S. P. cereals	<10	10–30	30–100	100–240	240–500	> 500
R. G. rice	<10	10–30	30–100	100–300	300–1000	>1000
M. G. corn	<10	10–30	30–100	100–300	>300	n.a.
Ala. sug.	<10	10–50	50–125	125–300	300–1000	>1000
Per. sug. IAA	<10	10–30	30–100	100–300	300–1000	>1000
S. P. sugar	<10	10–30	30–100	100–300	300–1000	>1000
S. P. cattle/gen.	<20	20–50	50–100	100–300	300–500	> 500
Cea. cattle	<15	15–30	30–100	100–300	300–500	> 500
E. S. cattle	<10	10–30	30–100	100–300	>300	n.a.
S. P. cattle	<30	30–50	50–100	100–300	300–1000	>1000
M. G. cattle	<10	10–30	30–100	100–300	300–800	> 800
R. G. Sul cattle	<10	10–50	50–125	125–300	300–1000	>1000

within a sector, or that effective pasture represent equally intensive land use as cultivated land.

Of the crop sectors, only Rio Grande do Sul rice shows an important shift from crops to effective pasture as farm size rises. In the cattle sectors, all sectors show a shift from cultivated area to effective pasture after the smallest size group, with a relatively constant mix of the two land uses for sizes above the smallest group. This phenomenon would probably represent the fact that small cattle farms raise forage crops for feeding cattle on a 'feedlot' basis.

In model IV.2, below, the problem of a shift from cultivated area to effective pasture as farm size rises, is avoided, since land use intensity within each sector is based on output per area without regard to source, from crops or cattle.

Third, in table 12 the percent of unusable land does not rise as farm size rises. This point would support the same point made with census data in the discussion on land quality, in chapter 2.

Fourth, 'effective pasture' falls relative to declared pasture as farm size rises, which indicates that grazing intensity falls as farm size rises. This trend is consistent with the general hypothesis of declining land use intensity as farm size rises.

4.3.2. Model IV.2

The second model of this chapter examines value added per hectare of total farm size. This model examines directly what model IV.1 examines indirectly – net production per hectare. Land use 'intensity' is presumably of interest only to the extent that it represents 'production' intensity of land use. Furthermore, whereas model IV.1 accounts for land quality by considering only farm area net of declared 'unproductive area', model IV.2 incorporates land quality into the analysis by use of land price as a proxy variable for quality.

If there were no market imperfections or institutional rigidities, and if land quality did not vary with farm size, one would expect value added per farm area to be constant over all farm sizes. In a given sector, all farm sizes would have the same percent of their land under production. This would be true because all farms would find it profitable to bring less and less productive land into use until the point where the quality of the most 'marginal' land used would be identical for all farms.[1] Factor combinations employed on the

---

[1] This point assumes random distribution of land quality among farms but non-homogeneous land quality within each farm. It is also assumed that the rate of decline in quality of land within the farm is identical for all farms.

land used would be identical for all farm sizes, assuming production function homogeneity. Thus, production per cultivated area, and therefore production per total farm area, would be constant across all farm sizes.

However, the market imperfections discussed in section 2.4, would cause falling production and value added per farm area as farm size rises. Labor market dualism would cause small farms to exploit land to a margin of lower quality and this, to a higher percent of farm area, than would large farms since the small farms would be willing to accept a lower marginal product of labor, while this 'marginal land' could not be profitably farmed on large farms with higher-cost labor. Higher output per farm area would be associated with the higher percent of area used on small farms.[1]

Landholding for speculative reasons would cause output per farm area to be low simply because little or no production would take place on land held for portfolio asset motives alone. It is likely that properties owned by persons concerned with holding wealth would be larger farms whereas the owners of small farms would be earning their living from the land. Therefore speculative land holding would cause output per farm area to be lower on large farms than on small farms.

The non-economic behavior of the '*latifundista*' would also be associated with low output per farm area. Furthermore, production by the small farm for 'own consumption' in addition to the commercial market would cause output per farm area to be higher on small farms than large.

Monopsony control by large farms would cause output per farm area to be low relative to the output which would occur in a competitive equilibrium. However, the competitive equilibrium would not be observed. For the observed data, output per farm area would be higher on small farms than on large, assuming that only large farms have monopsony power.

In sum, all of the mentioned causes of 'low land use' would cause a decline in output per farm area as farm size rises.

The hypotheses tested in model IV.2 are the same as in model IV.1: land-use intensity falls as farm size rises; owners use land more intensively than non-owners; and, land-use intensity falls as farm size increases even when the influence of land quality is removed. The data used are the same as for

---

[1] However, the assumption that the quality of marginal land declines as a higher percent of farm area is used, implies that the ratio of small farm output per total area to large farm output per total area would be less than the ratio of the percent of area used (cultivated) on small farms to the percent of area used (cultivated) on large farms.

PRINTED MATTER
IMPRIMÉS

Please put your stamp here

NORTH-HOLLAND PUBLISHING COMPANY

P.O. BOX 3489

AMSTERDAM - The Netherlands

Please note my continuation order for following series:

☐ **Studies in Mathematical and Managerial Economics,** from vol. .... onwards.
☐ **Contributions to Economic Analysis,** from vol. .... onwards.

Please send prospectuses in the following fields:

Name .... Full Address (*block letters please*):

☐ Economic Planning, Statistics
☐ Economic Theory, Mathematical Economics
☐ Econometrics
☐ International Economics, Economics of Developing Countries
☐ Welfare Economics
☐ Monetary Economics, Banking, Business Finance
☐ Industrial and Labour Economics
☐ Transport Economics
☐ Distribution and Consumer Research
☐ Business and Industrial Administration
☐ Personnel Management Commercial Studies

Please mention your institute or organisation and position held.

P 20 M 270 E

§4.3 HYPOTHESIS TESTS

model IV.1, in addition to the IAA sugar cane data of chapter 3, which are adequate since physical livestock information is not required for the present test.

Again only the general hypothesis is tested, that land use intensity, measured by value added[1] per farm area, declines as farm size rises, with the influence of land quality eliminated. This model does not permit a statistical test separating the individual hypotheses that the decrease in land use intensity is caused by (a) labor market dualism, (b) speculative land holding, (c) land market imperfections, (d) the 'own-consumption market' on small farms, (e) monopsony considerations, (f) non-economic behavior.

The following forms of model IV.2 are tested:

(1) $VA/X = a + b\log X + c(\log X)^2 + d(T) + e(P)$
(2) $VA/X = a + b\log X + c(\log X)^2 \qquad + e(P)$
(3) $VA/X = a + b\log X \qquad + d(T) + e(P)$
(4) $VA/X = a + b\log X \qquad + e(P)$
(5) $VA/X = a \qquad + e(P) + f(X)$

where

X = farm size, hectares;
VA = value added, or production minus expense on seeds, fertilizer, animal feeds, vaccines;
T = 1, owner; = 0, non-owner;
P = land price per hectare = total land value/X.

For each sector, the 'best' of the five forms is chosen, on a basis of multiple correlation coefficient, parameter significance, and F ratio.

The specific regression forms chosen are selected for the same reasons that the identical forms are used in model IV.1, as described above. However, to permit investigation for 'steps' in the decline in land use intensity, rather than for gradual decline as forced by the regression forms, data are shown by size group in table 14. Furthermore, table 15 shows value added per area standardized for land price. In this table, farm land value divided by average land price is used as the denominator in the ratio of value added to 'farm land'.

---

[1] The concept of 'value added' used here is gross, in that it does not deduct capital depreciation. A 'net' concept might find greater decline in value added per farm area as farm size rises, to the extent that capital increases relative to other factors as farm size rises. 'Value added' would be expected to parallel gross output. Some divergence might occur, to the extent that greater relative expenditures on improved seeds and chemical fertilizer occur on larger farms.

TABLE 13

Relationship of value added per hectare of farm area with farm size, tenure type, and land price

Sector	Best run	a	Log X b	(Log X)² c	T d	P e	X f	R^2
Ceará cotton	2)	994.0	−404.0 (67.2)	42.3 (9.0)	—	−0.044 (0.54)	—	0.4286
Pern. cotton	1)	664.4	−278.2 (39.7)	26.95 (5.0)	81.7 (42.1)	−0.055 (0.023)	—	0.7289
E. San. coffee	4)	185.7	−24.8 (12.7)	—	—	−0.0045 (0.009)	—	0.0598
S. P. coffee	5)	476.5	—	—	—	0.0386 (0.032)	−0.0296 (0.046)	0.0290
Pern. sugar FGV	4)	612.5	−63.0 (22.0)	—	—	−0.052 (0.040)	—	0.2276
S. P. cereals	3)	975.5	−132.2 (29.3)	—	−269.8 (86.4)	0.0687 (0.033)	—	0.2878
R. G. rice	4)	509.5	−65.5 (19.0)	—	—	0.242 (0.145)	—	0.3749

§4.3 HYPOTHESIS TESTS

M. G. corn	2)	2584.5	−1015.0 (260.0)	98.73 (37.7)	—	0.04625 (0.182)	—	0.5809
S. P. cattle/gen	2)	1971.1	−704.2 (182.5)	63.2 (19.7)	—	0.0758 (0.033)	—	0.5099
Alag. sugar	4)	2.98	0.1076 (0.324)	—	—	0.01381 (0.0094)	—	0.02705
Per sug. IAA	2)	32.50	−5.5592 (2.47)	0.3441 (0.192)	—	−0.00188 (0.0024)	—	0.08808
S. P. sugar	4)	21.50	−1.1339 (0.566)	—	—	0.00132 (0.0006)	—	0.0600
Ceará cattle	4)	368.5	−62.04 (14.0)	—	—	0.1161 (0.068)	—	0.3730
E. San. cattle	3)	315.0	−31.28 (13.0)	—	−72.18 (34.9)	0.00136 (0.019)	—	0.2935
M. G. cattle	2)	2043.4	−574.0 (184.4)	39.84 (16.8)	—	−0.0403 (0.110)	—	0.3401
R. G. cattle	2)	590.8	−194.1 (45.0)	14.22 (4.8)	—	0.2212 (0.101)	—	0.6537
S. P. cattle	4)	445.5	−50.27 (28.4)	—	—	0.04651 (0.022)	—	0.2471

This presentation thus assumes that n hectares of price p are equivalent for production purposes to m hectares of price w so long as $np = mw$.[1] In the continuous function of table 13, land quality is accounted for in the land price term.

The results in table 13 show that in every sector except Alagoas, sugar, there is a negative relationship between value added per hectare and farm size, even when land quality is accounted for by the land price term. The negative relationship of production intensity to farm size is statistically significant at the 5% level for all sectors except São Paulo coffee and São Paulo cattle.

The second degree of the logarithm of farm size is used in only five sectors. In these sectors, this term has a positive coefficient. Numerical investigation of the functions, however, shows that only in two sectors – Ceará cotton and São Paulo cattle/general – does value added per hectare recover to the sectoral average level, at the maximum value of farm size observed. Therefore, in the five sectors with positive coefficients for '(log size)^2' the term represents a 'flattening out' of the negative relationship of value added per hectare with farm size, rather than the existence of large farms with high value added per area. This point may be seen in tables 14 and 15 with regard to the five sectors in question; the largest size group in these tables does not show high value added per hectare.

The coefficients of 'land price' in table 13 are significant and positive, as expected, for only five sectors. Four of these are in São Paulo: cereals, cattle/general, sugar, cattle. The fifth is Rio Grande do Sul, cattle. The lack of influence of land price in the other sectors could represent various possibilities. Land quality may not be accurately represented by land price. Or, the use of other factors on land might compensate for quality in achieving standard output per total area. Finally, it is possible that land quality is very homogeneous within each product sector, except for the sectors mentioned.

Farm tenure shows negligible influence on production per area. The variable is significant in only three of seventeen sectors, where it is negative in two and positive in one.

The low multiple correlation coefficients indicate that influences other than farm size, land price, and tenure type affect value added per farm area.

---

[1] This assumption should be valid so long as land price represents the present value of the future stream of marginal product of the land.

TABLE 14

Value added* per hectare of farm area (by farm size group)

Sector	Size group					
	I	II	III	IV	V	VI
Ceará cotton	338	149	85	95	77	16
Pern. cotton	347	135	69	15	36	—
E. S. coffee	145	99	84	41	92	—
S. P. coffee	562	578	508	428	880	416
Pern. sugar (FGV)	—	371	276	250	150	199
S. P. cereals	644	481	369	244	207	68
R. G. rice	423	630	180	391	124	96
Minas G. corn	1491	358	194	100	14	—
S. P. cattle/gen	793	248	117	248	73	48
Alagoas sugar	—	4.29	9.29	9.81	7.18	8.38
Pern. sugar (IAA)	34.4	16.8	23.4	9.9	12.1	10.0
S. P. sugar	18.4	25.6	22.8	16.4	20.4	17.4
Ceará cattle	252	302	91	83	36	21
E. S. cattle	—	118	140	105	48	—
M. G. cattle	—	738	214	125	40	28
M. G. cattle	709	107	29	63	20	19
S. P. cattle	754	421	240	336	126	148

* 100 cruzeiros of 1962 for all sectors except: São Paulo and Minas Gerais sectors: 100 cruz. of 1963; Alagoas sugar, Pern. sugar IAA, and S. P. sugar: tons of sugar cane.
Size groups: see table 12.

Nevertheless, in regard to the hypothesis to be tested, the results in table 13 are statistically significant: intensity of production per farm area falls as farm size rises, even after the influence of farm land quality is taken into account. This conclusion is similar to that of the first model of this chapter although the present model is more direct and therefore more meaningful than the previous model. In the present model, land use intensity is measured directly by output per farm area rather than indirectly by the percent of farm area 'used' as in the previous model. In the present model, land quality is considered directly through the land price variable rather than indirectly through the exclusion of 'unproductive land' as in the previous model.

Table 14 shows value added per hectare by farm size group. The only apparent new information in table 14 is that in some sectors – E. S. coffee,

TABLE 15

Value added per 'constant quality' hectare of farm area*

Sector	Size group					
	I	II	III	IV	V	VI
Ceará cotton	311	80	112	90	53	67
Pern. cotton	140	120	97	22	83	—
E. S. coffee	297	144	88	71	132	—
S. P. coffee	867	681	520	648	534	422
Per. sug. FGV	—	298	125	250	147	305
S. P. cereals	845	461	308	219	228	97
R. G. rice	433	471	241	447	106	89
M. G. corn	683	265	228	75	75	—
S. P. cattle/gen	775	243	131	202	127	81
Ala. sug	—	4.61	9.48	10.33	7.16	8.31
Per. sug. IAA	8.36	10.74	28.78	6.41	11.7	11.13
S. P. sug.	16.64	24.97	24.22	19.80	20.93	15.02
Ceará cattle	149	181	95	104	66	8
E. S. cattle	—	40	110	123	72	—
M. G. cattle	—	400	139	79	22	120
R. G. cattle	290	74	46	52	20	21
S. P. cattle	508	182	138	321	148	193

* In place of land area, land value divided by sectoral average land price is used. Size groups: see table 12.

Note: Wide variance of land price, combined with a small number of observations in each size group, causes great discrepancy between value added per hectare (table 14) and value added per constant quality hectare (in this table) for the following sectors: E. S. cattle (size group II), Pernambuco sugar IAA (size groups I, II, III).

Per. sug. (IAA), S. P. sugar – the first size group (farms of less than 10 ha, in most cases) shows an especially high value added per hectare, while the subsequent size groups show a more constant value added per area than would be expected from a continuous function.

Table 15 shows value added per 'standard quality' area based on land value. Value added per 'standard quality area' does not drop as fast as value added per area, in Pernambuco sugar (FGV), M. G. corn, Ceará cattle, M.G. cattle, R.G. cattle, and S.P. cattle, although the trend is still a decline as farm size group rises. It is informative that in São Paulo coffee, value of land appears higher on large farms than on small. The performance of the smallest size

§4.3   HYPOTHESIS TESTS   97

group appears improved when 'constant quality' land is examined and the performance of size group V falls markedly.

Finally, the data of model IV.2 are plotted in the diagrams below. In these diagrams, the vertical axis shows value added per hectare of farm area, while the horizontal axis shows the natural logarithm of the hectares of farm area. The scatter diagrams are useful for three types of informal tests: a test for the general fall in land use intensity as farm size rises; a test for dichotomy between *latifúndios* and 'rural enterprises'; and tests to discriminate among the various explanations for falling land use intensity.

In the first test, the diagrams show the general decline in land use intensity as farm size rises. Only São Paulo coffee, and sugar cane in São Paulo and Alagoas seem to be exceptions to this rule. The diagrams thus permit visual confirmation of the regression results of model IV.2, that value added per farm area declines significantly as farm size rises.

A second test which may be made informally, with the use of the scatter diagrams, is for the existence of a sharp distinction between *latifúndios* or large farms that use their land inefficiently, and 'rural enterprises', large farms that are efficient in land use. The land reform literature and legislation make much of this distinction, and the 'large efficient farms' are exempted from expropriation in Brazilian legislation.[1]

A rigorous test for a latifundium – rural enterprise split could be formulated by testing for an increasing deviation of observed land use intensity around the curve of predicted land use intensity, as farm size rises. Thus, while land use intensity would fall generally as farm size rises, the larger farms would increasingly be of two types: 'efficient' with high positive deviation from expected land use intensity, and 'inefficient' with large negative deviation from expected land use intensity.

While the scatter diagrams (figs. 2–6) show that for some sectors there do exist large farms with output per farm area of about the sectoral average, inspection does not reveal any increasing deviation around the trend line as farm size increases. Thus, an informal test based on the diagrams would reject the notion that large farms fall into two distinct types, the inefficient *latifúndio* and the efficient 'rural enterprise'.

The third use of the scatter diagrams, discrimination among the various causes of falling land use intensity, is discussed below, in section 4.4.

---

[1] The 'rural enterprise' is a large farm meeting certain criteria of yield per area cultivated, accounting techniques, social conditions on the farm, and others.

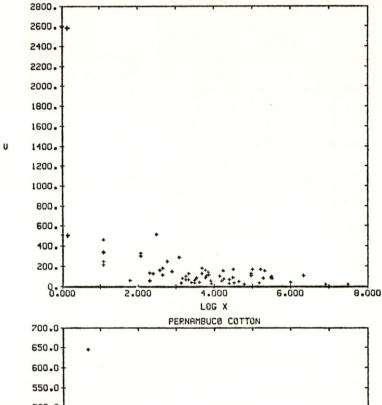

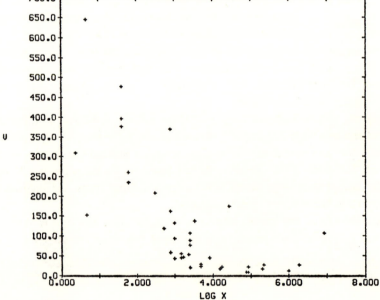

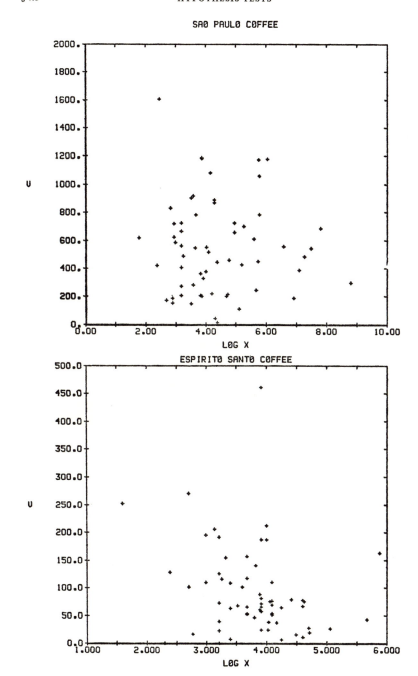

Fig. 2.

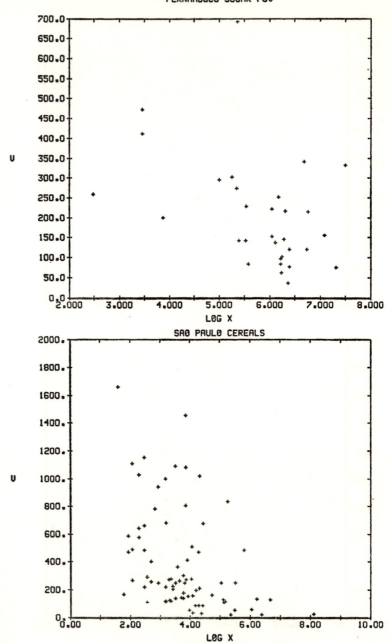

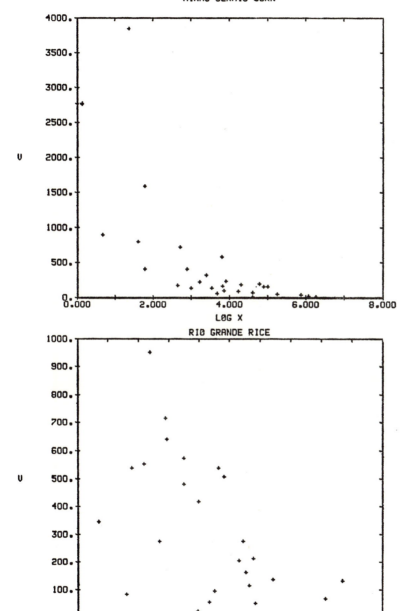

Fig. 3.

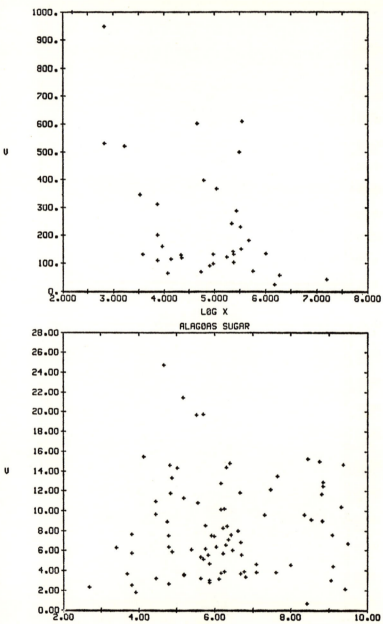

§4.3 HYPOTHESIS TESTS 103

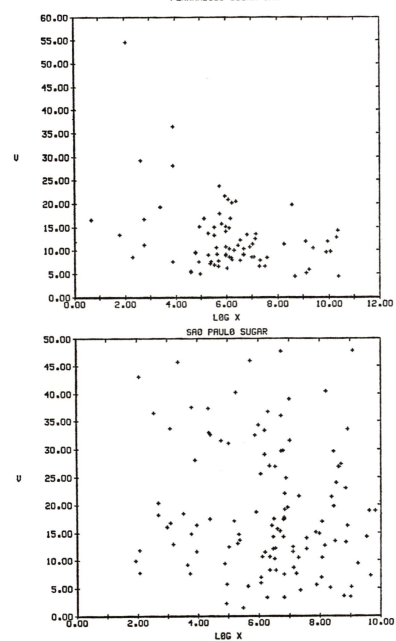

Fig. 4.

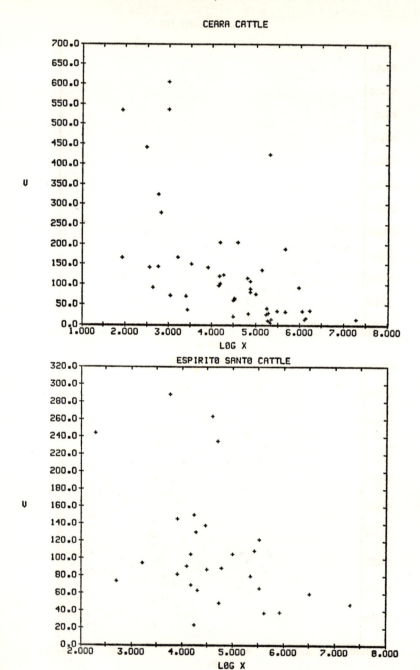

§4.3 HYPOTHESIS TESTS 105

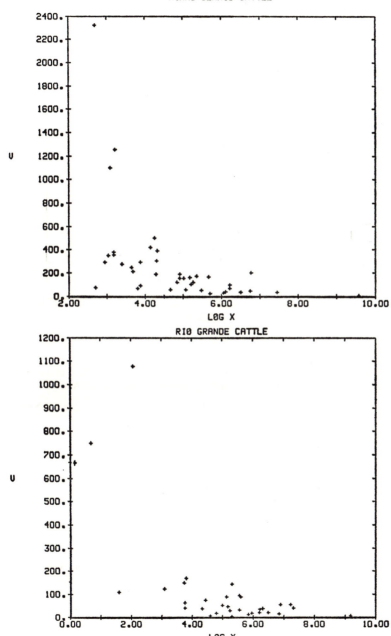

Fig. 5.

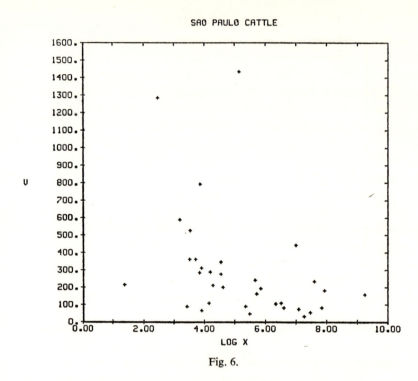

Fig. 6.

Figs. 2–6. Units for scatter diagrams. 1. Horizontal axis: natural logarithm of number of hectares, farm size. a) Note: number corresponding to logarithm:

Logarithm	Number	Logarithm	Number	Logarithm	Number
0	1.0	4	54.6	8	2980.4
1	2.7	5	148.4	9	8108.2
2	7.4	6	403.6	10	22054.2
3	20.1	7	1096.4		

2. Vertical axis: value added per hectare farm area.

Unit	Sectors
100 cruzeiros of 1962	Ceará cotton, Pernambuco cotton, Espírito Santo coffee, Pernambuco sugar FGV, Rio Grande rice, Ceará cattle, Espírito Santo cattle, Rio Grande cattle
100 cruzeiros of 1963	São Paulo coffee, São Paulo cereals, Minas Gerais corn, São Paulo cattle-general, Minas Gerais cattle, São Paulo cattle
Tons of sugar cane*	Alagoas sugar, Pernambuco sugar IAA, São Paulo sugar

* Intermediate inputs subtracted in units of sugar cane ton equivalents to obtain value added.

§4.3   HYPOTHESIS TESTS   107

Two more questions may be examined, regarding the hypothesis that some large farms are efficient while others are inefficient. One assertion common in Brazil is that large farms in the Northeast are archaic and inefficient, but those of the South are modern and efficient. This view implies that land redistribution should be limited to the Northeast. A second common view is that the large cattle ranches are the primary instances of the large inefficient farm, or *latifúndio*, and that large crop farms are efficient.

To investigate these two questions, tables 16 and 17 have been constructed. Table 16 shows the ratio of value added to total farm land value, for small farms (farms under 30 ha, in most sectors) and for large farms (farms over 300 ha, in most sectors). The table also shows the ratio of these two figures: the figure for large farms is divided by the figure for small farms. Table 17 shows a ranking of the sectors from 'worst' to 'best' in intensity of land use on large farms relative to intensity of land use on small farms. The ranking is shown on a basis of the ratio of value added per farm area for large farms, to value added per farm area on small farms; and on a basis of the ratio of value added per land value for large farms, to value added per land value, for small farms.

It is evident in table 17 that the problem of low land use by large farms is not limited to the Northeast.[1] Of the seven 'worst' sectors, on a basis of value added per farm area, five are sectors of the South.

It also appears, in table 17, that there is some validity to the hypothesis that cattle sectors are the primary locus of poor use of land by large farms. For the states in which both cattle and crop sectors are shown, the cattle sectors (in most states) show poorer land use intensity of large farms relative to small farms, than do the crop sectors. This distinction appears even stronger when value added per land value is the basis for the comparison. However, there appears to be a distinction even within crop sectors between products with relatively poor land use by large farms and products with relatively good land use by large farms.

Coffee and sugar cane are crops in which large farm land use is relatively

---

[1] Sectors in this study, from the Northeast are: Alagoas, Ceará, Pernambuco. From the South are: Minas Gerais, Rio Grande do Sul and São Paulo. Espírito Santo is in an intermediate zone.

Table 16
Ratio of value added to total land value: small farms and large farms*

Sector	A. Small farms (size groups I, II)	B. Large farms (size groups V, VI)	C. Ratio (B/A)
Cea. cot.	0.615	0.319	0.51
Pern. cot.	0.705	0.441	0.35
E. S. coffee	0.952	0.605	0.64
S. P. coffee	0.474	0.308	0.64
Pern. sug. (FGV)	0.820	0.514	0.63
S. P. cereals	0.458	0.144	0.32
R. G. rice	2.295	0.472	0.21
M. G. corn	0.875	0.145	0.17
S. P. cat./gen	0.319	0.095	0.27
Ala sug.**	0.0139	0.0240	1.73
Per. sug. IAA**	0.0204	0.0237	1.16
S. P. sug.**	0.0080	0.0064	0.80
Cea. cattle	1.020	0.156	0.15
E. S. cattle	0.117	0.213	1.71
M. G. cattle	1.450	0.162	0.11
R. G. cattle	0.528	0.109	0.20
S. P. cattle	0.174	0.142	0.83

* Small: Most sectors – up to 30 ha. Large: Most sectors over 300 ha. See table 12.
** Tons of sugar cane per 100 cruzeiros of 1963.

good compared to small farm land use; whereas in other crops – cotton, rice, corn, and 'cereals' (rice, corn, and beans), large farm land use intensity is poor relative to that of small farms. Therefore the concept of the 'efficient large farm' or 'plantation' appears to be most true in the sugar cane and coffee sectors. Note that in these sectors large farm land use intensity relative to that of small farms appears much better when analysis is based on value added per land value than when analysis is based on value added per farm area.[1]

---

[1] With the exception of São Paulo coffee, where large farms appear to have better land quality than small.

§4.3　　　　　　　　　　　HYPOTHESIS TESTS　　　　　　　　　　　109

TABLE 17

Ratio of large farm land use intensity to small farm land use intensity*

Sector	A. Value added per farm area basis **	B. Value added per land value basis†
M. G. corn	0.02	0.17 (3)
M. G. cattle	0.04	0.11 (1)
Ceará cattle	0.11	0.15 (2)
R. G. cattle	0.13	0.20 (4)
Pern. cotton	0.15	0.35 (8)
S. P. cattle/gen.	0.17	0.27 (6)
R. G. rice	0.19	0.21 (5)
Ceará cotton	0.20	0.51 (9)
S. P. cereals	0.25	0.32 (7)
S. P. cattle	0.30	0.83 (14)
E. S. cattle	0.41	1.71 (16)
Per. sug. FGV	0.45	0.63 (10)
S. P. sug.	0.48	0.80 (13)
Per. sug. IAA*	0.51	1.16 (15)
E. S. coffee	0.82	0.64 (12)
S. P. coffee	1.01	0.64 (11)
Ala. sug.	1.86	1.73 (17)

* 'Small farm' and 'Large farm' definition: see table 16.
** Column A: (value added/farm area – large farms)/(value added/farm area – small farms).
† Column B: (value added/land value – large farms)/(value added/land value – small farms). Rank, from lowest to highest, shown in parentheses.

4.3.3. Model IV.3

A third approach to the question of 'intensity of land use' is an examination of the relationship between inputs used and farm size. The theoretical expectation of declining intensity of land use, for the reasons given in section 2.4, implies a decline in inputs per farm area as farm size rises. The previous model showed declining output per farm area as farm size rose. Given constant returns to scale in the production function, found in chapter 3, declining output per farm area would be associated with declining inputs per farm area.

Thus, model IV.3 measures the relationship of each input with farm size. It is expected that all inputs rise more slowly than farm size, such that intensity of input use per farm area falls as farm size rises.

One additional insight may be gained from the present model, over the findings of models IV.1 and IV.2. Since each factor input is related to farm size separately, any tendency for factor combinations to change as farm size increases may be seen in the present model. The major change one would expect is a fall in labor relative to other inputs.

The expected relationship of inputs per farm area to total farm size is shown in fig. 7.

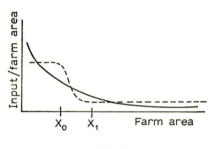

Fig. 7

The solid line indicates the general relationship expected. If labor market dualism alone were the causal influence, the dotted line would be the expected relationship. In that case, X_0 would be the maximum farm size on which only family labor is used, X_1 would be the minimum farm size on which only hired labor is used, and a mixture of family and hired labor would be used on farms in between size X_0 and X_1. Intensity of land use would be higher only for family farms, where 'cheap family labor' would be associated with production on the more marginal land within the farm. All farms with only hired labor would have constant intensity of land use.

The relationship estimated is:

$$\log(\text{input}) = a + b(\log \text{size})$$

This form yields the hypothesized relationship shown in the graph, for the solid line curve[1].

$$\log L = \theta + \phi \log X$$
$$\log N = \lambda + \mu \log X$$
$$\log K = \pi + \rho \log X$$
$$\log S = \sigma + \tau \log X$$

where

L = land input (cultivated land, crops; pasture, cattle);
N = labor, value;
K = capital stock, value;
S = seeds, fertilizer, and insecticides, value.

For cattle, there were two different inputs:

$$\log A = \sigma + \tau \log X$$
$$\log V = \psi + \omega \log X$$

where A = animal capital stock, V = feeds and vaccines, value.

A version of the model was attempted in which land price was included as well; thus,

$$\log \text{input} = a + b \,(\log \text{size}) + c \,(\log \text{land price}).$$

Thus, a shift in land price would have the effect of shifting upward or downward, proportionally, the curve in fig. 7 above. However, land price was significant in only two of the seventeen sectors, so it was omitted from the final model.[2]

The results of the regression model relating inputs to farm size are shown in table 18. These results show a decreasing intensity of inputs used per farm size as size increases. That is, in almost every factor of every sector, the coefficient of 'log size' is less than unity. This coefficient represents the elasticity of 'input use' with respect to farm size.

---

[1] That is, the curve shown is of the form $y = Ax^{-B}$ where y is the ordinate and x the abcissa. This form is identical to $\log(I) = a + b\,(\log X)$ where I = input and X = farm size, since $I = e^a X^b$ and $I/X = e^a X^{b-1}$. So long as coefficient b is less than unity, this equation is of the same form as $y = Ax^{-B}$.

[2] Furthermore, a theoretical case could be made for both an expected negative and positive land price coefficient. A negative coefficient would indicate that the farmer was using high input to compensate for poor quality land. A positive coefficient would indicate that the farmer did not bother to conduct an operation on low quality land.

TABLE 18

Relationship of inputs to farm size

Sector*	Constant	Coefficient	Std. error	R^2
Ceará cotton				
L	0.0129	0.7243	0.055	0.7275
N	6.7242	0.3193	0.082	0.1873
K	6.7576	0.4930	0.093	0.2994
S	1.3104	0.6824	0.088	0.4747
Pernambuco cotton				
L	0.3692	0.4472	0.084	0.4359
N	6.3532	0.3540	0.080	0.3462
K	6.4215	0.5260	0.090	0.4708
S	2.9300	0.2680	0.112	0.1338
E. Santo coffee				
L	—0.3452	0.7983	0.107	0.4747
N	6.1501	0.3945	0.155	0.0943
K	4.4708	1.0279	0.182	0.3401
S	2.9926	0.4875	0.219	0.0742
S. Paulo coffee				
L	0.1110	0.7993	0.060	0.7429
N	6.9063	0.5579	0.070	0.5061
K	6.5155	0.9015	0.077	0.6895
S	1.7867	1.2829	0.101	0.7226
Pernambuco sugar FGV				
L	0.4856	0.7881	0.073	0.8020
N	5.7304	0.8292	0.092	0.7362
K	7.5291	0.7308	0.098	0.6572
S	2.3645	1.1843	0.261	0.4147
S. Paulo cereals				
L	0.4078	0.6397	0.066	0.5585
N	7.3534	0.3194	0.089	0.1462
K	7.1448	0.6401	0.099	0.3559
S	4.0204	0.6265	0.130	0.2378
R. G. Sul Rice FGV				
L	0.1559	0.6489	0.056	0.8265
N	6.7134	0.4739	0.067	0.6382
K	6.9717	0.8028	0.056	0.8485
S	4.4512	0.6969	0.091	0.6770

Table 18, continued

Sector*	Constant	Coefficient	Std. error	R^2
M. Gerais corn				
L	0.4002	0.4254	0.092	0.4433
N	8.0528	0.0717	0.018	0.0160
K	7.8353	0.3930	0.081	0.4655
S	4.1142	0.3144	0.152	0.1364
S. Paulo cattle/gen.				
L	−0.0109	0.9752	0.023	0.9813
N	7.1690	0.3847	0.102	0.2876
K	6.8983	0.8729	0.089	0.7340
S	4.8554	0.7635	0.133	0.4858
Alagoas sugar				
L	−1.3948	1.0097	0.040	0.8842
N	2.7581	1.0750	0.051	0.8408
K	−0.4253	1.2018	0.051	0.8689
S	−1.1386	1.1081	0.060	0.8015
Pernambuco sugar IAA				
L	−0.2842	0.9043	0.020	0.9633
N	4.2661	0.9362	0.024	0.9495
K	1.7403	1.0119	0.037	0.9043
S	0.6686	0.9715	0.049	0.8321
S. Paulo sugar				
L	−0.5497	0.9729	0.023	0.9381
N	3.0340	1.0039	0.027	0.9231
K	2.1159	1.0357	0.033	0.8942
S	0.0030	1.1065	0.038	0.8731
Ceará cattle				
L	−0.7766	1.0272	0.088	0.7416
N	7.1154	0.2337	0.126	0.0669
K	6.9879	0.5507	0.115	0.3246
A	6.7301	0.6048	0.094	0.4635
V	4.6300	0.4245	0.134	0.1724
E. Santo cattle				
L	−0.7016	1.0537	0.070	0.8962
N	7.0551	0.2809	0.114	0.1895
K	6.5969	0.6360	0.177	0.3331
A	7.5192	0.5774	0.141	0.3936
V	3.1663	0.6439	0.213	0.2605

Table 18, continued

Sector*	Constant	Coefficient	Std. error	R^2
M. Gerais cattle				
L	0.0020	0.9277	0.044	0.9163
N	6.5608	0.4657	0.095	0.3722
K	7.9143	0.4920	0.104	0.3524
A	6.3469	0.7421	0.109	0.5309
V	5.0387	0.5618	0.153	0.2478
R. G. Sul cattle				
L	—0.6432	1.0599	0.036	0.9647
N	6.2995	0.3687	0.084	0.3842
K	7.1732	0.5484	0.102	0.4834
A	6.1477	0.7657	0.082	0.7384
V	4.7376	0.3812	0.132	0.2120
S. Paulo cattle				
L	—0.3476	0.9910	0.038	0.9543
N	7.3978	0.3607	0.069	0.4502
K	6.8553	0.6384	0.146	0.3675
A	6.8327	0.8361	0.067	0.8241
V	5.3276	0.4680	0.124	0.3031

* L = land input (crops = area cultivated, cattle = pasture); N = labor; K = capital; S = seeds, fertilizer, insecticides; A = animal capital; V = feed, vaccines.

Besides the general fact of declining input intensity with respect to farm size, two noteworthy phenomena are shown in table 18. First, the elasticity of labor use with respect to size is much lower than the elasticity of land input, capital, and seeds and fertilizer use with respect to farm size. This fact would tend to confirm the hypothesis that labor market dualism is present. Small farms use family labor intensively, and large farms economize on hired labor. The second expectation based on labor-market dualism, however, was not clearly borne out. The hypothesis that inputs per farm area would be high over the range of 'family size farms', and then would drop to a lower constant shelf for 'hired labor fams', was not supported. This question was investigated by calculating the average percentage deviation of actual 'log input' from estimated 'log input'. There was no trend for positive deviation over the lowest two or three size groups, and no trend of negative deviation in the fourth or fifth size groups as would have been expected in the case of labor-market dualism.

§4.4 DISCRIMINATION AMONG CAUSES OF LAND USE PATTERNS 115

Table 18 contains other useful information. The exceptions to the general rules are of interest. Seeds and fertilizer inputs rise more rapidly than farm size ($\tau > 1$) in these sectors: São Paulo coffee, and sugar cane in Alagoas, Pernambuco, and São Paulo. The same is true of capital in Espírito Santo coffee, and in all three IAA sugar sectors. These patterns would point to a greater 'modern' or 'technical' orientation of large farmers than of small farmers, in these sectors, or else an easier access of large farmers to credit for these inputs. A second 'exception' is that pasture input on cattle farms rises as fast or faster than farm size. The explanation of this fact is that the cattle owner considers nearly his whole farm to be grazing area, regardless of the density of cattle per area – which probably declines as farm size rises. Furthermore, there is still some crop activity even in cattle sectors, and this crop activity tends to occur on small farms, so a shift toward pasture as farm size increases gives the appearance of increasing 'land input' or pasture land in relation to farm size.

A final important point is that sugar cane sectors from the IAA Survey show very little decline in input use per area as farm size rises, that is, the coefficients of 'log size' are nearly unity. These coefficients are nearly as high in the FGV Pernambuco sugar sector, so that the peculiarity of sugar is probably not a question of divergence caused by separate data sources. Even more intriguing is the fact that the elasticity of labor input with respect to farm size exceeds the elasticity of 'land input' with respect to farm size in all four sugar sectors but in none of the other sectors. This fact suggests that sugar cane requires a technology that allows little substitution of land for labor,[1] and furthermore, that organizational forms require more labor on larger farms than on small, because overseers and clerical staff are required.[2]

4.4. Tests for discrimination among alternative causes of land use patterns

The first three models of this chapter tested only for an overall decline in land use intensity as farm size rises. Of the seven reasons given for this decline, only

---

[1] Harvesting in all three sugar areas shown is still done by hand and is very labor intensive.
[2] When the IAA data were broken down into direct field labor and administrative or overhead labor, it was found that in São Paulo, farms under 1000 ha had about 90% of labor on 'direct' field work, whereas farms 1000 to 3000 ha had 85% and farms over 3000 ha, only 68%. In Pernambuco, farms under 1000 ha had about 90% of labor 'direct', while farms over 1000 hectares had only 81%. In Alagoas, however, direct labor was about 80% of labor for all size groups.

one, land quality, was examined, in contradistinction to the supposed combined influences of the others. This separation was made by the exclusion of 'unusable' land in the land use analysis of model IV.1, and by the use of average land price as a proxy variable for land quality, in model IV.2. In this section, informal tests are made to differentiate more finely among the six influences other than land quality which cause land use intensity to fall as farm size rises. Three elements are considered in these tests: the trend in factor ratios as farm size rises; the existence or non-existence of a two-step pattern in land use intensity, for family versus non-family farms; and the degree of concentration in the distribution of farm area among farm owners.

It should be emphasized at the outset that the author considers the tests of this section to be of only secondary importance. For the question of the effect of land redistribution on agricultural production, the primary issue is whether or not low land use on large farms is caused by low quality of land on large farms. This issue has already been investigated statistically in models IV.1 and IV.2. The attempts of this section to discriminate among the other possible influences on land use are included for the sake of completeness. Furthermore, it is the author's feeling that the attempts of this section are generally inconclusive, but that no further discrimination among the influences on land use is possible with the data available.

4.4.1. Factor ratios

Labor market dualism and land market imperfection are two of the six influences to be considered. Both of these influences would cause changing factor combinations as farm size rises. 'Own consumption' on small farms, speculative land holding, and non-economic behavior would not, by themselves, cause changes in the combinations of labor, capital, and cultivated area, although these influences would cause a fall in area utilized, relative to farm size, as farm size rises.[1]

Labor market dualism implies higher marginal product of labor on larger farms, and thus less labor relative to the land input (cultivated land, for crops, or pasture, for cattle) and relative to capital. Land market imperfection implies an increased use of cultivated (or pasture) land relative to labor and capital, as farm size rises, since it is hypothesized that larger farms pay a

---

[1] Monopsony would cause somewhat smaller intensity of labor use relative to other inputs, on farms extremely large and capable of exercising monopsony power.

§4.4   DISCRIMINATION AMONG CAUSES OF LAND USE PATTERNS   117

lower price for land of a given quality than do small farms. It is assumed that in factor combination decisions, the 'price' assigned by the farmer to his 'land input' parallels the price he faces for purchase of farm area. Finally the capital market may also be imperfect. The bargaining power of large farms makes it likely that there will be cheaper credit available to large farms than to small farms. Capital market imperfection is not one of the six influences causing falling land use intensity; instead, it would cause greater intensity of land use as farm size rises, *ceteris paribus*.

TABLE 19

Expected trend in factor combinations as farm size rises, for various market situations

Market	Labor	Land	Capital	N/L	N/K	K/L
1	I	I	I	↓	↓	—
2	I	I	P	↓	↓	↓
3	I	P	I	↓	↓	↑
4	I	P	P	↓	↓	—
5	P	I	I	↓	↓	—
6	P	I	P	↓	—	↓
7	P	P	I	—	↓	↑
8	P	P	P	—	—	—

I = Imperfect   ↑ = Increases as farm size rises N = Labor
P = Perfect   ↓ = Decreases as farm size rises L = land input
                                                     K = capital

Table 19 shows the eight possible combinations of imperfection versus perfection in the three factor markets. In each of the eight situations, an arrow indicates the trend of the factor ratio as farm size rises.[1] It may be seen that three of the situations give identical factor ratio trends (situations 1, 4, and 5).

A test for the existence of labor market dualism, and/or land market imperfection, and/or capital market imperfection, may be made by comparing observed factor ratio trends against the factor ratio trends which would be expected in each market situation of table 19. Factor ratios for each farm size

---

[1] Note that when both capital and land markets are imperfect (situations 1 and 5), it is assumed that no change in the capital/land input ratio occurs, and thus, that the relative increase in the use of land due to the falling price of land occurs at the same rate as the relative increase in the use of capital due to the falling cost of capital.

Table 20

Factor ratios by farm size groups: sample survey data (100 cruzeiros/ha)*

	Labor/ farm area	Labor/ cultiv. area	Capital/ cultiv. area	Seeds, fert., insecticides/ cultiv. area	Production/ cultiv. area
Ceará cotton					
I	553.9	697.4	651.6	5.1	430.3
II	230.7	360.5	486.7	2.8	236.1
III	68.1	207.3	509.1	5.2	265.2
IV	47.9	136.1	397.3	5.1	274.0
V	12.7	50.0	284.9	4.9	307.1
VI	11.5	77.1	237.8	1.6	111.5
Pernambuco cotton					
I	303.2	350.5	429.2	11.1	412.0
II	140.2	322.1	513.2	12.1	323.4
III	55.1	300.9	679.5	8.2	386.7
IV	19.0	292.2	1123.5	11.3	237.8
V	20.4	204.9	588.6	2.2	373.0
Espírito Santo coffee					
I	193.6	188.6	183.6	13.8	155.2
II	102.6	255.5	378.0	25.0	272.3
III	57.8	162.0	362.2	12.9	249.4
IV	30.4	106.1	487.5	9.0	153.0
V	29.9	84.1	586.1	7.6	265.4
São Paulo coffee					
I	808.8	1060.1	1079.3	40.4	776.6
II	250.0	432.1	961.6	54.4	1053.4
III	134.9	233.4	1097.5	69.3	947.6
IV	76.8	217.2	1605.7	109.1	1318.2
V	163.4	254.4	1354.3	184.2	1553.2
VI	43.3	165.6	980.5	164.8	1756.5
Pernambuco sugar (FGV)					
I	0.0	0.0	0.0	0.0	0.0
II	226.9	260.2	920.0	94.0	519.0
III	110.6	198.2	889.4	138.4	632.2
IV	172.4	313.7	1295.4	70.2	524.8
V	105.5	212.8	728.7	110.4	413.4
VI	132.6	408.0	749.7	101.5	715.2

§4.4 DISCRIMINATION AMONG CAUSES OF LAND USE PATTERNS   119

Table 20, continued

	Labor/ farm area	Labor/ cultiv. area	Capital/ cultiv. area	Seeds, fert., insecticides/ cultiv. area	Production/ cultiv. area
São Paulo cereals					
I	509.9	807.4	745.1	32.7	1052.6
II	354.3	597.0	1741.8	80.8	891.6
III	162.8	315.5	1099.5	87.2	802.9
IV	103.8	349.4	600.4	68.7	889.5
V	40.2	171.1	1265.4	45.1	924.1
VI	19.1	113.9	926.2	55.1	460.8
Rio Grande do Sul rice (FGV)					
I	466.4	734.3	969.9	73.2	739.2
II	305.6	564.7	1365.2	124.9	1288.8
III	88.2	393.2	2439.0	126.2	928.1
IV	118.8	278.8	1509.7	91.3	1009.0
V	43.2	267.3	2667.2	126.2	892.6
VI	16.6	162.4	1776.1	145.2	1082.3
Minas Gerais corn					
I	1380.7	1845.0	1935.4	48.2	2041.1
II	396.8	886.7	1088.8	63.1	862.5
III	77.1	388.8	1450.7	34.3	1012.6
IV	48.3	374.4	1455.8	34.6	809.4
V	13.3	303.6	1125.1	17.7	340.0
Alagoas sugar (IAA)[†]					
I	0.0	0.0	0.0	0.0	0.0
II	17.9	87.7	4.7	2.4	23.5
III	38.1	102.4	6.7	2.4	27.4
IV	35.3	98.5	8.1	3.1	30.5
V	25.7	96.6	10.8	3.2	30.2
VI	35.3	107.7	14.1	3.1	28.7
Pernambuco sugar (IAA)[†]					
I	87.3	116.3	13.0	2.8	48.6
II	46.2	107.8	14.7	2.4	41.4
III	76.6	103.3	11.4	4.3	35.8
IV	52.7	110.9	11.5	8.8	25.2
V	51.4	116.1	20.0	4.7	32.0
VI	41.9	134.5	21.3	5.7	37.7

Table 20, continued

	Labor/ farm area	Labor/ cultiv. area	Capital/ cultiv. area	Seeds, fert., insecticides/ cultiv. area	Production/ cultiv. area
São Paulo sugar (IAA)[†]					
I	92.4	35.6	35.0	4.8	25.0
II	25.5	29.1	28.1	5.1	33.0
III	26.1	46.4	17.0	2.4	44.2
IV	16.5	40.9	23.0	7.6	35.4
V	26.1	50.9	23.3	5.2	43.6
VI	23.8	44.6	26.7	10.1	36.2
São Paulo cattle/general crops					
I	581.0	658.1	999.1	121.3	1019.1
II	91.9	101.7	774.0	68.8	343.4
III	83.0	89.8	492.0	41.7	168.6
IV	68.0	77.0	764.8	70.3	351.1
V	27.5	32.7	388.1	39.0	125.9
VI	32.1	41.0	598.3	15.4	76.6

	Labor/ farm area	Labor/ pasture area	Capital/ pasture area	Animal capital/ pasture	Vaccines and feed/ pasture	Production/ pasture area
São Paulo cattle						
I	467.7	708.9	602.4	1581.7	119.4	1262.1
II	165.4	223.2	835.4	871.2	87.5	655.8
III	98.9	142.2	390.3	453.7	35.7	381.0
IV	113.6	149.8	433.0	836.3	64.7	507.8
V	46.8	81.4	338.9	296.4	27.1	247.1
VI	12.0	15.9	170.3	501.4	6.4	202.9
Ceará cattle						
I	389.9	710.3	859.0	776.5	72.3	531.1
II	111.0	189.4	457.6	448.8	31.4	546.4
III	84.7	140.6	500.4	403.3	24.9	176.7
IV	35.6	55.2	232.8	208.7	18.3	147.1
V	21.2	32.5	239.5	115.4	5.9	61.1
VI	11.1	25.6	199.7	168.0	1.3	48.7
Espírito Santo cattle						
I	0.0	0.0	0.0	0.0	0.0	0.0
II	150.8	278.9	336.2	1351.3	16.0	233.9
III	69.0	95.4	516.8	622.6	12.4	206.6
IV	49.5	73.8	291.2	451.5	10.6	166.6
V	8.2	13.7	135.4	240.7	6.2	86.4

Table 20, continued

	Labor/ farm area	Labor/ pasture area	Capital/ pasture area	Animal capital/ pasture	Vaccines and feed/ pasture	Production/ pasture area
Minas Gerais cattle						
I	0.0	0.0	0.0	0.0	0.0	0.0
II	235.9	279.9	1104.9	318.5	108.1	983.1
III	87.1	119.4	738.0	379.3	66.3	360.2
IV	74.1	86.8	353.4	287.2	35.0	181.1
V	24.0	46.9	352.9	262.3	22.5	100.9
VI	10.7	14.9	70.4	136.9	8.8	48.3
Rio Grande do Sul cattle						
I	431.0	995.7	3329.1	1049.6	579.6	2218.0
II	53.5	90.7	415.9	468.2	39.2	220.3
III	35.2	38.1	187.3	170.6	1.6	33.4
IV	24.1	30.2	322.9	207.1	15.1	94.7
V	9.5	11.0	63.8	154.0	4.4	27.2
VI	5.2	8.6	79.7	179.6	1.9	34.0

* Size groups I–VI: see table 12. Entry of '0.0' means no observations in size group or else no such size group.
† IAA sectors: see table 4 for units.

group are shown in table 20. The trends of change in factor ratios, as farm size rises, are shown in table 21.

The factor combination trends shown in table 21 are consistent with labor market dualism (situations 1, 2, 3, and 4) in all sectors except sugar cane. In all of the cattle sectors and in three out of twelve crop sectors, it appears that labor market dualism and land market imperfection exist, but that the capital market is not substantially imperfect (situation 2). Capital market imperfection with lower cost of capital to large farms would appear to exist in Espírito Santo coffee, Rio Grande do Sul rice, and sugar cane in Alagoas and Pernambuco (IAA). The data are consistent with land market imperfection (situations 1, 2, 5, and 6) in eleven of the seventeen sectors.

In sum, the factor combination trends are consistent in most sectors with the hypothesis that labor market dualism exists, and with the hypothesis that imperfection exists in the land market. The data do not show similar frequency of capital market imperfection. It is important to note that both labor market imperfection ('dualism') and land market imperfection seem to exist. For if the labor market alone were imperfect, a decline of labor

TABLE 21

Factor ratio trends as farm size rises

Sector	Factor ratio			Possible situations (table 19)
	N/L	N/K	K/L	
Cea. cot.	↓	↓	↓	2
Per. cot.	↓	↓	—	1, 4, 5
E. S. coffee	↓	↓	↑	3
S. P. coffee	↓	↓	—	1, 4, 5
Per. sug. FGV	↑	↑	—	none
S. P. cerls.	↓	↓	—	1, 4, 5
R. G. rice	↓	↓	↑	3
M. G. corn	↓	↓	↓	2
S. P. cat./gen.	↓	↓	↓	2
Al. sug.	—	↓	↑	7
Per. sug. IAA	—	↓	↑	7
S. P. sug	—	—	—	8
Cea. cat.	↓	↓	↓	2
E. S. cat.	↓	↓	↓	2
M. G. cat.	↓	↓	↓	2
R. G. cat.	↓	↓	↓	2
S. P. cat.	↓	↓	↓	2

N = labor K = capital L = land input
↑ = increase ↓ = decrease

relative to both land and capital would occur, with no decline in capital relative to land (situation 4). But this case is observed in only 3 sectors. If the land market alone were imperfect, both labor and capital would decline relative to the land input, with no decline in labor relative to capital (situation 6). But this case does not occur in any of the sectors. In contrast, in eleven of the 17 sectors the data are consistent with joint imperfection of the land and labor markets (situation 1 or 2).

4.4.2. Rate of decline of land use intensity

A second way of testing the alternative explanations of land use is to search for a phenomenon of two-step land use intensity – one level for family farms and another, lower level for capitalist farms – in support of the hypothesis of labor market dualism. Thus, if family versus non-family labor is the only market imperfection one would expect more intensive use of land on family farms, but constant intensity of land use over the whole size range of

§4.4   DISCRIMINATION AMONG CAUSES OF LAND USE PATTERNS   123

TABLE 22

Adult equivalent workers per farm, by farm size group

Sector	Farm size group*					
	I	II	III	IV	V	VI
Ceará cot.	0– 6.2	2.6– 7.8	2.3– 7.6	5.4–16.2	4.3–14.2	> 12.8
Per. cot.	0– 4.4	2.0– 6.1	2.4– 8.0	2.8 – 8.4	>9.0	n.a.
E. S. cof.	0–3.2	1.8– 3.4	1.9– 6.4	3.4– 8.5	>8.4	n.a.
S. P. cof.	0–11.6	3.6– 8.9	4.8– 9.6	5.5–16.5	35.1–117	> 30.9
P. sug. FGV	n.a.	3.3–13.2	6.6–32.4	50.2–75.3	46 –155	>194
S. P. cerls.	0– 3.6	2.5– 7.5	3.4–11.6	7.4–17.8	7.0–14.3	> 7.0
R. G. rice	0– 5.6	3.7–11.1	3.1–10.5	14.3–32.9	15.4–51.5	> 20.3
M. G. corn	0– 9.9	2.8– 8.4	1.6– 5.5	3.4–10.5	>2.8	n.a.
S. P. cat./gen.	0– 8.3	1.3– 3.3	2.9– 5.9	4.9–14.7	6.0– 9.8	> 11.5
Al. sug.	n.a.	0.6– 3.0	6.4–15.9	14.8–34.4	25.7–85.7	>117.7
Per. sug. IAA	0– 2.9	1.5– 4.5	7.8–25.5	17.6–52.8	51.3–171.3	>140.0
S. P. sug.	0– 0.8	0.8– 2.6	2.6– 8.7	5.5–16.5	25.1–87.0	> 79.3
Ceará cat.	0– 6.5	1.8– 3.6	2.8– 9.5	4.0–12.0	7.0–23.6	> 12.4
E. S. cat.	n.a.	1.7– 4.1	2.3– 7.7	5.6–16.8	>2.7	n.a.
M. G. cat.	n.a.	1.7– 4.1	1.8– 6.2	5.3–15.9	4.1–13.6	> 6.4
R. G. cat.	0– 5.2	0.6– 3.2	2.1– 5.2	3.6– 8.7	3.4–11.3	> 6.2
S. P. cat.	0–10.0	3.6– 5.9	3.5– 7.1	8.1–24.3	10.0–33.6	> 8.6

* See table 12.

capitalist farms. This pattern would also be consistent with the 'own consumption market' consideration, however, since the own-consumption influence would be expected to be greatest on family farms.

The ratios of labor to farm size shown in table 20 serve as a basis for determining the size range of family farms, in each sector. Table 22 shows the number of workers per farm in each farm size group, based on the labor value per farm area, of table 20. The range of workers in each size group is found by multiplying the floor and ceiling farm sizes in the group by the average number of workers per farm area in the group.

It is clear from table 22 that a unique mapping of farm area to number of workers is not accurate, since the labor density falls so fast that a higher farm size group may have no more workers than a lower size group. Nevertheless, there is an overall correspondence of farm size with number of workers. For an informal test of the 'labor–market dualism' hypothesis it is desirable to separate farms into 'family', 'mixed', and 'capitalist' size

TABLE 23

Informal test for existence of labor-market dualism: two-step intensity of land use

Sector	Farm size groups of type:			Two-step land use intensity	
	Family (<5) workers	Mixed (5–10) workers	Capitalist (>10) workers		
	A	B	C	D	E
Cea. cot.	I, II, III	—	IV, V, VI	R	C
Per. cot.	I, II, III	IV, V	—	R	R
E. S. cof.	I, II, III	IV, V	—	R	R
S. P. cof.	I, II	III, IV	V, VI	R	R
P. sug. FGV	II	III	IV, V, VI	U	R
S. P. cerls.	I, II	III, IV	V, VI	R	R
R. G. rice	I	II, III	IV, V, VI	R	R
M. G. corn	I, II, III	IV	V	R	C
S. P. cat./gen.	I, II, III	IV	V	R	R
Al. sug.	II	III	IV, V, VI	R	R
Per. sug. IAA	I, II	III	IV, V, VI	U	C
S. P. sug.	II	III, IV	V, VI	U	R
Cea. cat.	I, II	III, IV	V, VI	C	R
E. S. cat.	II, III	IV, V	—	R	R
M. G. cat.	II, III	IV, V, VI	—	R	C
R. G. cat.	I, II, III, IV	V, VI	—	R	C
S. P. cat.	I, II, III	IV	V, VI	R	R

R = reject two-step pattern; C = confirm; U = unclear.

groups of, respectively, up to five workers, five to ten workers, and above ten workers. It is expected that intensity of output per farm area will be high for the first, falling for the second, and low but constant for the third type of farm.

In table 23, the size groups corresponding to each type of organization (family, mixed, capitalist) are shown, along with a judgment as to whether the 'step' fall in intensity of output per farm area is confirmed (C), rejected (R), or unclear (U). In column D, the analysis is based on the data of table 14, where value added per farm area is shown by size group. In column E, the analysis is based on examination of the scatter diagrams of model IV.2.

The conclusion of table 23 is that, on a basis of value added per farm area by size group (from table 14), there exists no clear two-step pattern of land use intensity, corresponding to a high shelf for family farms and a low, constant shelf for capitalist farms.

The same question may be investigated in the scatter diagrams of model IV.2. None of the diagrams shows a two-shelf pattern as such. However, five of the sectors show a flattening of output per area above certain farm sizes. These sectors, and the logarithm of farm size at which value added per area becomes constant, are: Ceará cotton (3.0), Minas Gerais corn (3.8), Pernambuco sugar IAA (7.0), Minas Gerais cattle (4.5), and Rio Grande do Sul cattle (5.5). The corresponding absolute farm sizes are, in hectares: 21, 45, 1092, 89, and 240. These farm sizes are consistent with the ceiling of 'family farms', as may be seen in table 22, except for Pernambuco sugar IAA. In this sector, the turning point is too large to represent the ceiling of family farms, since farms of 1000 ha employ roughly 140 workers.

Since only four sectors appear to show a constant output per area for farms above 'family' size, it would seem that influences other than labor market dualism alone are operative. Also, the influence of the 'own consumption market' would not be the only explanation of land use patterns, since this influence too would cause high land use intensity for family farms and lower but constant land use intensity for the whole size range of capitalist farms.

4.4.3. Further scatter diagram analysis

The scatter diagrams are of further use in distinguishing among the possible causes of falling land use intensity. If the tendency to hold land for speculative reasons grows gradually with farm size, as suggested earlier, then one would expect a gradual decline in land use intensity, to very low levels on the largest farms. While this description is not rigorous, it is nevertheless useful to examine the scatter diagrams for such a pattern. The diagrams show a gradual decline in land intensity, to very low levels on the largest farms, relative to smaller farms, for eight sectors: Pernambuco cotton; São Paulo cereals; Rio Grande do Sul rice; Minas Gerais corn; São Paulo cattle/ general, and cattle in Ceará, Espírito Santo, and São Paulo. Thus in these sectors, speculative land holding may be responsible for the fall in land use intensity. From the previous analysis of factor ratio trends, the influences of labor market dualism and land market imperfection are probably also present in these sectors.

Non-economic behavior would cause extremely low output per area on the largest farms, and thus would be difficult to distinguish from speculative holding. Land market imperfection would cause a pattern similar to that described for speculative landholding in that intensity of land use would fall gradually; but land market imperfection would not necessarily cause extremely low land use on the largest farms. Since almost all of the scatter diagrams show declining land use intensity to some degree, land market imperfection would be consistent with almost all of the diagrams.

Monopsony of large farms over labor should be observable in the scatter diagrams. There would be a two-step pattern for intensity of land use: one higher level for the whole range of competitive farms, and one lower level for the farms large enough to exert monopsony influence. The 'step' would occur at a much larger farm size than the expected 'step' for family vs. non-family farms. The size of 10,000 ha might arbitrarily be chosen as the minimum size necessary for exertion of monopsony influence. This size corresponds to a value of roughly 8.5 on the X axis of the diagrams. In none of the diagrams does there appear to be a two-step-pattern of land use with no decline in the intensity of land use until this large farm size is reached. Thus, if monopsony power is exerted, it is not the only influence affecting land use.

In sum, almost all of the diagrams are consistent with land market imperfection; some are consistent with speculative holding and non-economic behavior; and few if any are consistent with 'own market consumption' or 'labor–market dualism' as unique influences. However, the strong likelihood of labor market dualism, based on the factor ratio analysis above, suggests that this influence exists in combination with other influences, probably primarily land market imperfection and speculative holding. Similarly, if monopsony action exists, it is not the only operative influence, since land use intensity declines for farm sizes smaller than the sizes which would be necessary for the existence of monopsony power.

4.4.4. Concentration of land ownership

A necessary but not sufficient condition for monopsony behavior to have an important effect on the sector's land use is that land ownership be relatively highly concentrated. It is therefore useful to examine briefly the degree of land concentration in the sectors of this study. Table 24 shows the percent of total sectoral area in each farm size group.

It may be seen that the sectors with the highest concentration of land in farms over 1000 ha are Pernambuco sugar; Alagoas sugar; Rio Grande do

§4.4   DISCRIMINATION AMONG CAUSES OF LAND USE PATTERNS   127

TABLE 24

Distribution of farm area by farm size group (universe, by product sector)

Sector	Percent of area in farms of size (ha)			
	<10	10–100	100–1000	>1000
Cea. cotton*	2.9	45.6	38.6	12.4
Per. cotton[†]	20.1	39.6	36.2	4.1
E. S. cof.[†]	1.1	59.0	36.5	3.6
S. P. cof.[†]	3.3	26.7	47.3	22.3
Per. sug.**	1.0	4.3	30.5	64.0
S. P. cerls.[†]	6.3	33.3	40.1	20.6
R. G. rice[†]	1.0	21.3	37.5	40.3
M. G. corn*	5.2	35.6	59.2	0.0
Al. sug.**	0.3	5.3	38.4	56.0
S. P. sug.**	0.7	13.3	59.4	26.6
Cea. cat.*	1.6	17.8	73.9	6.7
E. S. cat.[†]	0.5	24.7	58.9	16.4
M. G. cat.*	0.0	13.6	40.0	46.4
R. G. cat.[†]	0.5	8.1	40.0	51.0
S. P. cat.[†]	0.2	12.3	44.8	42.2

Source: [†] 1960 agricultural census
  * Weighted sample, see appendix C.
  ** IAA data, see appendix C.

Sul cattle; and Rio Grande do Sul rice. The São Paulo sectors – cattle, sugar, coffee, cereals – all show substantial concentration of area in farms over 1000 ha, from 20% to 40%. These sectors probably meet the necessary concentration for importance of monopsony influence of large farms over labor. However, while monopsony power is not exercised as a unique influence in these sectors (as discussed above) it is impossible to determine whether or not monopsony action exists in combination with some of the other influences on land use. Furthermore, in two of the sectors with high land ownership concentration in large farms (Alagoas sugar and São Paulo coffee) land use[1] is not low on large farms; and therefore neither monopsony action nor other causes of low land use seems to exist.

4.4.5. Summary

The attempts to differentiate among the various causes of falling land use

---

[1] On a basis of model IV.2.

intensity may be summarized in the following way. First, on a basis of factor ratio trends, it appears that labor market dualism and land market imperfections are both important. Second, the scatter diagrams show the very low land use on large farms which would be expected for speculative holding or non-economic behavior for half of the sectors. Third, labor–market dualism must coexist with other influences, primarily land market imperfection and speculative holding of land. If labor dualism were the only influence, a two-step pattern of land use would be observed, corresponding to family versus non-family farms, and this split is not observed in the data. Finally, monopsony may be of importance in sectors where the necessary condition of land concentration exists, but the methods of this section do not permit detection of actual exertion of monopsony power.[1]

4.5. 'Social efficiency' and farm size

At this point in the study, Brazilian data have been used to test the hypotheses that increasing returns to scale exist in agriculture (chapter 3) and that land use intensity declines as farm size rises (in this chapter). It was found that returns to scale are constant for inputs used. It was also found that the intensity of inputs used per farm area declines as farm size rises. These two results, combined with the assumption that unemployed rural labor exists, imply that land redistribution from large farms into smaller farms could increase intensity of inputs per farm area and equalize this intensity across farms. Therefore production increases could be achieved through land redistribution.

Before land redistribution's impact on agricultural production is estimated (in chapter 5), it is useful to reconsider the findings in terms of 'social efficiency'. In section 2.5 above, it was suggested that analysis using social shadow prices for factors would be useful to supplement the analysis of 'production efficiency' of chapter 3 and the analysis of 'farm efficiency' of this chapter. 'Social production efficiency' would be measured by the ratio of

---

[1] That is, while monopsony power in isolation could be observed in the scatter diagrams, the diagrams do not show patterns compatible with monopsony as a sole influence. On the other hand they do show patterns consistent with the joint existence of monopsony and other influences such as land market imperfection and speculative land holding: yet is is impossible to demonstrate that monopsony influence is exerted in these cases, since the other influences could cause the observed patterns even if monopsony were not present.

output to social cost of inputs utilized, with only the land 'input included in cost. This measurement would be used to qualify the results regarding returns to scale in production. 'Social farm efficiency' would be measured by the ratio of output to social cost of resources available, and would be identical to 'social production efficiency' except that total farm area would be included as the land cost in 'social farm efficiency'. 'Social farm efficiency' would be used to identify an optimal farm size in each sector of agriculture at present.

The absence of valid economy-wide 'shadow prices' makes an analysis of the relationship of 'social production efficiency' and 'social farm efficiency' to farm size impossible. However, inferences about social efficiency may be drawn from the trends of factor combinations. The analyses of sections 4.3.3. and 4.4.1. above demonstrate large shifts in factor combinations from labor toward cultivated land and capital, as farm size rises. The various reasons for this shift have been discussed. However, the consistent shift in factor combinations implies that:

1. 'constant returns to scale' should be qualified with the observation that 'social production efficiency' would probably not be constant over all production scales;

2. 'social farm efficiency' would go beyond the 'farm efficiency' (of this chapter), because it would show not only the influence of declining land use intensity, but also the influence of a shift from labor to cultivated land and capital as farm size rises.

In the absence of factor shadow prices only two general conclusions may be drawn about 'social farm efficiency'.

The first conclusion is that factor misallocation exists in Brazilian agriculture, and this misallocation is systematically related to farm size. This conclusion requires the reasonable assumption that production functions are homogeneous. If the production functions are homogeneous, only one factor combination is socially efficient for each product. The misallocation of factors used in agriculture implies a possible production gain from land reform.[1] If reform equalizes factor ratios across farms, production will increase. This increase will be partially additional to the production gain to be expected from post-reform use of farm area previously idle, and from use of previously unemployed labor.

---

[1] This gain may possibly be achieved by measures other than land redistribution. See section 6.1 below.

The second conclusion, which is more tenuous, is that if shadow prices were available for factors, one would find a relatively small farm size to be 'optimal' since labor's 'shadow price' is likely to be low and the smaller farms are the more labor intensive. Nevertheless, one would expect the optimal size to be greater than the smallest size; one would expect that the very smallest farms use too much labor even given its low shadow price. Finally, it would be possible for no farm size in the sector to have a 'socially optimal' factor combination, if the entire sector used too much (or too little) of a factor considering its opportunity cost to the rest of the economy.

To summarize, in theory a 'socially optimal farm size' could be determined if shadow prices were available because the factor combination consistently shifts away from labor toward capital and land as farm size rises. In this study, however, this optimal size is not identified. The major conclusion to be drawn from observed factor combination shifts is that there exists a potential production gain from land reform, through equalization of combinations of factors already utilized in agriculture. In part, this gain would be additional to the gain from new use of formerly idle land, but the two gains would not be completely independent. For example, part of the 'excess labor' on the smaller farms would be shifted onto land used by large farms before the reform (factor combination equalization) and part of that excess labor would be shifted onto formerly idle land (increase in the 'land input' factor, i.e., increased land utilization).

4.6. Conclusion

The principal findings of this chapter are:

1. Three different tests show a statistically significant decline in 'land use intensity' as farm size rises, for almost all of the 17 sectors examined. The first test uses the percent of 'usable' farm area cultivated or grazed at normal rates as the measure of land use intensity; the second test uses 'value added per farm area' as the measure of land use intensity; the third test estimates the relationship between inputs and farm size. The 'elasticity of input use with respect to farm size' is found in most cases to be less than unity.

2. The influence of land quality does not account for all of the decline in land use intensity as farm size rises. In the first statistical test, only 'usable' farm area is considered, so that the influence of changing land quality is to some extent removed. In the second test, the influence of land quality is

removed by the use of 'land price' as an independent variable, under the assumption that land price reflects both the physical and locational 'quality' of the land.

3. The land tenure situation (operation of the farm by tenants versus operation by the owner) does not have any consistent, statistically significant effect on land use intensity.

4. Scatter diagrams of value added per farm area do not show, within each sector, any clear dichotomy for large farms between large 'efficient' farms ('rural enterprises') and large inefficient farms ('*latifúndios*'), despite the existence of this distinction in the literature and legislation. Nevertheless it would be rational in any land expropriation process to proceed from the least productive farms (in terms of output per farm area) to the more productive large farms, so long as the set of farms considered for expropriation had good land quality.

5. The common view that agrarian structure is only a problem in the Northeast, not in the South, of Brazil, is not found to be true on a basis of comparison of value added per farm area or per land value, between small farms (less than 30 ha) and large farms (over 300 ha). Using the same criteria, there does seem to be some validity to the idea that poor use of land on large farms is primarily found in cattle sectors. However, of the crop sectors, only sugar cane and coffee sectors appear to have relatively good land use on large farms, while rice, cotton, and corn sectors have relative land utilization by large farms that is as poor as that for cattle sectors.

6. Informal tests are made to discriminate among alternative possible explanations of poor land use on large farms. Factor ratio trends suggest that both 'labor-market dualism' and 'land market imperfection' are important; the scatter diagrams, of value added per hectare against farm size, do not show a two-step pattern which would be expected if only labor market dualism were important; monopsony action by large farms does not appear to be the sole influence, although it could exist in combination with other influences; and the very low relative land utilization by large farms in half of the sectors suggests speculative land holding or non-economic behavior by large farms in these sectors. These informal tests are considered inconclusive by the author, and it is emphasized that, for the purpose of predicting the output effect of land redistribution, the most important distinction is between the 'land quality' influence and the other influences combined.

7. The absence of economy-wide shadow prices for factors precludes

measurement of 'social production efficiency' and 'social farm efficiency'. However, the observed shift from labor to cultivated land and capital, as farm size rises, has two implications for 'social efficiency'. First, misallocation of inputs now used exists across farms, and an equalization of factor combinations across farms could increase production. This statement assumes that the production functions are homogeneous. Second, since it is likely that labor's shadow price is very low, and since small farms are more labor intensive than large farms, it is likely that the optimal farm size in terms of 'social farm efficiency' is small.

CHAPTER 5

PREDICTION OF THE IMPACT OF LAND REFORM ON BRAZILIAN AGRICULTURAL PRODUCTION

5.1. Introduction

This chapter attempts to measure the change in agricultural production to be expected from land redistribution. The production functions of chapter 3 and the relationships of inputs to farm size of chapter 4 are the basis for the predictions. The production changes represent the once-for-all impact of increased land and labor use, and of factor re-allocation in land reform.[1] Any short-run effects due to uncertainty caused by reform are ignored (partly because they would be difficult to estimate, partly because they could be either positive or negative, depending on the announced land reform procedures). The purpose of the prediction is to see whether production would rise or fall due to reform; to find the general magnitude of the change, and to identify the specific regions and products in which output would increase most greatly. These three points are investigated because of their crucial policy implications. Respectively, they will tell whether land reform should be opposed because it will injure production; whether potential gains in production are large and therefore are likely to exceed the costs of land reform; and, finally, where the reform should begin.

Two reform calculations are made, each with varying assumptions. In the 'total reform' calculation, the entire sector is divided into family farms of equal size. In the 'partial reform' calculation, only farms over 300 ha with above-average land quality are considered eligible for expropriation.

The reform calculations are limited to redistribution of land within each product sector. Thus, no calculation is made for shifts in the principal product on land in a given product sector. Such inter-sectoral shifts would probably

---

[1] Specifically, the impacts of: (a) an increase in the percent of available land actually used as a productive input; (b) the use of labor formerly unemployed; (c) equalization among farms of the combinations of factors used. Note that any long run changes due to shifts in agricultural savings and receptivity to technical change, are excluded from the calculations of this chapter, since data are unavailable for analysis of such shifts.

be most important in the case of transformation of cattle land into crop production.[1] It is also assumed that no shift occurs in the product mix within a given 'product sector'. Each product-sector is defined on a basis of the major product, but each member farm produces minor crops as well. In reality, it is likely that after a land reform there would be some shift from the major crop in the sector toward the minor crops in cases in which the major crop is an industrial crop (such as cotton, coffee, sugar cane) and the minor crops are foodstuffs. Nevertheless, for simplicity of analysis, crop mix within each product sector is assumed not to change after land reform.

In both the 'total reform' and the 'partial reform', the size of the farm unit created by reform – the 'parcel' – is the total land area in the sector divided by the number of 'families' in the sector (assuming 2.5 adult-equivalent workers per family). Unemployed workers allocated to the sector are included in determining the number of 'families'. Since unemployment data are not available, alternative assumptions are made about the number of unemployed workers, in both the 'total 'and 'partial' reforms. In the total reform, two additional alternative assumptions are made: that total capital and intermediate inputs in the sector do not change after land reform; and that these input totals may change after land reform.

The reform calculations are made for each of the 17 sectors investigated in chapters 3 and 4. Percentage changes in production and inputs are calculated for each sector, and the relative production gains of the sectors after land reform may be compared. The sectors are weighted by their relative importance in current national production, in order to determine the percentage increase in Brazilian agricultural output that would result from land reform applied to all sectors.

Finally, although the expected percentage increase in output, resulting from land redistribution, is quite high in some sectors (the highest is 60%), no adjustment is made for possibile decline in product prices. Price elasticities of demand are not available. However, it is likely that much of the increased production would be consumed by the farm families themselves, so that there need be no great concern about decreased market prices. Furthermore,

---

[1] Table 14 gives some indication of the level of output per farm area on cattle farms in comparison with crop farms in the same state. Rio Grande do Sul seems to be the main case in which a large difference exists between output per area on crop farms and that on cattle ranches. Inter-sectoral shifts of products or of factors are excluded from the land reform calculations because of limits to the feasible scope of the study.

the level of food consumption is low for urban workers, and food expenditures comprise a high percent of their budgets. Therefore the income effect of slightly decreased food prices would add heavily to the substitution effect and the increased food consumption would prevent large declines in food prices.

5.2. Assumptions

There are six major assumptions made in the land reform calculations of this chapter.

The first assumption is that production functions after the reform will be identical to those before the reform. On the basis of this assumption the functions estimated in chapter 3, for agriculture in Brazil at present, are applied to the inputs on post-reform farms to determine the output on these farms.

The second assumption is that land quality may be represented by land price. This assumption is necessary in the conservative 'partial reform' calculation, in which large farms with 'poor land' are excluded from expropriation. While the land price may not always accurately represent quality because of land market imperfections, it is the only index of land quality for which data are available. In the less conservative 'total reform' calculation, it is implicitly assumed that all land is of identical quality.

The third assumption is that the post-reform units are private rather than state farms. The reason for the assumption is that large state farms are most attractive if there are prospects of important economies of scale; but is has been found (in chapter 3) that returns to scale are constant in Brazilian agriculture. Therefore post-reform units can be relatively small scale private farms without loss of efficiency.

The fourth assumption is that post-reform units, or 'parcels', are 'family' units, arbitrarily set at 2.5 adult-equivalent workers. Given the 'private' basis of reform, and given the falling intensity of land use as farm size rises, it may be concluded that the optimal 'parcel' size is the smallest farm size consistent with two constraints: that all the land is in farms, and that all the labor is absorbed in farms. The smallest feasible size is assumed to be the 'family' size. Therefore the reform 'parcel' size in land area, is the total farmland of the sector divided by the number of families in the sector, including unemployed workers.

It is important to note that the choice of the family unit is not the planner's value judgment, or preference for family farm organization. Instead, it is a logical conclusion since intensity of land use declines as farm size increases. With constant returns to scale, this relationship between land use and farm size implies that the smallest feasible farm unit will maximize production. The family unit is assumed to be the smallest feasible unit.

Selecting the family farm as the post-reform unit is consistent with the statement in section 2.5.2 that the socially optimal unit should be larger than the smallest size, since the post-reform farm would have more land than the smallest pre-reform farms.[1] If the 'socially optimal' farm size could be measured, it would be the appropriate unit for the calculations of this chapter, but this measurement is not possible because 'shadow prices' for factors are not available.

The fifth assumption in the land reform calculations is that on post-reform units of a given area, inputs of cultivated (or pasture) land, capital, seeds and fertilizer are identical to the inputs of pre-reform farms of the same size. Therefore the relationships of inputs to farm size, estimated in section 4.3.3, are used in order to determine the amounts of inputs applied on the post-reform parcel.[2] The labor input on the parcel is assumed to be 2.5 adult-equivalent workers.[3]

---

[1] The higher amount of land available to the post-reform family unit implies one of two things. Either there is a strict pre-reform labor/farm area ratio for a level of 2.5 workers and that ratio is broken in the reform calculations, or there is in reality no unique labor/farm area relationship before reform, but instead families (of 2.5 workers) may be found with, for example, 2 ha, other families with 10 ha, others with 30 ha, etc. The second case is the more valid, and the point here is that the 'family unit' after reform is patterned after the pre-reform family unit with 30 ha (for example) rather than the 2 ha family unit. Thus the post-reform unit is larger than the smallest pre-reform farms even though it is based on the smallest feasible labor organization.

[2] This procedure is used for the land input in all of the reform calculations. The procedure is used for capital, and for seed and fertilizer inputs, in the 'partial' reforms, and in two of the four versions of 'total reform'. In the other two versions of total reform, it is assumed that total capital, seeds, and fertilizer inputs in the sector cannot increase. Therefore, in these two versions, the capital input (for example) on the land reform parcel equals the total amount of capital in the sector before reform, divided by the number of parcels.

[3] It may be asked whether the pre-reform relationship of input to farm size should be assumed for the land input, capital seeds, and fertilizers, while the labor on the parcel is not derived from the pre-reform labor–farm size relationship. In practice this question is not very important, since the labor on the reform parcel would be close to 2.5 workers even if the labor input were determined by the pre-reform relationship (see section 5.4.1, table 25).

§5.2 ASSUMPTIONS 137

The assumption that the farm size-input relationship will remain constant after land reform requires that the post-reform units be privately owned. There would be no reason to expect inputs to be as low on large state farms as on pre-reform large farms. The levels of inputs applied on large state farms could be determined by executive fiat. In the case of private post-reform farms, however, pre-reform practices on a farm of a given size would be the best available guide to post-reform practices on a parcel of that size.[1]

There is a second basis for the use of the pre-reform farm size–factor input relationship. Six major market imperfections and behavioral rigidities cause a decline in land use intensity as farm size rises. The influences are: (1) 'labor-market dualism', (2) speculative landholding by large owners, (3) land market imperfection, (4) production for 'own consumption' on small farms, (5) non-economic behavior of large farm owners, and (6) monopsony power of large farms. Ideally, a function would be estimated relating inputs to all six of these influences, with one variable to represent each influence, and the post reform parcel would have inputs predicted by the changed values of these six variables. The use of a single input-farm size relationship is a simplifying step, in which farm size is used as the independent variable to represent the joint effect of the six influences mentioned.[2] In section 2.5 it was argued that all of these influences cause land use intensity to decline as

---

[1] This assertion implicitly assumes that the pre-reform set of market imperfections and behavior patterns would remain unchanged after reform and that only the relative frequency of large and small farms would be changed by reform. This description would be accurate only if land redistribution alone were carried out, without increased credit for general land purchase, without land taxation, in other words, without complementary measures to improve factor markets. While the rigidity of preference for work on the family farm could be expected to continue after reform, other market imperfections could in fact be expected to be improved by correct policy. Nevertheless, the distortion involved in assuming that pre-reform input–size relationships apply to post reform farms is minimized if the 'reform parcel' in question is of an intermediate size range. The very smallest and very largest pre-form farms are those with the most distorted factor combinations, such that if market imperfections were removed, their inputs could be expected to change the most. For some intermediate pre-reform farm size, however, pre-reform inputs are such that general market improvements would not change the farm's input pattern. The closer the 'parcel' is to this farm size, the less distortion there will be in assuming that the post reform parcel inputs will be the same as inputs on pre-reform farms of size equal to the parcel.

[2] The implications of the six influence for land reform are all similar: large farms have unused land that could be used after land redistribution. However, the influences do not have identical implications for other policy measures such as land tax, credit for land purchase, etc. (see section 6.1).

farm size rises. There should be little distortion when the 'proxy' input-farm size relationship is used in place of a function relating inputs directly to the six influences. Furthermore, data is lacking for some of the influences, and it would be difficult to specify a model accurately representing the six influences even if data were available for all of them.

Finally, land quality is the only influence incompatible with the simple relationship of inputs to farm size. Only this influence might reverse the production implications of the inverse relationship between land use intensity and farm size. For this reason, the 'partial reform' predictions explicitly account for land quality (both physical quality and the influence of market accessibility) by excluding from expropriation farms with low land price.

The sixth assumption in the land reform calculations is that the rural unemployed workers are absorbed onto land reform parcels. The use of formerly unemployed labor is one of the sources of increased production expected from land redistribution. Furthermore, the absorption of unemployed workers is a policy goal in itself.

It is necessary to estimate the amount of unemployed labor, since no rural unemployment data exist for Brazil. It is assumed that 'temporary workers' defined in the census as workers who are not on the farm year-round, represent the rural unemployed. While temporary labor may be employed at peak seasons only,[1] it is assumed that most of the temporary workers could find employment for the whole year on farms of their own.[2] High and low estimates of unemployment are made, as 1/2 and 1/10 of temporary labor.

5.3. Sample expansion

In order to use the sample data of this study for projection of the effect of land reform, it is necessary to weight the sample information so that it resembles

---

[1] This assumption would be invalid if temporary workers merely followed the harvest season across a large area so as to be employed continually. However, it is unlikely that the harvest seasons are timed in this way.

[3] Note that if all temporary workers are fully employed at exactly the same peak season, and if it is impossible to stagger peak employment periods by changes in planting time, then the increase in the 'labor' applied due to land reform will be overstated in the estimates below. Nevertheless the 'low unemployment' versions of the calculations assume very small increases in labor inputs, and approximate estimates which would assume no increase in labor inputs.

the universe. The data of the FGV sample are dominated by large farms, as may be seen in table 32, appendix B, which shows the percentage of total area by farm size in the sample as opposed to census information.[1] The reason for the undue weight of large farms is probably the 'cluster' method of sampling used in the Getulio Vargas Foundation sample. In the first stage farms were chosen at random from the census rolls. Then, a 'cluster' of farms adjacent to each chosen farm was surveyed. This procedure permitted random sampling while keeping actual traveling costs within reason. However, in a situation in which small farms are intermixed with large farms, the sampling procedure would be biased in favor of selecting large farms. The bias results from the fact that, given the farm chosen at the first stage, the probability that a large farm will be among those chosen at the second stage is higher than the share of large farms in the total number of farms, since the large farm's greater area increases its chances of being adjacent to a farm selected at random. In two distinct areas, one strictly of small farms and the other strictly of large, with no intermixture, the 'cluster' sample would not be biased.

Adjustment of the sample data is of great importance, since the possible gains from land reform could be grossly overestimated if the data represented a severe overstatement of the percent of area in large farms.

The data have therefore been adjusted by expansion multiples. These multiples are the ratios: A_j/a_j where A_j is the percent of total area in farms of size group j, from census information, and a_j is that percent for the sample. The 1960 census provides size group data by principal product, for each state and these data are used directly for the expansion multiples for the identical product sectors of this study. For those product sectors of this study for which census data are not yet published, generalized expansion factors are used, based on the average of expansion factors for the sectors for which census information is available.

The values of all variables for each sample observation, are multiplied by the expansion factor for the size group of which the observation is a member. The transformed data then have two necessary properties: the total farm

---

[1] For all farms together, this comparison is only possible for Pernambuco and Rio Grande do Sul, the only two states in which the entire set of sample observations are available to the author. For the other five states, only 'product-sector' observations are available.

area of the sample is unchanged; and the percentage composition of the data, by size group, is now identical to that of the census data.[1]

The 'expansion factors' for each size group are given, by sector, in appendix B (table 33).

For data from the IAA sugar cane survey, the same expansion technique is used. In this case 'cluster sampling' was not used in the original sample. Instead, a stratified random sample was taken, based on production size groups. Nevertheless, expansion of the sample by the method described above is used in this study. The census data are not relied upon entirely for this expansion, since data from the Institute of Sugar and Alcohol imply substantial errors in the census data. The census seems to register as independent farms the sub-units *(fundos)* composing the land of each sugar mill. Since these sub-units are operated jointly, they should be viewed as one large farm per sugar mill. Thus, the Census grossly understates the number of extremely large sugar farms in all three states examined – Pernambuco, Alagoas, and São Paulo. The methods used for construction of the 'universe', and for derivation of the expansion factors, are shown in appendix B.

In summary, values of variables – production, farm area, inputs, etc. – are multiplied by expansion factors. These factors 'blow up' the small farms and 'shrink' the variables for the large farms, since the latter are over-represented in the sample. The transformed data can then be used as a basis for calculations of the effect of land reform on production.

5.4. Land reform calculations

5.4.1. 'Total reform'

In chapter 3, the production functions estimated showed constant returns to scale (with the exception of increasing returns in São Paulo, coffee). In chapter 4 it was found that in most sectors, the intensity of inputs used per

---

[1] Proof: Let $s = \Sigma_j s_j$ and $S = \Sigma_j S_j$ where s_j = sample area in size group j, and S_j = census area in size group j. Then $a_j = s_j/s$ and $A_j = S_j/S$. Let x_j = area of transformed sample, in size group j. $X = \Sigma_j x_j$. Then $x_j = (A_j/a_j)s_j$.

$$X = \sum_j \frac{A_j}{a_j} s_j = \sum_j \frac{S_j/S}{s_j/s} s_j = s \sum_j \frac{S_j}{S} = s.$$

Thus, total area of transformed data equals total area of raw data. Also $x_j/X = [(A_j/a_j)s_j]/S = A_j s_j/a_j S = A_j s_j/s_j = A_j$. Thus, percentage composition of the area of transformed sample data, by size group, equals that of the census.

hectare of farm area, declines as farm size rises. The implication of these two phenomena is that reorganization of production on a small farm size basis would increase production. The family unit would be the logical floor to farm size. The 'total reform' calculation thus assumes complete reorganization of sectors into family farms of equal size.[1] It represents the maximum level of potential gain from land reform, under the restrictive assumption of no change in product composition for land in a given product sector.

The amount of unemployed labor to be absorbed in each sector is based on the amount of 'temporary labor' in the region, as discussed above (section 5.2). The 1950 census showed temporary labor constituted 32% of the labor force in the Northeast, 28% in the East, and 13% in the South. Since the Northeast is Brazil's region of most severe unemployment, the temporary labor data do seem to parallel unemployment levels. Thus, the high estimates are that the unemployed workers, as a percent of observed employed, were 19% in sectors of the Northeast, 16% in the East, and 7% in the South.[2] The low estimates are 3.4%, 2.9%, and 1.3%, respectively.

Four total reform calculations are made. These correspond to the four combinations of two variable assumptions: high (H) and low (L) levels of unemployment; and, no change (A) in sectoral capital, seeds, and fertilizer, versus change (B) in these inputs.

Sectoral levels of capital, seeds, and fertilizer are allowed to change in two of the four 'total reform' calculations, in order that the post-reform 'parcels' may have levels of these inputs equal to the levels on pre-reform farms of parcel size (see section 5.2). However, to provide for the contingency that it would be impossible to increase capital, seeds, and fertilizer, due to investment limitations in the land reform, two alternative 'total reform'

---

[1] The choice of the 'family farm' as the post-reform unit is discussed above, in section 5.2.
[2] For example: northeastern sectors: high unemployment is 0.16 of total labor force. Therefore, high unemployment is $0.16/(1-0.16) = 0.19$ of observed employed. That is: let temporary labor in the Census be called the fraction t of the total labor force. High and low estimates of unemployment as a fraction of the total labor force are $1/2\ t$ and $1/10\ t$. Consider only the high estimate; $u_h = 1/2\ t$. This fraction cannot be applied directly to sample labor data to determine the sample sector's unemployed, because the sample shows employed only – not total labor force. Instead, the fraction applied to the sample sector's employed must be: $u_h/(1-u_h)$. Let L be the unknown sectoral total labor; E = observed total employment in the sector. U = unemployed to be estimated for the sector. Then $E+U = L$. It is desired that $U = u_h(L)$. Thus, $E+u_h(L) = L$, and $L = E/(1-u_h)$. Therefore $U = u_h(L)$ becomes $U = (u_h) [E/(1-u_h)]$. Therefore unemployed equals the fraction $u_h/(1-u_h)$ of observed employed.

calculations are made in which sectoral totals of these inputs do not change.

The relationship of the land input to farm size, from chapter 4, is used to determine land input on the parcel. In the case of 'no change' in capital and seeds and fertilizer (SFI), the parcel simply receives a share of $1/m$ of the pre-reform totals of capital and SFI in the sector, where m is the number of 'families' and therefore the number of 'parcels' in the sector. In the case of change in capital and SFI, each parcel uses capital and SFI according to the relationship of these inputs to farm size before the reform.

The four reforms, thus, are calculated as follows:

(a) High Unemployment, no change in Capital, SFI

$$\text{Number of parcels} = m = \frac{U_h + N}{2.5}$$

where U_h = the number of unemployed workers in the sector, high estimate; and N = the number of employed workers in the sector. Thus, the number of land reform parcels equals the number of workers available, divided by 2.5 workers per family.

$$\text{Size of parcel} = x = X/m,$$

where X = total sectoral area.

Thus, the size of the parcel equals the total sectoral area divided by the number of parcels.

$$\text{Land input on parcel} = l = e^\theta x^\phi$$
$$\text{Labor input} = n = 2.5(W)$$
$$\text{Capital on parcel} = k = K/m$$
$$\text{SFI on parcel} = s = S/m,$$

where θ, ϕ are parameters from section 4.3.3; W = imputed wage, K = sectoral total capital, S = sectoral total SFI.

$$\text{Production on parcel} = q = e^\alpha l^\beta n^\gamma k^\delta s^\varepsilon$$

where $\alpha, \beta, \gamma, \delta, \varepsilon$ are the production function coefficients of chapter 3.[1]

$$\text{Total production} = Q = mq.$$
$$\text{Total land input, post reform} = L = ml$$

---

[1] Throughout this chapter, the 'constrained' production functions are used except for São Paulo coffee (increasing returns to scale), and São Paulo cattle/general and Minas Gerais cattle (decreasing returns to scale).

§5.4   LAND REFORM CALCULATIONS

(b) Low unemployment, no change in capital, SFI.[1] This calculation is the same as (a) except that U_L replaces U_h.
(c) High unemployment, change in capital and SFI (all variables same notation as above).

$$m = \frac{U_h + N}{2.5} \qquad x = \frac{X}{m} \qquad l = e^\theta x^\phi$$

$$n = (2.5)(W)$$

$$k = e^\pi x^\rho \qquad s = e^\sigma x^\tau$$

$$q = e^\alpha l^\beta n^\gamma k^\delta s^\varepsilon$$

$$Q = mq \qquad L = ml \qquad K = mk \qquad S = ms$$

where L, K, and S are post-reform sectoral total land input, capital, and seeds and fertilizer. The parameters π, ρ, σ, τ are those estimated in section 4.3.3.
(d) Low unemployment, change in capital and SFI. Same as (c) except that U_L replaces U_h.

Two important assumptions underlie the total reform calculations.[2] It is implicitly assumed that land quality is homogeneous, for the total reform calculations, whereas allowance is made for varying land quality in the 'partial' reform calculation, below. It is assumed that pre-reform input size relationships prevail on the parcel, in determining the land input (cultivated

---

[1] It should be noted that an alternative calculation was tried in which capital, seeds, and fertilizer on the parcel were based on parcel size multiplied by the ratio of these inputs to farm size for 'size group II', and, secondly, for 'size group III'. In crops, as expected, these two calculations gave production changes that were greater (group II) and smaller (group III) than the results of table 26. The differences between these 'group II' and 'group III' results were quite large in some cases. For cattle sectors, since 'parcel size' is close to the ceiling of size group III, application of size group II and III input ratios gave larger increased production than the increases shown in table 26. The most extreme example of discontinuity caused by the size group ratio approach was Rio Grande do Sul cattle, where the high unemployment reform at group II ratios gave 287% rise in production, and, at group III ratios, 29% decline in production.

[2] It may be noted that an earlier version of the 'total reform' calculation set up a maximization problem,

$$\text{Max } m \cdot q.$$

Subject to

$$m \cdot n = N + U$$
$$m \cdot x \leq X$$

where the notation was as above except that N and U here are in value terms. When all land for crop sectors, pasture for cattle sectors) in all four 'total reform' calculations and capital and 'SFI' in two of the four calculations.

Since the reform calculations depart from the exact pre-reform relationship of labor to farm size it may be asked whether the other inputs should be determined by their pre-reform relationships to farm size. However, a great amount of variance exists in the pre-reform relationship of labor to farm size, as is shown by the low R-square levels in the regressions of the logarithm of labor on the logarithm of farm size (table 18). This wide variance implies that a large number of alternative labor to farm size ratios are consistent with the 'pre-reform relationship of labor to farm size'. Also, in practice the

---

inputs, including labor, are assumed related to farm size by the pre-reform functions, the problem has an immediate solution so long as land constraint is binding. That is, since

$$n = e^\lambda x^\mu$$

and

$$q = e^\alpha l^\beta n^\gamma k^\delta s^\varepsilon$$
$$= e^\alpha (e^\theta x^\phi)^\beta (e^\lambda x^\mu)^\gamma (e^\pi x^\rho)^\delta (e^\sigma x^\pi)^\varepsilon$$

and $m = X/x = (N+U)/n$ with the land constraint binding, it followed that the 'optimal parcel size' would be

$$x = \frac{Xn}{N+U} = \frac{Xe^\lambda x^\mu}{N+U}$$

so that

$$x^{(1-\mu)} = Xe^\lambda/(N+U)$$

and

$$(1-\mu)\log x = (\log X) + \lambda - \log(N+U)$$

and

$$x = \exp \frac{\log X + \lambda - \log(N+U)}{1-\mu}$$

This formulation, in which an 'optimal parcel' was found, was rejected. The total reform approach described in the text had more intuitive appeal in that the smallest farm size was deemed 'optimal' if the returns to scale were constant and intensity of input use fell with farm size. Also, the calculation described here gave absurd results in the sugar sectors, where one sector showed the entire sector in one farm and another sector showed an extremely large number of 'optimal parcels' of close to zero size. These extreme results were due to the fact that the value of μ in the sugar sectors approached unity, such that x approached $e^{\pm\infty}$.

It may be noted that rejection of the 'maximization' approach to total reform, described here, implies rejection of a rigid relationship of labor to farm area. If the labor-farm size regression estimated in section 4.3.3 above were strictly adhered to, there would be only one 'farm size' which would exactly absorb all sectoral labor – and this farm size would not necessarily be that for 2.5 workers or one 'family'.

§5.4 LAND REFORM CALCULATIONS 145

TABLE 25

Pre-reform number of workers on farm of size equal to post-reform 'parcel' size ('high unemployment' parcel size)

Sector	Parcel size (ha)	Number of workers*	Sector	Parcel size (ha)	Number of workers*
Ceará cotton	20.9	2.4	Alagoas sugar	19.5	1.3
Pern. cotton	15.2	2.2	Per. sug. IAA	13.6	2.7
E. San. coffee	32.3	2.0	S. P. sugar	27.3	2.0
S. P. coffee	19.3	3.8	Ceará cattle	41.5	3.2
Per. sug. FGV	11.8	3.0	E. San. cattle	43.9	3.7
S. P. cereals	22.2	3.0	M.G. cattle	80.1	3.9
R.G. rice	29.0	4.9	R.G. cattle	139.3	3.9
M.G. corn	21.9	2.8	S.P. cattle	55.8	4.9
S. P. cattle/gen.	47.6	4.0			

* Based on estimated relationship: $\log(\text{labor}) = \lambda + \mu (\log(\text{size}))$.

labor/farm size ratio used in the reform calculation is very close to the labor/farm size ratio that would be determined by the more rigid pre-reform regression of labor on farm size.[1] The number of workers that would be associated with a given parcel size if the pre-reform regression relationship were used is shown in table 25. The table shows that this number of workers is close to the number 2.5 used in the reform calculation, with the possible exception of the sectors of R.G. rice and S.P. cattle.

The results of the four total reforms are shown in table 26. Most sectors show substantial increases in production in all four calculations. One surprising result is that the two versions in which total capital, seeds and fertilizer are allowed to change show decreases in these inputs in several sectors, rather than the expected increases. In the case of seeds and fertilizer, for example, only São Paulo coffee and Pernambuco sugar would be expected to show input declines, since only in these sectors are elasticities of seed and fertilizer use with respect to farm size greater than one. The other sectors show seeds and fertilizer decreasing after reform, not because small

---

[1] The former is 2.5 workers per parcel, and parcel area equals total sectoral area divided by the number of '2.5 worker families'. The latter would be $e^\lambda x^\mu / W$ workers for a parcel of identical size, where x is farm size, W is the imputed wage, and λ and μ are the parameters estimated in chapter 4.

TABLE 26

Results of 'total' land reform based on family units (2.5 adult-equivalent workers).
Percentage change of inputs and production

						Percentage change		
Sector	Unemp. assump.*	Cap. SFI assump.**	Parcel size (ha)	Product	Land input	Labor	Capital	SFI
Ceará cotton	H	A	20.9	25.6	19.2	19.0	0.0	0.0
	L	A	24.0	22.2	14.7	3.4	0.0	0.0
	H	B	20.9	26.5	19.2	19.0	9.9	—12.1
	L	B	24.0	19.6	14.7	3.4	2.3	—15.9
Pernambuco cotton	H	A	15.2	7.7	9.7	19.0	0.0	0.0
	L	A	17.5	1.7	1.5	3.4	0.0	0.0
	H	B	15.2	2.3	9.7	19.0	8.5	—15.0
	L	B	17.5	—7.0	1.5	3.4	1.5	—23.3
E. Santo coffee	H	A	32.3	5.9	—8.2	16.0	0.0	0.0
	L	A	36.4	1.5	—10.4	2.9	0.0	0.0
	H	B	32.3	—5.2	—8.3	16.0	—35.2	—22.7
	L	B	36.4	—9.7	—10.4	2.9	—35.0	—36.7
S. Paulo coffee	H	A	19.3	—9.2	35.0	7.0	0.0	0.0
	L	A	20.4	—10.5	33.5	1.3	0.0	0.0
	H	B	19.3	—27.7	35.0	7.0	—7.1	—74.1
	L	B	20.4	—28.5	33.5	1.3	—7.6	—73.7
Pernambuco sugar FGV	H	A	11.8	63.1	106.7	19.0	0.0	0.0
	L	A	13.6	56.1	100.6	3.4	0.0	0.0
	H	B	11.8	74.3	106.7	19.0	158.6	—66.4
	L	B	13.6	66.2	100.6	3.4	149.0	—65.6
S. Paulo cereals	H	A	22.2	22.8	28.6	7.0	0.0	0.0
	L	A	23.5	20.2	26.1	1.3	0.0	0.0
	H	B	22.2	9.9	28.6	7.0	—7.9	—38.0
	L	B	23.5	6.7	26.1	1.3	—9.7	—39.2
R.G. rice FGV	H	A	29.0	34.2	66.6	7.0	0.0	0.0
	L	A	30.6	33.3	63.4	1.3	0.0	0.0
	H	B	29.0	52.9	66.6	7.0	36.5	25.3
	L	B	30.6	51.1	63.4	1.3	35.1	23.2
M.G. corn	H	A	21.9	—3.7	33.0	7.0	0.0	0.0
	L	A	23.2	—5.1	28.8	1.3	0.0	0.0
	H	B	21.9	11.5	33.0	7.0	40.8	—9.7
	L	B	23.2	7.0	28.8	1.3	36.2	—13.0

§5.4   LAND REFORM CALCULATIONS   147

Table 26, continued

Sector	Unemp. assump.*	Cap. SFI assump.**	Parcel size (ha)	Product	Land input	Percentage change Labor	Capital	SFI
S. Paulo	H	A	47.6	27.6	3.5	7.0	0.0	0.0
cattle/gen.	L	A	50.4	25.3	3.4	1.3	0.0	0.0
	H	B	47.6	30.1	3.5	7.0	4.6	1.2
	L	B	50.3	26.8	3.4	1.3	3.8	0.0
Alagoas	H	A	19.5	—13.2	—18.1	19.0	0.0	0.0
sugar	L	A	22.5	—14.2	—18.0	3.4	0.0	0.0
	H	B	19.5	—18.1	—18.1	19.0	—68.4	—53.6
	L	B	22.5	—18.9	—18.0	3.4	—64.5	—52.9
Pernambuco	H	A	13.6	29.4	57.0	19.0	0.0	0.0
sugar IAA	L	A	15.6	23.8	54.9	3.4	0.0	0.0
	H	B	13.6	25.7	57.0	19.0	—17.5	—12.5
	L	B	15.6	20.3	54.9	3.4	—17.3	—12.9
S. Paulo	H	A	27.5	—2.1	—1.4	7.0	0.0	0.0
sugar	L	A	29.0	—5.5	—1.5	1.3	0.0	0.0
	H	B	27.5	0.0	—1.4	7.0	—25.5	—44.1
	L	B	29.0	—3.4	—1.5	1.3	—25.39	—43.8

Sector	Unemp. assump.*	Cap., anim., vac. assump.**	Parcel size (ha)	Product	Pasture	Percentage change Labor	Capital	Animal	Feed and vaccines
Ceará	H	A	41.5	15.9	—17.2	19.0	0.0	0.0	0.0
cattle	L	A	47.7	10.7	—16.8	3.4	0.0	0.0	0.0
	H	B	41.5	31.6	—17.2	19.0	15.7	37.6	20.4
	L	B	47.7	20.4	—16.8	3.4	8.6	30.1	11.0
E. Santo	H	A	43.9	17.8	—6.4	16.0	0.0	0.0	0.0
cattle	L	A	49.5	15.8	—5.8	2.9	0.0	0.0	0.0
	H	B	43.9	20.5	—6.4	16.0	—3.4	23.9	—2.9
	L	B	49.5	15.6	—5.8	2.9	—7.5	17.7	—6.9
M. Gerais	H	A	80.1	49.4	3.3	7.0	0.0	0.0	0.0
cattle	L	A	84.6	44.4	2.9	1.3	0.0	0.0	0.0
	H	B	80.1	65.2	3.3	7.0	44.6	17.0	19.2
	L	B	84.6	58.1	2.9	1.3	40.6	15.4	16.4

Table 26, continued

Sector	Un-emp. as-sump.*	Cap., anim., vac. as-sump.**	Parcel size (ha)	Product	Pasture	Percentage change			
						Labor	Capital	Animal	Feed and vac-cines
R.G. Sul cattle	H	A	139.3	27.7	—0.5	7.0	0.0	0.0	0.0
	L	A	143.1	26.9	—0.2	1.3	0.0	0.0	0.0
	H	B	139.3	35.6	—0.5	7.0	36.2	9.7	0.2
	L	B	143.1	31.6	—0.2	1.3	32.9	8.3	—3.2
S. Paulo cattle	H	A	55.8	6.9	—3.4	7.0	0.0	0.0	0.0
	L	A	58.9	5.5	—3.4	1.3	0.0	0.0	0.0
	H	B	55.8	17.7	—3.4	7.0	0.0	22.5	13.7
	L	B	58.9	15.1	—3.4	1.3	—2.0	21.4	10.4

* Unemployment as % of employed. High assumption, 19% in Northeast, 16% in East, 7% in South. Low assumption: 3.4% in Northeast, 2.9% in East, 1.3% in South.
** A = No change in sectoral total capital and seeds, fertilizer. Pre-reform totals spread evenly across reform parcels. B = Post-reform capital and seeds, fertilizer allowed to change such that parcels use inputs according to pre-reform input-size relationship.

farms use these inputs less intensively per farm area than do large farms, but because the very small farms with intensive seed and fertilizer use comprise a large percentage of the sectoral total for the input, and these farms are replaced by larger, less intensive, parcels. (The weight of each size group in pre-reform input and production totals is shown in table 36, appendix C.)

São Paulo coffee and Alagoas sugar are the only two sectors in which production seriously declines in all four total reforms. In the case of São Paulo coffee the decline in production occurs because there are increasing returns to scale, with elasticities summing to 1.2, so that fragmentation of large farms into small units reduces production. Furthermore, seeds and fertilizer inputs fall drastically after reform, since they are used more intensively on large farms ($\tau>1$). In the case of Alagoas sugar, the decline in production is caused by a reduction in the land input, and in capital and

§5.4 LAND REFORM CALCULATIONS 149

seed inputs when these inputs are allowed to vary. The data for Alagoas sugar simply show greater intensity of land use on large farms.[1]

The small decrease in production for Minas Gerais corn is due to a negative land coefficient in the production function, which is statistically insignificant. São Paulo sugar cane shows small declines in production in three of the four reforms. These declines are caused partly by the slight decline in the land input after reform.[2] The production declines are also due, ironically, to the equalization of combinations of capital with other factors, after land reform.[3] However, the magnitudes of these perverse production responses are small and therefore not troublesome. A final point regarding São Paulo sugar is that while capital, seeds and fertilizer decline roughly 30% after reform (when allowed to vary), production declines less than 5% so while reform does not increase production it does reduce input cost in the sector.

The cattle sectors have two unusual features, as shown in table 26. First, the 'land input' or pasture area declines after reform, because the large cattle ranches (before reform) have a higher percent of their area declared in pasture than do small cattle ranches (see table 18, chapter 4). This pattern apparently represents a shift from crop activities to grazing as farm size rises, even within the 'cattle sector'. The production impact of the decline in pasture after land redistribution is small, however, since the production coefficients of pasture are extremely low or negative.

Second, the sizes of 'land reform parcels' for cattle sectors are much larger than those for crop sectors, because labor density per farm area is much

---

[1] It is possible that this fact reflects non-specialization of smaller farms. The IAA data are for the sugar operation only. However, the questionnaires had provision for 'other production' and the entry was blank in almost all cases. It seemed generally true that all farms surveyed, regardless of size, specialized entirely in sugar cane.

[2] This decline is spurious. Cultivated land should increase slightly after reform, since the elasticity of its use, with respect to farm size, is slightly less than unity (see table 18) and fragmentation of large farms should cause the land input to rise. Therefore its decline apparently represents error of estimation; that is, the actual total cultivated land before reform is greater than the sum of estimated land inputs (from the relationship of table 18 applied to each pre-reform farm) would be. However, the error is small.

[3] The production coefficient of capital is negative. When capital is concentrated on large farms, its negative effect is less pronounced than when it is combined more evenly with land and labor on post-reform parcels. That is, capital's negative marginal product is larger in absolute value on post-reform parcels than on pre-reform large farms, because land and labor inputs are larger relative to capital on post-reform parcels.

higher for crop sectors. The higher labor density in crops is mainly due to the fact that 'extensive grazing' uses little labor relative to land, capital, and animal capital. The higher labor density in crops may also be caused by better quality land in crop sectors than in cattle sectors.

An implication of the large size of cattle reform parcels is that product shifts from cattle to crops could be of major importance in land reform. Conversion of cattle land to crop production would permit a greater number of smaller parcels and therefore greater possibility of labor absorption, provided the former cattle land were of sufficiently good quality for crop production. However, in this study no calculation is made of the effect of a product shift from cattle to crops. In general, inter-sectoral shifts of products or of factors are not considered in this study.

The level of income per worker on post-reform parcels is an important variable. An objective stated in the Brazilian land reform law is to achieve income on reform parcels of the legal minimum wage plus ten percent. Table 27 shows the net income per worker after reform in the 'total reform' calculation. The net income figure for the farm is gross production, minus expenditure on seeds and fertilizer, minus 6% interest and 5% depreciation on capital, minus 3% of land value.[1] The last 'land cost' represents the average interest cost for land repayment when interest is 6% paid on the 'declining balance'. The 'principal' on land repayment is not subtracted from income, on the grounds that it constitutes saving and thus part of income.

In eleven of the seventeen sectors, net income per worker on land reform parcels would exceed the target income specified in the reform law. On the remaining sectors, and particularly in Pernambuco cotton, special efforts would have to be made to increase capital seeds and fertilizer inputs in order to raise the parcel worker's income to the target level.

To summarize the results of the 'total reform' calculations, the sectors may be divided into three groups. In the first group are those sectors with large production gains, of over 20%: Ceará cotton; Pernambuco sugar (both FGV and IAA); São Paulo cereals; R. G. rice; São Paulo cattle/general; and cattle in Ceará, E. Santo, M. Gerais, and R. G. Sul. In the second group, those sectors with small production gains (under 20%) are Pernambuco cotton, E. Santo coffee, M.G. corn, S. Paulo sugar, and

---

[1] Both capital and land value are first deflated to account for the difference between 'crop year' and date of capital and land data, in the FGV sample.

TABLE 27

Net income per worker on land reform parcels,
as a fraction of target income (regional minimum wage + 10%)

Sector		Net income per worker/ target income	Sector		Net income per worker/ target income
Ceará cotton	H	0.96	Alagoas sugar	H	0.79
	L	1.06		L	0.89
Pern. cotton	H	0.47	Per. sug. IAA	H	1.05
	L	0.49		L	1.04
E.S. coffee	H	0.69	S.P. sugar	H	2.40
	L	0.73		L	2.40
S.P. coffee	H	0.97	Ceará cattle	H	1.35
	L	1.01		L	1.65
Per. sug. FGV	H	1.27	E.S. cattle	H	0.96
	L	1.38		L	1.03
S.P. cereals	H	0.90	M.G. cattle	H	1.43
	L	0.91		L	1.42
R.G. rice	H	2.02	R.G. cattle	H	0.89
	L	2.12		L	0.90
M.G. corn	H	0.61	S.P. cattle	H	1.29
	L	0.61		L	1.33
S.P. cat./gen.	H	1.32			
	L	1.34			

S. Paulo cattle. In the third group are those sectors with serious production loss from reform: São Paulo coffee and Alagoas sugar. The first group represents major incidence of the potential gains from reallocation of land which this study has hypothesized. The second group represents sectors in which the incidence of large farms is small and therefore potential gains are limited (Pernambuco cotton, E. Santo coffee, M.G. corn) or sectors in which large farm intensity of production differs little from small (São Paulo sugar). The third group represents the two exceptions to the two rules – increasing returns to scale (São Paulo coffee) and increasing intensity of land use (Alagoas sugar).

The importance of each sector's production change, relative to total Brazilian agricultural production, can be derived by multiplying the percent

152   PREDICTION OF THE IMPACT OF LAND REFORM

TABLE 28

Production change from land reform, by sector,
as a percent of Brazilian agricultural production

| Sector | Weight | Increase (%) of Brazilian total agr. product | | | | | |
| | | Total reform | | | | Partial reform | |
		A, H	A, L	B, H	B, L	H	L
Cea. cot.	1.06	0.271	0.235	0.281	0.208	0.034	0.028
Per. cot.	0.44	0.034	0.008	0.010	—0.031	0.0	0.0
E.S. cof.	0.32	0.019	0.005	—0.017	—0.031	—0.018	—0.021
S.P. cof.	2.53	—0.233	—0.266	—0.701	—0.721	—0.405	—0.415
*Per. sug. FGV	0.29	0.86	0.166	0.219	0.200	0.086	0.079
S.P. cereals	5.41	1.234	1.093	0.536	0.362	0.022	—0.038
R.G. rice	1.99	0.682	0.663	1.052	1.016	0.531	0.517
M.G. corn	2.03	—0.075	—0.104	0.234	0.142	0.0	0.0
*S.P. cat./gen.	2.13	0.590	0.540	0.643	0.572	0.094	0.088
Al. sug.	0.36	—0.047	—0.051	—0.065	—0.068	—0.020	—0.021
*Per. sug. IAA	0.60	0.174	0.140	0.152	0.120	0.072	0.058
S.P. sug.	2.19	—0.046	—0.120	0.000	—0.076	—0.050	0.0
Ceará cat.	0.53	0.084	0.057	0.168	0.108	0.061	0.048
E.S. cat.	0.25	0.045	0.039	0.051	0.039	0.0	0.0
M.G. cat.	5.82	2.874	2.585	3.795	3.382	1.054	0.926
R.G. cat.	2.04	0.565	0.549	0.726	0.644	0.090	0.067
*S.P. cat.	2.13	0.147	0.117	0.378	0.322	0.095	0.071
Total	30.13	6.504	5.656	7.462	6.186	1.645	1.384

* Duplicate sectors. Pernambuco sugar: 1/3 weight, FGV; 2/3 weight, IAA; S.P. cattle: 1/2 weight, 'cattle/general', 1/2 weight, 'cattle'.

output change in table 26 by the weight of the sector in Brazilian production, given in table 6, chapter 3. The percentage change in total agricultural production that would occur in a land reform applied to all sectors, may be inferred from the sum of the weighted percentage changes in production in the individual sectors. Table 28 shows the production increase of each sector as a percent of total Brazilian agricultural production.[1] The sectors of this study represent only one-third of Brazilian agricultural production. Thus if the excluded sectors have potential gains from reform similar to the gains of the sectors here, then the aggregate increase in production from land

---

[1] Note that for convenience, table 28 includes the production results of the 'partial reform', discussed below.

reform applied throughout Brazilian agriculture would be three times the figures of table 28, or about 20% to 25% of total production.

It is useful to note that about half of the production gains, for the sectors in this study, would occur in one sector: Minas Gerais cattle. São Paulo cereals, and Rio Grande do Sul rice, show the second and third most important gains in production as a result of land reform.

5.4.2. 'Partial reform'

The 'total reform' calculations represent a maximum estimate of the gain from land reform, given the limiting assumption of no change in the 'principal product' of each sector. The 'partial reform' calculations are designed to simulate the land reform process more realistically and to reflect more conservative assumptions about possible production gains from land redistribution. In general, the 'partial reform' exempts from expropriation large farms with 'poor land'. The rest of the large farms are expropriated in ascending order, from those with the lowest output per area to those with the highest. The procedure continues until all eligible land is expropriated, or until all labor to be absorbed is placed on land reform parcels. The labor to be absorbed includes labor previously on expropriated farms, the unemployed, and the 'excess' labor on sub-parcel farms (explained below).

In comparison to the 'total reform', the first new assumption of the 'partial reform' is that only 'large' farms of over 300 ha would be subject to expropriation. This assumption is more realistic than the assumption that all farms would be expropriated and reorganized. The orientation of the land reform movement in Brazil has been towards expropriating large farms and converting them into medium-sized family farms. A second new assumption is that only land with land price above the sectoral average land price (defined as total land value divided by total land area) would be considered eligible for expropriation. This assumption is made to assure that the land on expropriated farms is of good quality – since a standard argument against reform is that idle land in large farms is of poor quality and could not be used. The assumption is quite conservative. Even if land quality were totally homogeneous, the assumption would exclude from expropriation an expected one half of all farms over 300 ha, thus limiting the area available for creation of reform parcels.

The unemployment and parcel size assumptions are identical to those of the total reform calculations. The parcel size could not logically be larger than that used in the total reform, since a larger size (more land area per family settled) would imply the creation of a privileged class of parcel recipients. It would be impossible to settle all families on parcels of this larger size even if the whole farm area of the sector became subject to expropriation.[1] Smaller parcels are not considered in the 'partial reform' calculation, because in most sectors the net income of parcel recipients is just barely at the target income level. Smaller parcel area would mean that the units created by land reform would be too small to permit attainment of the target income. Nevertheless, it is possible that smaller area per family would give higher reform production increases, since the constraint in the calculation is almost always availability of expropriated land for settlement. Smaller parcels would permit the settlement of a larger portion of the unemployed and of excess labor on small farms.[2]

Capital, seeds, and fertilizer inputs on the land reform parcel are determined in the same way as in the third and fourth calculations in the 'total reform' model. That is, the pre-reform relationships of input to farm size are used to find the levels of inputs, other than the labor input, on the reform parcel.

In the partial reform, there are two sources of labor to be settled on parcels: the unemployed, and 'surplus' or 'excess' labor on small farms. Surplus labor does not refer to the amount of labor that could be withdrawn before marginal product of labor rises to the level of its remuneration (as the term is used by Lewis and by Ranis and Fei). Here, the term denotes the amount of labor on farms of sub-parcel size, in excess of the amount of labor these farms would have at the labor/land ratio of the parcel.

---

[1] If cross-sector reform were permitted, it would be logical to transfer labor out of low income, labor-dense sectors into the closest labor-sparse sectors. In that case, parcel sizes would be above those in the present calculations for labor-dense sectors and below those in labor sparse sectors.

[2] Note that in effect the 'partial land reform' calculations do imply the creation of a privileged class of parcel recipients, even though the parcel size used is no larger than that of the 'total reform'. The reason is that because of restrictions on area subject to expropriation it is impossible in most sectors to absorb all of the eligible labor – unemployed, workers on farms to be expropriated, and 'excess' workers on farms below parcel size. The implication is that either smaller parcels would be in order, or that restrictions on land subject to expropriation would have to be eliminated. Where the land excluded from expropriation is actually of poor quality, the only alternative would be creation of smaller parcels.

§5.4 LAND REFORM CALCULATIONS

Thus, the amount of labor to be transferred to reform parcels is

$$U + \left(\sum_i n_i - \frac{n^*}{x^*} \sum_i x_i\right)_{i \in [x_i < x^*]}$$

where U = unemployed labor, n_i = labor on farm i, x_i = size of farm i, n^* = labor on reform parcel, and x^* = size of reform parcel, and $\in$ means 'is a member of the set'. The second term is 'surplus labor' on small farms.

The concept of 'surplus labor' on farms smaller than the parcel is based on the idea that once land is made available to small farms on a credit-purchase basis, some of the laborers on smaller farms would migrate to reform parcels. The main barrier to their migration would have been removed, because they would now be able to work the land as owners, rather than as salaried laborers. It is also assumed that the use of capital, seeds, and fertilizer would decline on these small farms, to the point where these farms would resemble the 'parcels' in all inputs.[1] In this way factor ratios after reform would be equated across the set of newly created parcels and previous 'small farms' below parcel size, so that previous 'sub-parcel' farms would resemble parcel farms in inputs and output per farm area. However, the process of equalization of factor ratios would be limited by the availability of land subject to expropriation.

It is assumed that the workers on an expropriated farm would receive parcels. However, if these workers remained on the expropriated farm, they would not receive its entire area in parcels, since much of this land would be transferred to formerly unemployed workers and 'excess' laborers from small farms.

The partial reform calculation is calculated in the following way. First, the parcel size is determined, as the total sectoral area divided by the number of families (including unemployed laborers). Second, surplus labor is estimated, as described above. Third, the area in farms over 300 ha is found.

---

[1] That is, as the 'excess' workers moved from sub-parcel farms to new parcels, they would take part of their complementary inputs – capital, seeds, fertilizer – with them. Note that there is an alternative view of the reason why sub-parcel farms would become identical to parcels after reform. That is, the land reform agency could pursue a conscious policy of grouping subparcel farms into farms of parcel size and transferring excess labor and inputs from the very small farms onto new parcels created from expropriated large farms – if the expected automatic flow of labor and inputs from sub-parcel farms to parcels failed to materialize.

Fourth, the area, inputs, and production on farms over 300 ha with land price above average land price, are found. These farms are considered eligible for expropriation. Fifth, the amount of 'net land' on the set of eligible farms is found. 'Net land' is defined as the amount of land in excess of land required to absorb labor already on the expropriated farms at the 'parcel' labor/size rate.

At this point, the calculation follows one of four alternatives. The first alternative (referred to as reform 1 or R1) is the case in which 'net land' on expropriated farms exceeds 'required parcel area' for the unemployed and 'surplus labor' to be settled. In this case, the eligible large farms are ordered by output per farm area, and expropriation proceeds from 'least productive' to 'more productive' farms until total 'net land' on expropriated farms equals or exceeds required parcel area. The second alternative (R2) is the case in which total 'net land' on farms subject to expropriation falls short of required parcel area for unemployed plus surplus labor, but exceeds required parcel area for unemployed labor alone. Here it is assumed that all eligible area would be expropriated, and 'parcels' would be created for: (a) all labor previously on the expropriated farms; (b) all unemployed labor; (c) as much of the 'surplus labor' as possible. In the third alternative (R3), the area eligible for expropriation does not have enough 'net' land to permit settlement of the unemployed labor alone. In this case, all eligible farms are expropriated and parcels are created to absorb (a) all labor previously on the expropriated farms; (b) part of the unemployed labor. In the fourth alternative (R4), the 'net land' which may be expropriated is zero or negative. This means either there are no farms subject to expropriation, or the eligible farms already have greater labor density than that of the proposed reform parcel. In the fourth case, no reform calculation is made.

The calculations for post reform product and inputs are shown below. In the notation subscript 1 refers to farms below parcel size, subscript 2 to parcels created, 3 to farms above parcel size and below 300 ha, 4 to farms subject to expropriation but not expropriated, and 5 to farms over 300 ha but not eligible for expropriation. Subscript 6 refers to variables for farms actually expropriated. The asterisk refers to 'parcel' variables, and the variables q, l, n, k, s, x represent product, land input, labor, capital, seeds and fertilizer, and farm size, respectively. SURLAB refers to surplus labor, calculated as described above. In reform R2, the variable n_s refers to the amount of surplus labor which is removed from small farms, and γ refers

§5.4 LAND REFORM CALCULATIONS

to the coefficient of labor in the production function. Note that n_s is only a part of total excess labor on small farms; the rest cannot be absorbed on reform parcels in reform R2. Thus, in the first reform (R1):

$$Q = (q^*/x^*) \sum_i x_{ie1} + [(U + \text{SURLAB} + \sum_i n_{ie6})/n^*] q^* + \sum_i q_{ie3} + \sum_i q_{ie4} + \sum_i q_{ie5}$$

The first element is the production on farms smaller than parcel size, which are now converted to farms similar to parcels by an outflow of 'surplus labor', and an outflow or inflow of other inputs such that the ratios of inputs to size are identical to those ratios on parcels. The second element is production on reform parcels. The number of parcels is shown in parentheses as the coefficient of q^*. The remaining elements represent unchanged production on farms not expropriated.

In the second reform (R2):

$$Q = \sum_i q_{ie1} - \left[\frac{n_s}{\sum_i n_{ie1}} \right] \gamma \sum_i q_{ie1} + q^* \left[\frac{U + n_s + \sum_i n_{ie6}}{n^*} \right] + \sum_i q_{ie3} + \sum_i q_{ie5}$$

where

$$n_S = \left(\sum_i x_{ie6} \right)(n^*/x^*) - (U + \sum_i n_{ie6}).$$

Here, the first element represents original production on sub-parcel farms, the second element represents the percentage withdrawal of labor from sub-parcel farms, multiplied by the labor elasticity of production times original sub-parcel production. That is, the fall in small farm production in this case is accounted for by application of the labor production elasticity to labor withdrawal. The small farms in this case do not become identical to 'parcels', they only lose part of their surplus labor. The third element represents 'parcel' production, and the other elements are self-explanatory. The term n_S is the amount of labor which the expropriated land can absorb in excess of unemployment plus labor already on the expropriated farms.

In the third reform, there is no change at all in production on farms below parcel size, since none of their surplus labor can be removed. Here,

$$Q = \sum_i q_{ie1} + q^* \left(\sum_i x_{ie6}/x^* \right) + \sum_i q_{ie3} + \sum_i q_{ie5}.$$

In the reform a part of unemployed is left unabsorbed, equal to

$$U - \left[\left(\sum_i x_{ie6} \right)(n^*/x^*) - \sum_i n_{ie6} \right].$$

TABLE 29

Partial reform. Expropriation of farms over 300 ha with above-average land quality. Reform parcel of family unit (2.5 adult-equivalent workers)

Sector	A Un-emp. as-sump.	B Parcel size (ha)	C Surp. lab.	D >300 ha as % area	E >300 ha $p > \bar{p}$ as % area	F 'E' on net basis	G Required parcels as % area	H Exprop. as % area	I Prod.	J Land input	K Labor	L Cap.	M SFI	N	O Type re-form
												Percentage change			
Ceará	H	21	37.8	19.1	6.7	5.9	47.8	6.7	3.2	3.4	7.0	4.5	0.7		R3
cotton	L	24	39.6	19.1	6.7	5.9	41.5	6.7	2.6	3.1	3.4	4.0	0.5		R2
Pern.	H	15	34.6	22.0	0.0	0.0	45.0	0.0	—	—	—	—	—		R4
cotton	L	18	37.6	22.0	0.0	0.0	41.1	0.0	—	—	—	—	—		R4
E. San.	H	32	11.6	5.9	5.9	2.5	22.6	5.9	−5.8	−1.2	3.2	−8.1	−0.5		R3
coffee	L	36	14.3	5.9	5.9	2.0	16.1	5.9	−6.1	−1.4	2.7	−8.1	−0.8		R3
S. Paulo	H	19	31.6	52.0	30.5	16.7	36.2	30.5	−16.0	12.5	7.0	0.9	−34.3		R2
coffee	L	20	32.4	52.0	30.5	15.9	33.3	30.5	−16.4	12.1	1.3	0.7	−34.2		R2
Per. sug.	H	12	0.0	83.0	30.3	6.6	15.9	30.3	29.2	38.3	7.8	54.8	−13.3		R3
FGV	L	14	0.6	83.0	30.3	3.0	3.9	30.3	26.7	36.4	3.1	51.8	−13.0		R3
S. Paulo	H	22	27.1	29.5	7.5	6.1	31.8	7.5	0.4	−0.5	6.6	−1.1	−0.5		R3
cereals	L	24	28.0	29.5	7.5	6.1	28.9	7.5	−0.7	−0.7	1.3	−1.3	−0.6		R2
R.G. rice	H	29	16.9	59.0	33.3	16.5	22.4	33.3	26.7	26.7	7.0	20.5	7.0		R2
FGV	L	31	17.1	59.0	33.3	15.6	18.2	33.3	26.0	25.7	1.3	20.0	6.3		R2
M.G. corn	H	22	57.5	22.0	0.0	0.0	56.8	0.0	—	—	—	—	—		R4
	L	23	58.3	22.0	0.0	0.0	58.7	0.0	—	—	—	—	—		R4

Table 29, continued

Sector	A Un- emp. as- sump.	B Parcel size (ha)	C Surp. lab.	D >300 ha as % area	E >300 ha $p > \bar{p}$ as % area	F 'E' on net basis	G Required parcels as % area	H Exprop. as % area	I Prod.	J Land input	K Labor	L Cap.	M SFI	N	O Type re- form
										Percentage change					
S. Paulo cat./gen.	H	48	15.6	29.5	5.1	3.5	21.1	5.1	4.4	1.2	3.7	2.1	1.5		R3
	L	50	16.3	29.5	5.1	3.4	17.4	5.1	4.1	1.2	1.3	2.1	1.4		R3
Al. sug.	H	20	−0.7	84.5	39.0	7.3	15.3	39.0	−5.5	−4.8	8.6	−27.9	−23.4		R3
IAA	L	23	−0.6	84.5	39.0	2.4	2.6	39.0	−5.8	−4.8	2.5	−27.6	−23.2		R3
Per. sug.	H	14	0.2	86.4	41.9	7.2	16.2	41.9	12.2	26.8	8.5	−6.4	−7.5		R3
IAA	L	16	0.6	86.4	41.9	2.0	3.8	41.9	9.9	26.0	2.2	−6.5	−7.6		R3
S.P. sug.	H	27	−0.5	70.7	29.4	0.1	6.0	29.4	−2.3	−1.6	0.1	−11.9	−20.9		R3
	L	29	0.1	70.7	29.4	−1.5	1.4	0.0	—	—	—	—	—		R4

Table 29, continued

Sector	A Unemp. assump.	B Parcel size (ha)	C Surp. lab.	D >300 ha as % area	E >300 ha $p > \bar{p}$ as % area	F 'E' on net basis	G Required parcels as % area	H Exprop. as % area	I Prod.	J Land input	K Labor	L Cap.	M Anim.	N Vac.	O Type reform
													Percentage change		
Ceará	H	42	21.4	33.0	10.6	8.4	33.9	10.6	11.4	1.3	10.0	7.0	9.0	12.1	R3
cattle	L	48	22.7	33.0	10.6	8.1	25.2	10.6	9.0	1.3	3.4	6.3	8.2	11.1	R2
E. Santo	H	44	23.9	37.5	0.0	0.0	34.4	0.0	—	—	—	—	—	—	R4
cattle	L	50	25.3	37.5	0.0	0.0	34.4	0.0	—	—	—	—	—	—	R4
M.G.	H	80	25.7	67.8	15.2	5.4	30.4	15.2	18.1	3.0	5.8	13.8	3.0	8.4	R2
cattle	L	85	26.4	67.8	15.2	4.9	28.5	15.2	15.9	2.9	1.3	13.2	2.7	7.9	R2
R.G.	H	139	27.0	74.5	17.8	7.6	31.7	17.8	4.4	−4.8	7.0	2.4	−15.5	11.9	R2
cattle	L	147	27.5	74.5	17.8	7.0	28.4	17.8	3.3	−4.7	1.3	1.9	−15.8	11.3	R2
S. Paulo	H	56	15.6	66.9	17.4	8.1	21.1	17.4	4.4	−0.8	7.0	0.7	8.6	1.5	R2
cattle	L	59	16.0	66.9	17.4	7.6	17.2	17.4	3.3	−0.8	1.3	0.3	8.4	1.0	R2

Notes: C = 'Surplus labor as' % of employed. D = area in farms over 300 ha as % of sectoral area. E = area in farms over 300 ha with above average land price, as % of sectoral area. F: see text. G = area in parcels required to absorb 'surplus labor' plus unemployed. O: R1 = expropriable land sufficient to absorb surplus labor and unemployed. R2 = expropriable area sufficient for unemployed and part of surplus labor. R3 = expropriable area adequate for part of unemployed only. R4 = no net land available for expropriation.

§5.4   LAND REFORM CALCULATIONS

In the fourth case, no calculation is made, as no reform occurs.

The post-reform sectoral levels of inputs are calculated in a manner similar to the calculation of production. The reforms described are calculated once with the high unemployment assumption and once with the low assumption.

Table 29 shows the results of the partial reform analysis. The first striking result is that in none of the sectors is 'reform 1' possible. Thus, when expropriation is limited to farms over 300 ha with above average land price, there is in no case sufficient 'net' land on farms subject to expropriation to absorb all unemployed and all surplus labor. Correspondingly, in no case is it possible to allow the 'luxury' of expropriating the least productive farms first and exempting the 'efficient' large farms. Instead, the large farms exempted are those with below-average land price.

A second informative result in table 29 is the high incidence of surplus labor on sub-parcel farms. In most sectors the surplus labor represents from 20 to 30 percent of the sector's total employment. Sugar cane is a clear exception. In sugar cane, the weight of small farms is so miniscule that surplus labor on sub-parcel farms is a negligible fraction of total employment.[1] Still, if unemployment is assumed to exist, there would be production gains through greater use of land on large expropriated sugar cane farms.

The major results of the partial land reform experiment are that only Pernambuco sugar, Rio Grande do Sul rice, cattle in Minas Gerais and Ceará remain as clear cases of large gains from land reform. Other sectors which showed major gains in the 'total reform' show reduced gains in the partial reform. Ceará cotton, São Paulo cereals, São Paulo cattle/general, and cattle in Espírito Santo, Rio Grande do Sul, and São Paulo are examples of these sectors. In all of these cases the reason for the change is that much of the large farm area has below-average land price and on the stricter grounds of the 'partial reform' does not qualify for expropriation.

The partial reform should be viewed as a conservative estimate of gains from reform, as opposed to the maximum estimate of the 'total reform'. Thus, even on conservative grounds, four of the seventeen sectors present prospects for major production increases through land redistribution.

---

[1] Furthermore in Alagoas and São Paulo the density of labor per farm area is as high on large sugar farms as on small, so that small farms have little or no 'surplus' labor.

5.5. Costs

It is beyond the scope of this study to estimate the costs which would be involved in Brazilian land reform. Nevertheless, it is useful to consider the types of costs which could arise. Six types of cost could be expected.

The first type of cost would be that of increased capital and intermediate inputs (seeds, fertilizer, insecticides). However, it is not clear *a priori* that such inputs would have to increase in order for output to rise, for the 'excess' levels of these inputs on the very smallest farms could cause total production to rise when transferred to unused land on large farms.

A second possible cost of reform would be the labor cost. To the extent that the additional labor absorbed in agriculture were to come from labor employed in secondary industry or the services, and not from unemployed labor, the economy would bear the cost of land reform's labor absorption.[1]

The third major cost is the expense of land clearing. It is possible that increased cultivation (or grazing) of land formerly 'unused' would come at the expense of clearing forest area.

The fourth major cost is administrative expense. This category would include the costs of the personnel and equipment necessary to compile records, carry out land surveys, handle the claims of expropriated owners and of new parcel owners, and carry out other administrative tasks.

The fifth major cost would be compensation costs. Compensation could be a cost in terms of capital available for investment for economic growth. That is, government revenue available for investment would be lowered by the amount of compensation payments net of new owner repayments. Investment in the economy would drop to the extent that compensated landlords used their new funds for consumption or capital export, rather than for investment, assuming that those net funds would have been used by the government for investment. In the Brazilian case, it has been recognized that full immediate compensation would be impossible. The law provides for payment in government bonds, to be redeemed in installments over a twenty year period. Since funds would flow into the reform agency from yearly land

---

[1] In the estimates of increased output, given above, it is assumed that only unemployed abor increases the agricultural labor input. While absorption of workers elsewherel employed would mean additional labor costs, it would also mean increased agricultural production over the estimates of this study.

purchase payments by new small owners, the net drain of 'compensation' on the government's budget could be held very low.

The sixth type of cost would be expenditure on health and education for new 'parcel' owner families. This cost would not be directly attributable to the land reform, since these expenditures would represent welfare transfers and could conceivably be made without the occurrence of land reform. Such costs would therefore not be included in a cost–benefit analysis of land reform.[1]

In regard to the actual costs of land reform in Brazil it is not likely that land clearing costs would be important, for the sectors examined in this study. On a basis of census data for area presently under forest, no forest area would have to be cleared to permit the expected levels of cultivated and pastured area after reform.[2]

5.6. Alternative methods of analysis

Due to limitations on the scope of this study, certain additional ways of predicting gains from land reform are not attempted. One approach would be an inter-sectoral extension of the sector-by-sector analysis of this chapter. Specifically, it seems likely that cattle sectors would offer higher gains in production if they were converted to crop production in the reform process. This conversion would also permit much greater absorption of unemployed and 'surplus' labor, than would installation of cattle parcels of the size used in the reforms shown above. However, land quality on expropriated cattle farms should be examined carefully to assure that the land would be of adequate quality to support crop production.

An alternative approach to that used in this chapter would be to consider the reform prediction from a linear programming viewpoint. Pre-reform sectors would be broken into size groups. The aggregate inputs and output in each size group would be used to calculate technical coefficients for an activity. The unit level of activity would be one hectare of farm land in a specific size group. Then the linear programming problem would be to maximize production subject to the constraints of total factor availability.

---

[1] These costs might be included as costs and also as benefits. They would thus subtract out, unless the benefits somehow were computed to exceed market costs, as for example, in the case that increased health caused higher worker productivity.
[2] With the exception of Pernambuco sugar cane, the FGV sector only.

Since the number of activities (size groups) in the solution could not exceed the number of factor constraints, some of the size groups would be run at zero activity level, in other words, farms in these size groups would be expropriated and replaced by farms in other size groups. Those size groups whose activity levels were smaller than their pre-reform area would represent partially expropriated size groups; those with higher post-reform levels would represent the reform 'parcel' sectors into which new farms were placed.

The primary danger of the linear programming approach would be that the number of data observations would have to be quite large to ensure that the size group technical coefficients were valid. Otherwise, one size group could dominate the others, although it really represented an aberration from general input and output relationships to farm size. Changes in factor availability could be specified to allow for comparison of the linear programming results with results from the method used in the present chapter, in which sectoral inputs are allowed to change in the reform.

It is likely that the results of a linear programming approach would be similar to the results of this study. Differences would arise if the production function did not, in reality, have constant returns to scale over the whole scale range, or if the intensity of input application per farm area were not a smoothly declining function of farm size. If data were accurate the linear programming approach would single out any farm size group that deviated favorably from these general tendencies. In the programming approach, the 'optimal farm size' would be found empirically – although this size would be optimal from the standpoint of the sector and not necessarily optimal for the economy as a whole. A disadvantage of the programming approach is that it would have to employ arbitrary farm size boundaries. Furthermore, the solution could have the number of activities equal to the number of constraints, and thus could have perplexing results from the policy viewpoint. For example, a small farm activity might be chosen to operate along with a large farm activity, but this result would be less reasonable than the choice of a unique post-reform farm size and would occur only because of the rigid production coefficients assumed for each activity.

5.7. Conclusion

The first conclusion of this chapter is that on 'optimistic' assumptions of 'total reform', production would increase by substantial amounts (ranging

§5.7   CONCLUSION   165

from roughly 5% to some 60%) in all sectors but São Paulo coffee, sugar, and Alagoas sugar. It is a useful insight, however, that small farms are such a large percent of total output and inputs in some sectors, that total intensity of capital, seed, and fertilizer inputs might actually fall in these sectors, if all farms were converted to a medium-sized 'parcel' on which intensity of land use were lower than that in the smallest pre-reform farms.

On more conservative assumptions about the size and land quality of farms which could be expropriated – with expropriation limited to farms over 300 ha with above average land price – land reform shows substantial production gains (ranging from 10% to 30%) in only four of the seventeen sectors. Furthermore, in the conservative estimate, land available for expropriation would be insufficient to permit the elimination of all (or, in some sectors, any) of the 'excess labor' on sub-parcel farms.

The conservative 'partial reform' estimate is useful in that it singles out four sectors in which land reform would very probably increase production. These sectors are: Pernambuco sugar, Rio Grande do Sul rice, Ceará cattle and Minas Gerais cattle. Since land reform can be a piecemeal process, it is useful to have a ranking of sectors from highest production increase to lowest, as the two reform calculations of this chapter permit. Furthermore, since the impact of reform even on conservative assumptions is not negative except in two sectors, it may be said that if land redistribution were to be undertaken for reasons of social equity alone, the production results would not be injurious to the economy.[1]

---

[1] It would be likely, however, that the marketed surplus to the cities would fall in a land distribution to small family farms, if total production did not rise (see the discussion and data of section 2.4.4).

CHAPTER 6

CONCLUSION

6.1. Alternative policy measures

Before the summary and conclusions of this study are presented, it is appropriate that land redistribution be compared with several alternative policy measures toward agriculture.

6.1.1. Measures to increase production

There are two primary differences between land redistribution and conventional policies for increasing agricultural production. First, land redistribution would increase output by improving the efficiency of the agricultural structure; conventional policies, instead, increase output by inducing the application of more inputs onto a structurally inefficient base. Thus, it may be expected that conventional policies, without land redistribution, will be less efficient than they would be after structural reform. Second, land redistribution operates simultaneously to achieve two targets: equity in income distribution and increase in the production level. Conventional policies are directed toward increasing production but only incidentally affect equity in income distribution.

The 'conventional policies' toward agriculture include policies toward product prices, 'modern input' prices, extension services, farm credit, storage, and transport. The use of these policies to increase agricultural output increases the level of inputs into agriculture with no change in the structure of land ownership. The additional inputs are chiefly capital: machinery, seeds, fertilizer, pesticides; and skilled labor-extension workers. Any increased use of unskilled labor resulting from conventional policies comes from the rural pool of unemployed and thus does not represent an opportunity cost of the economy.[1]

---

[1] However, the case of a large pool of rural unemployed is more true for the Northeast of Brazil, and less true for the South.

Where the structural distortion in resource use in agriculture is severe, increased production may be expected to come with lower opportunity cost through land redistribution than through application of conventional policies. Land reform does involve administrative costs, and a crucial question is whether or not these costs are so high that the 'return to investment in land reform', net of costs, is higher than the net return to investment caused by use of conventional policies.

6.1.2. Measures to improve the use of land and labor

The policies other than land reform which might improve the use of land and labor resources in agriculture would be: an increase in land taxation, an increase in long-term credit for land purchase, the improvement of the financial assets market, and the elimination of minimum wages and rental controls.

Land taxation has been negligible in Brazil. The land reform law of 1964 calls for land taxation as a stimulus to effective land use. No tax is to be charged for farms under 20 ha, while the tax rate for other farms rises with farm size and with non-use of land. The maximum rate is 2.7% of land value. The effectiveness of taxation depends on the realism of assessed land valuation, on the level of the tax rate, and on the degree of honesty in administration of collection. The fact that land may be expropriated at its value declared for tax purposes is a great incentive for realistic valuation by the owner. However, the expropriation threat under present Brazilian law applies only in limited 'priority' areas, and so widespread undervaluation of land may be expected to continue. As for the tax level, the maximum rate of 2.7% of land value would be high enough to encourage 'use' of land, if annual reassessment were made to account for inflation.[1] However, with annual price level increases of 25% to 40%, the tax of 2.7% on an outdated land valuation would become negligible. In regard to administration, the great influence of local landlords on collection of the taxes is a hindrance to effective collection.

In sum, while land taxation theoretically could increase efficiency of land use in Brazil, in practice the measure may have little effect. At its best, taxation would work toward the production objective by encouraging

---

[1] Annual income from a capital asset of infinite life should be $r\%$ of the asset's price, where r is the discount rate. Assuming a 15% discount rate for Brazil, 2.7% of land value would represent about one sixth of the annual income generated by the land.

owners of unused land to produce, or to sell their land to farmers who would use it more effectively. Land taxation would work indirectly toward the objective of increased welfare for the rural poor, through increasing the supply of land for sale or rent in the land market.

Long term credit for land purchase would increase the 'access' of small farmers to land. However, it would have the disadvantage of driving up the land price drastically, as small farmers increased their competition for land purchase.

Improvement of the financial assets market – private and government bonds, corporate stocks, savings deposits, and money itself in the sense of reduced inflation – would work indirectly toward improvement of land use, if land were being held unused as a portfolio asset. Speculative landholders would begin to find alternative assets more attractive than land and would sell their land. The supply of land for sale would increase, its price would fall and land could become more easily available to small farmers. However, it is likely that a credit program would be necessary for land purchase; small farmers' land purchases might be much less sensitive to price than to credit availability.

Minimum wages and rent control are policy measures in which production effects run counter to equity effects. Misallocation of labor in agriculture – excessive labor on small farms and low labor/land ratios on large farms – might be reduced by the elimination of minimum wages.[1] A lower wage would presumably increase employment on large capitalistic farms. The agricultural workers as a group would lose, in welfare terms, if the elasticity of capitalists' demand for labor with respect to wage were less than unity. The previously employed workers would lose, as individuals, even if the wage bill of agricultural laborers as a group increased.

Rental restrictions similarly have contradictory equity and production effects. From the production viewpoint, there should be no rental restrictions such as maximum rent payments as a percent of land value (as provided by the 1964 law), enforced compensation to tenants for improvements, and guaranteed non-eviction after a number of years. These restrictions inhibit the allocation of land owned by large owners into use by rental arrangements. However, the elimination of these restrictions would cause a welfare transfer

---

[1] Minimum wages in agriculture were first legalized and introduced in Brazil in 1963. However, it is doubtful that their enforcement has been comprehensive.

away from present tenants toward landlords. Whether the low income farm population as a whole would benefit from the elimination of rental restrictions would depend on whether the gains of new tenants as a group outweighed the losses of previous tenants as a group.

Finally, it is useful to ask to what extent the 'conventional' policies toward agriculture will cause improvement in resource use. First, consider price policy: suppose that high support prices were put into effect for agricultural products.[1] This policy would only have a major effect in improving land use on large farms if the main cause of poor land use were a lack of market for large farms, relative to the stable market for 'own consumption' on the small farms. Yet this influence is probably not the most important influence on land use. In contrast, in the extreme case of 'non-economic behavior', higher prices would not induce higher output from large landowners. The influence of 'speculative landholding' would be such that some large areas held as portfolio assets might be converted to production, after product price increases, since the activity of 'production' would become more attractive relative to the activity of idle landholding. Yet price policy would be an extremely indirect measure to reduce speculative landholding, in comparison with either land redistribution or taxation of unused land. The influence of 'labor market dualism' would still keep output and inputs per farm area higher on small farms than on large farms, despite higher product prices. However, large farms might now find it profitable to hire unemployed landless labor and increase production, so that the differential of land use intensity between small and large farms would diminish. Similarly, monopsonistic farms would now produce more, yet there would still be a difference between their land use intensity and that of small, competitive farms. In short, price policy could only partly diminish the distorted allocation of land and labor caused by ownership structure and the behavior of owners, and would be a much less direct measure for this purpose than would land redistribution or land taxation.

Second, 'modern input' subsidization would have parallel effects to those of price policy, since it would increase profitability of production. It would seem inefficient for a program of input subsidization to be applied to an

---

[1] This policy would by no means necessarily be desirable, as it would raise food prices and therefore industrial wages. Alternatively, if the government bought food from farmers at high prices and sold to the urban population at low prices, a deficit would arise which would be a drain on government resources.

agrarian structure in which small farms already apply an excess of inputs per farm area, relative to large farms. The same inefficiency would exist with extension programs and short-term credit, since these programs are directed towards an increase in the use of modern inputs.

In sum, the conventional policies toward agricultural prices, input prices, short term credit, agricultural extension, and storage and transport would probably do little to correct structural distortion of land and labor use in agriculture. Instead, they would induce the agricultural system to expand further on the same base of factor misallocation. It is important to note that these policies are the very ones which have received the most governmental support in Brazil. From the production standpoint alone, the crucial question is whether long run agricultural growth will be greater if expansion continues on a 'distorted' base, or if instead the base is first corrected, at some cost.

6.1.3. Evaluation of alternative policies

The ideal basis for evaluation of the alternative policies would be the rate of return to investment in each policy activity. These rates would also tell whether any of the policies should be adopted, as opposed to investment elsewhere in the economy. The rates of return would show only production results. Some set of rates of 'social welfare' return would also be necessary to evaluate the relative efficacy of each policy in meeting the social equity target of increased welfare for the low income rural population.

A rate of return is not even available for the one policy examined in this study – land redistribution. Therefore, the comments here about relative efficiency of alternative policies are based on intuition, not quantitative analysis.

6.1.4. Policy choice as a function of diagnosis

The discussion in section 2.4 suggests alternative causes for poor use of land in agriculture. To some extent, the effectiveness of alternative policies depends on which cause or combination of causes is operative.

Table 30 shows a heuristic analysis of the responsiveness of production to alternative policies, depending on which 'state of nature' is true. Ideally, table 30 would have rates of return as its elements; instead, only signs for the direction of change are suggested. Policies 6 and 7 are in parentheses because they represent increased investment in agriculture without any improvement in previous factor misallocation, that is, with no structural change.

§6.1   ALTERNATIVE POLICY MEASURES   171

TABLE 30

Direction and magnitude of production change resulting from policy A if cause of misallocation of resources in agriculture is cause B

Causes B: Policies A:	1	2	3	4	5	6	7
1	++	++	++	++	++	++	0
2	+	+	+	++	+(?)	+(?)	0
3	+	+(?)	+	++	0	0(?)	0
4	0	++	0	0	0	0	0
5	0	0	0	+	0	0	0
6	(+)	(+)	(+)	(+)	(+)	(0)	(+)
7	(+)	(+)	(+)	(+)	(+)	(0)	(+)

Policies A:
1 = land redistribution
2 = land taxation
3 = land purchase credit
4 = improved assets market
5 = removal of rental restrictions
6 = increase in agricultural prices
7 = input packages *cum* extension efforts.

Causes B:
1 = 'dualism', family vs. capitalistic farms
2 = landholding for portfolio asset motives
3 = 'own consumption' land use on small farms
4 = land market imperfection
5 = monopsony power of large farms over labor
6 = non-economic behavior by large owners
7 = poor quality land on large farms

The results of policy 7 would depend on the distribution of input and extension efforts between small farms and large farms.

The responsiveness of the welfare of the low income farm population to each policy would parallel the response of production, shown in table 30, except for policy 5, rental restriction, in which the welfare effect could be negative. Although this study does not determine conclusively which of the possible causes of land use patterns are most important, it appears that labor market dualism and land market imperfection (causes 1 and 4 in the table) are the major influences on land use (see section 4.4). Therefore, land taxation and land purchase credit (policies 2 and 3 in the table) probably would improve land use. These two policies could be used to supplement a land redistribution program, or to substitute imperfectly for it so long as political reality would rule out land redistribution but would permit tax and credit measures.

6.2 Political considerations

A few words on the political likelihood of land reform in Brazil are necessary, to place this study in a realistic context. There are three considerations that are favorable to the possibility of land reform. First, the legislation has been passed providing for land redistribution. Even though it may not be implemented now, the very existence of the legislation will enable a future government to carry out land redistribution.[1] Second, the institutional organization to execute land reform has been established, in the Brazilian Institute of Agrarian Reform (IBRA). Third, a comprehensive cadastral survey was carried out in 1966. Therefore, the legislation, machinery, and information necessary for land redistribution exist, and they will facilitate land reform's execution once political forces favor it.

Despite these considerations favorable to land reform, virtually no land redistribution has occurred since the 1964 law. Given the political nature of the military regime[2], it appears unlikely that substantial land expropriation and redistribution will occur in the near future. While some elements of the political center have in the past recommended 'family farm' land reform as a measure to avoid Communism's appeal to the peasantry, most members of the right[3] view land expropriation as a Communistic threat to private property and a direct threat to their interests. Nevertheless, the government does seem to be seriously committed to economic development

---

[1] Hirschman emphasizes this point in his examination of Colombian land reform. Albert O. Hirschman, *Journeys Toward Progress: Studies of Economic Policy Making in Latin America* (New York: Twentieth Century Fund, 1963).

[2] In 1964 the military brought down the government of Goulart, in the belief that he was leading the country toward Communism. There was wide support for the coup in the middle and upper classes. Subsequent developments – such as wage control, credit restrictions, a shift to indirect elections, and the abolition of former student organizations – have eroded this support.

[3] It may be incorrect to assume the military is strictly rightist in orientation. The army recruits from the popular classes, and the military's conservatism may be due more to its reaction against the supposed or real threat of Communism, than to any natural alliance with the upper classes. Furthermore, there appears to be a faction within the military which strongly favors land reform and related social reform measures, as a means of consolidating national security. Finally, it should be noted that the military government since 1964 has accomplished more in the field of land reform legislation and implementation than previous governments. The lack of action under previous regimes was in large part due to the impossibility of passing land reform legislation in parliaments controlled by landed and traditional interests.

and has pledged itself to social reform.[1] Therefore, it is possible that the government would carry out at least limited land redistribution if it were convinced the measure would spur economic growth.

6.3. Summary of the study

This study may be summarized in three categories: theory, empirical results, and prediction.

6.3.1. Theory

The goals of land reform are to improve social equity and increase agricultural production. Land reform affects equity through redistribution of wealth and income toward the low income rural class, and through absorption of formerly unemployed rural labor. Concerning production, land reform's primary positive effect is on static efficiency. Long-run growth may be adversely affected by land redistribution if large farmers have a higher marginal propensity to save than small farmers, or if large farmers are more receptive to technical change. However, the effects of land reform on savings and innovation are not examined empirically in this study since relevant data are not available.

The effect of land reform on static efficiency is the main concern of this study. At the theoretical level, the first major consideration is that it is unlikely that economies of large scale production exist in agriculture in a country at Brazil's stage of economic development. The main reason why increasing returns to scale might exist is that farm machinery cannot be fully utilized on small farms. Yet in the early stages of development, the cheapness of labor relative to capital limits the relevance of farm machinery. The issue of whether or not increasing returns to scale exist is important in determining whether post-reform units should be relatively small scale 'family farms' or large scale cooperatives or state farms.

The second major theoretical point concerning static efficiency is that for several reasons larger farms tend to use their land less intensively – in terms of inputs and output per farm area – than do small farms. Seven influences causing this pattern may be distinguished:

1. 'Labor-market dualism' exists, in which the cost of labor is the going wage rate for large capitalistic farms but is implicitly lower for family labor on small farms. Family labor seems to leave the small farm for outside wages

---

[1] Land reform and tax reform were two of the major reforms pledged. The first has remained a paper phenomenon; the second has been implemented more effectively.

only when the prospective wage exceeds the average product of the family worker, rather than the marginal product. The theories of Sen and Chayanov are discussed in regard to this influence. The implication is that marginal product of labor on family farms is below that on capitalistic farms (using primarily hired labor) and thus that land is used to a point of greater intensity of output and inputs per area on the family farm than on the large farm.

2. The profit incentive of the large owner may lead him to hold land idle for purposes of speculation alone; especially if the future product price is uncertain but land prices habitually rise, if the owner's primary activities are in the city, and if assets alternative to land are unattractive.

3. The Brazilian land market seems to be imperfect, with small purchasers facing higher prices for a given quality land than large purchasers, and with poor credit availability for small purchasers. This differential in land price would cause more intensive use of land by small farmers than by large owners.

4. The family farm produces both for the market and for family consumption, and therefore has greater 'market certainty' for use of its output than do large commercial farms.

5. Large farms may have monopsony power over the local labor force, so that their profit maximization leads to production levels below those that competitive farms would reach, and to less intensive production per farm area than smaller, competitive farms in the sector attain.

6. There is the possibility that some large owners are not economic maximizers, but hold land for prestige.

7. Land quality and access to market may be poorer for large farms than for small; however, census data on 'unusable' land by farm size do not indicate this is so.

With the exception of the argument about land quality, these influences imply that poorly used land on large farms could be combined with unemployed and underemployed labor to increase agricultural production.

A third consideration concerning static efficiency is that land reform would tend to equalize the combinations of factors used, across farms. Before reform 'labor market dualism', land market imperfection, monopsony, and perhaps capital market imperfection cause large farms to employ little labor relative to capital and cultivated land, in comparison with smaller farms. Land redistribution would tend to create farms of uniform size within each product and therefore would reduce factor combination divergences associated with farm size divergences, and market improvements would tend to equalize factor combinations among farms of different sizes. Under the assumption of homogeneous production functions, this equalization would increase static efficiency and production, and this production effect would supplement the effect of new use of formerly unemployed land and labor.

A fourth theoretical consideration is the concept of 'social efficiency' as related to farm size. The best measure of efficiency would be the ratio of output to total factor cost evaluated at the factor's opportunity costs to the economy, or 'shadow prices'. Ideally, this measure would identify the socially optimal farm size for each good, and this size could be chosen as the post-reform organizational unit. In practice, 'shadow prices' are not available for this type of estimation.

A final consideration is that transformation of tenant farmers into owners could increase static efficiency, since certain tenancy arrangements impair certainty and incentives in production decisions. However, high rental payments may have a negative income effect on leisure which causes the tenant to produce more than an owner with similar land and labor resources so that transformation of tenants to owners would not cause increased production.

6.3.2. Empirical results

The hypothesis that increasing returns to scale exist in agriculture is tested first. The data used are some 1000 individual farm observations from three sample surveys, embracing seven states in Brazil. Cobb–Douglas type production functions are estimated (chapter 3), and it is found that the degree of homogeneity is not significantly[1] different from unity for fourteen of seventeen state-product sectors. Therefore it is concluded that returns to scale are constant, for inputs actually utilized. In this analysis, 'area cultivated' is the land 'input' for crop farms, and pasture area is the land input for cattle ranches.

A second production function model is used (in chapter 3) to determine whether or not deviations from constant returns to scale are found in specific farm size groups. Positive deviation in small farm size groups would indicate entrepreneurial superiority of small farm owners due to high incentive;

---

[1] In this summary, 'significant' refers to statistical significance at the 5% level.

positive deviation in larger farm size groups would indicate entrepreneurial superiority of large owners due to better technical knowledge. This model also examines the deviation from the general production function, associated with owner-operation as opposed to tenant-operation. This model is applied jointly to all observations from nine crop sectors, with appropriate intercept and factor elasticity 'dummy variables' to account for differences among sectors. This test finds that, given the inputs used, there is no significant difference in output among farm size groups or between tenure types.

Three formal statistical tests (in chapter 4) show that land use intensity declines as farm size rises. The first model tests the hypothesis that 'land used' as a percent of farm area declines as farm size (area) rises. Land 'used' is defined as area cultivated plus the 'effective pasture'[1] area. A significant negative relationship is found to exist between farm size and percent of farm area used, for all sectors examined. However, no significant relationship is found between 'percent land use' and tenure form (owner versus non-owner).

The second model of chapter 4 tests the same hypothesis, that land-use intensity declines as farm size rises, but the measure of 'land use intensity' is value added per hectare of farm area. Land price, farm size, and tenure form are included as the independent variables. Land price represents the quality of land, both inherent physical quality and access to market. It is found that for all but two of 17 sectors, a significant negative relationship exists between value added per farm area and farm size, even with the influence of land quality netted out by the land price variable. Tenure form is again found to have no significant relationship with land use intensity.

The third statistical model of chapter 4 tests the hypothesis that inputs used per total farm area decline as farm size rises. The logarithm of the input is regressed on the logarithm of farm area, for each input: land cultivated (or pasture land, for cattle sectors), labor, capital, and seeds and fertilizer. The estimated coefficient is the elasticity of the input's use with respect to farm size. This elasticity is less than unity for most inputs, for most sectors; thus, intensity of application of inputs per farm area declines as farm size rises.

Informal analysis (in chapter 4) indicates that there is no clear distinction between large efficient farms ('rural enterprises') and large inefficient farms

---

[1] Defined as the minimum of either declared pasture area, or livestock units divided by average livestock units per pasture area for the farms in the sector.

(latifúndios) within each state-product sector, despite the popularity of this distinction in the literature and legislation. Scatter diagrams of value added per farm area, against farm size, do not show that large farms are separated into these two classes. Similarly, informal analysis does not show a greater incidence of poor land use on large farms in Brazil's Northeast than in its South, despite the popularity of this view. However, similar analysis does suggest that low land utilization on large farms is a greater problem in certain products than in others. The problem seems greatest in cattle sectors, while the relative land utilization of large farms seems best in sugar cane and coffee sectors. Therefore, the concept of a dichotomy between efficient and inefficient large farms may have some validity in a comparison of large, sugar or coffee farms to large cattle ranches.

Informal tests are made (in chapter 4) to determine the relative importance of the several causes suggested for land use patterns. These tests refer to influences other than land quality, since the influence of land quality on land use is tested explicitly in earlier tests.

First, factor ratio changes associated with farm size are examined, and are found to be consistent in most cases with the influences of land market imperfection and 'labor–market dualism'. Specifically, labor per area cultivated declines as farm size rises, suggesting a rising cost of labor and/or a declining cost of land. Furthermore, capital per utilized area declines as farm size rises, in several sectors, indicating a declining effective price of land as farm size rises.

Second, scatter diagrams of value added per farm area, against farm size, are examined for a two-step pattern separating family farms from capitalistic farms, a pattern which would be expected if the consideration of family labor versus hired labor were the most important. Such a pattern is not generally found; that is, intensity of land use continues to decline over the whole range of 'capitalistic' large farms: thus, 'labor market dualism' does not appear to be the only influence on land use.

Third, the scatter diagrams are examined for a two-step pattern with higher land utilization for 'competitive' farms and lower utilization for monopsonistic farms, under the assumption that a farm size of roughly 10,000 ha is necessary for the existence of monopsony power over local labor. However, no distinct step is found for farms in the range of 10,000 ha.

Fourth, the scatter diagrams are examined to see whether or not large farms have almost no production, which could be expected if land were held for speculative reasons alone or for non-economic reasons. Eight of the seventeen sectors show extremely low output per area for larger farms.

In sum, the informal analysis arrives at no rigorous conclusion as to which of the possible influences actually cause land use intensity to decline as farm size rises, but the most likely causes are found to be 'labor market dualism' and 'land market imperfection'. The influence of land quality is rigorously tested, however, as discussed above.

Finally, the relation of 'social efficiency' to farm size is examined informally. Data are presented (in chapter 4) which show that factor combinations consistently shift away from labor toward cultivated land, and to a lesser extent, toward capital, as farm size rises. The implication of these data is that some intermediate farm size would be found to be socially optimal if economy-wide shadow prices were available for factors. These accounting prices are not available, so no estimate of 'socially optimal farm size' is made; instead, it is merely argued that shifting factor combinations imply inefficient factor allocation under the assumption of homogeneity in the production functions. Furthermore, given the likelihood of a low shadow price for labor, and given the intensive use of labor on small farms, it is argued that the 'socially optimal' farm size would be in the smaller farm size range.

6.3.3. Prediction of the impact of land redistribution on agricultural production

In chapter 5, the production effects of land reform are estimated. First, the sample data are weighted so as to correspond to universe data. Then two experiments are conducted: a 'total reform' and a 'partial reform'. In both experiments, the post-reform unit is the 'family farm'. This unit is chosen on the grounds that since smaller farms make more intensive use of land than larger farms, the unit which would maximize post-reform production would be the smallest realistic labor unit, the family farm, subject to full allotment of available land and labor into farms. Labor availability is determined for each sector as pre-reform labor in the sector plus an assumed percent for unemployed to be absorbed, based on the 'temporary labor' data from the agricultural census. The total number of workers in each sector is divided by 2.5 to find the number of families, and hence the number of post-reform farms. Then, the land area of the family unit, or 'parcel', is the total area of the sector divided by the number of family units. The cultivated land, capital, and seeds and fertilizer inputs on the family parcel are then determined from the pre-reform relationships of these inputs to farm size.[1] Then the inputs – including labor of 2.5 adult-equivalent workers – are applied to the production function estimated for the sector to determine output per 'parcel'. Output per parcel is multiplied by the number of parcels to determine post-reform output.

The 'partial reform' calculation is similar to that of 'total reform', just described, except that farms under 300 ha are exempted from expropriation, and only large farms with above average land prices are considered for expropriation. The first restriction reflects a possible political constraint; the second restriction is included to guarantee that the land expropriated is not of bad quality. The farms eligible for expropriation are ranked by output per area and expropriated in order from lowest to highest output per area, until either all unemployed labor plus 'excess labor'[2] on small farms is allocated to parcels on expropriated land, or until the eligible area is exhausted. The purpose of this method is to simulate what would probably be the practice of the reform agency, to leave the 'best' large farms unexpropriated if possible; but in none of the sectors is enough land eligible for expropriation to afford the luxury of exemption for the most efficient farms of the eligible set.

It is estimated in the total reform that an across-the-board land redistribution would increase Brazilian farm output by about 20%. The corresponding figure for the more conservative partial reform is roughly 6%. However, the percentage production increase would be much higher in some individual sectors – the highest increases are on the order of 60% for total reform (Minas Gerais cattle) and production would even decline in a few sectors (São Paulo coffee and Alagoas sugar cane). Since land reform would probably begin on a gradual basis, it is concluded that from a technical but not political viewpoint certain sectors, of those investigated in this study, would be the appropriate sectors in which to initiate land redistribution. Furthermore, it is found, in the total reform, that the land reform law's target income for parcel recipients – the minimum wage plus 10% – could be achieved or exceeded

---

[1] That is, from the regression estimates in chapter 4. However, in one 'total reform' version, capital and seeds and fertilizer inputs on the parcel are simply set equal to the fraction $1/m$ of the pre-reform sectoral totals, where m is the number of post-reform parcels.
[2] Defined as the excess of labor on small farms above that amount implied by the labor/land ratio of the reform parcel.

in most of the sectors. The reform calculations do not account for long run investment effects due to possible changes in agricultural savings, nor is the effect of product shifts due to reform calculated: labor is assumed not to shift from one product-sector to another, and farms are assumed to produce the same principal product after the reform as before.[1] Furthermore, costs of land reform are not estimated, although the post-reform levels of capital and seeds and fertilizer inputs are calculated.

It is necessary to make a final qualification on the predicted effects of land redistribution. It is likely that the gains of new smallholders after land reform would be offset partially by deterioration in agricultural prices, due to increased agricultural production and increased rural demand for industrial products. In this case part of the benefits of land redistribution would be transferred from the new smallholders to the urban workers through lower food prices. However, it seems unlikely that agricultural price deterioration would be severe. Given overall production increases of 6% to 20%, the increased 'own-consumption' of foodstuffs on the farms could very well leave little increment in the marketed surplus. Even with an increase in the marketed surplus, urban food consumption would very probably increase briskly in response to relatively small declines in food prices. The reason is that the urban workers are at income levels at which a large percent of their budget goes to purchase of foodstuffs. Thus a price decline for food would induce extra consumption both through the price-substitution effect and through a substantial income effect of higher real income due to lower food prices. Still, the possibility of agricultural price deterioration must be acknowledged.

6.4. Conclusion

There are three main conclusions of this study.
1. Returns to scale are constant in Brazilian agriculture, for inputs actually used. Therefore, land reform could create relatively small scale 'family farms' without loss of efficiency.
2. The intensity of land use declines as farm size rises. This decline is not caused primarily by declining land quality. Therefore, redistribution of

---

[1] Since output value gains might be possible if cattle ranches were shifted to crop production, gains from land reform could be understated in the calculations of this study.

land from large farms to small farmers and landless workers would increase land utilization and therefore agricultural production.
3. A simulation experiment shows that land redistribution could be expected to increase agricultural production substantially. However, production increases would be much greater in some state-product sectors than in others. The logical policy, from the technical standpoint alone, would be to begin land redistribution in those sectors which show the highest potential increases in production from land reform.

APPENDIX A

COLONIZATION

Colonization often is suggested as a solution to the problem of agricultural poverty. Migration to frontier regions has the advantage that it causes less political strife than land redistribution in traditional areas.

The difficulty with the colonization alternative is its high cost and the lack of interest of the population in migration. With regard to costs, two types of considerations are relevant. First, transport costs: one may investigate whether transport from frontier areas to consumer markets is sufficiently cheap to permit commercial production in frontier areas. Otherwise colonization can be only on a basis of subsistence farms not integrated with the economy. Secondly, the various costs of moving population, clearing land, building new roads, schools, and health facilities, must be considered.

The analysis of this section examines only transport costs. On a basis of truck and sea-shipping costs per kilometer-ton, given in a 1965 study of transport in the Northeast,[1] the costs are calculated for transport from three potential colonization areas[2] to their respective consumer markets. The transport expenses are compared with production costs[3] and final market prices. These costs have been calculated for colonization area suppliers and for traditional area suppliers with whom colonies would compete for the urban markets in question. While the calculations are extremely rough, the tentative conclusion is the following: the colonization area of Maranhão is feasible for commercial production and supply to Fortaleza and Recife. However, the two other areas most likely for colonization, Southern Pará (i.e. west of Tocantinópolis) and Rondônia-Mato Grosso, are not feasible commercial areas. These results may be seen in table 31.

---

[1] R. E. Lave and D. W. Kyle, *A Systems Study of Transportation in Northeast Brazil* (Stanford: Institute in Engineering-Economic Systems, 1966).
[2] As recommended by J. Hayne in R. Newberg and E. Miller, *Aspects of Frontier Settlement in Northern Brazil: Report of Interagency Reconnaissance Team*, (n.p.: United States Agency for International Development, 1964), mimeographed.
[3] In general, lower production costs in frontier areas – due to high yields and lower land prices – could permit competition with established areas, despite higher transport costs.

TABLE 31

Production and transport costs for some agricultural goods, Brazil. 'Frontier-colonization' areas versus traditional agricultural areas

Market	Land*	Labor**	Capital Animal	Capital Tractor, plows	Seeds, fertilizer, insecticides	Sum prod. cost	Transport***	Total cost	Retail market price****
					Costs per ton, 1965, cruzeiros				
I. *Rio de Janeiro*									
a) Rice									
A	1,850	64,180	243	21,670	27,760	115,703	213,800	329,503	297,000
X	45,141	67,445	5,801	3,683	41,642	163,712	31,300	195,012	297,000
b) Beans									
A	3,214	204,428	3,643	1,490	19,530	232,304	213,800	446,104	346,000
X	101,048	437,000	5,726	2,340	30,700	592,163	31,300	623,463	346,000
c) Cotton									
A	1,745	93,835	—	42,750	91,790	230,120	213,800	443,920	n.a.
X	34,910	127,610	—	42,750	91,700	296,970	31,300	328,270	n.a.
II. *Fortaleza*									
a) Rice									
B	826	69,500	—	—	2,370	71,870	77,000	148,870	289,000
C	2,500	152,000	—	—	3,935	155,935	116,100	272,035	289,000
Y	4,414	57,572	—	—	1,786	59,358	26,600	85,958	289,000

Table 31, continued

Market	Land*	Labor**	Capital Animal	Capital Tractor, plows	Seeds, fertilizer, insecticides	Sum prod. cost	Transport***	Total cost	Retail market price****
				Costs per ton, 1965, cruzeiros					
b) Beans									
B	1,923	224,230	5,230	2,140	56,488	290,011	77,000	367,011	327,000
C	3,160	245,780	4,772	1,952	51,532	307,196	116,100	423,296	327,000
Y	16,092	268,040	6,253	2,557	67,528	360,470	22,400	382,870	327,000
c) Corn									
B	1,405	163,832	3,822	1,563	17,564	188,186	77,000	265,186	n.a.
C	3,117	242,591	4,710	1,926	21,645	273,989	116,100	390,089	n.a.
Y	9,655	160,824	3,752	1,534	17,241	183,351	22,400	205,751	n.a.
d) Cotton									
B	2,880	405,166	12,719	4,640	16,306	441,711	77,000	518,711	n.a.
C	9,310	876,852	22,910	8,358	29,370	946,800	116,100	1,062,900	n.a.
Y	24,926	501,355	15,738	5,742	20,178	543,013	22,400	565,413	n.a.
III. *Recife*									
a) Rice									
B	826	69,500			2,370	71,870	110,400	182,270	243,000
C	2,500	152,000			3,935	155,935	140,775	296,710	243,000
Z	7,839	63,436			1,851	73,126	19,000	92,126	243,000

b) Beans								
B	1,923	224,230	5,230	2,140	56,488	290,011	110,400	400,411	492,000
C	3,160	245,780	4,772	1,952	51,532	307,196	140,775	447,971	492,000
Z	32,070	331,450	7,270	2,973	78,504	452,272	19,000	471,272	492,000
c) Corn								
B	1,405	163,832	3,822	1,563	17,564	188,186	110,400	298,586	120,000
C	3,117	242,591	4,710	1,926	21,645	273,989	140,775	414,764	120,000
Z	18,950	195,808	4,294	1,756	19,736	221,594	19,000	240,594	120,000
d) Cotton								
B	2,880	405,166	12,719	4,640	16,306	441,711	77,000	518,711	n.a.
C	9,310	876,852	22,910	8,358	29,370	946,800	116,100	1,062,900	n.a.
Z	56,916	710,312	20,964	7,648	26,877	765,801	19,000	784,801	n.a.

Colonization areas:

A = Mato Grosso and Rondônia
B = Maranhão (Pindaré-Mirim)
C = Pará (100 km west of Tocantinópolis)

Traditional agricultural areas:

X = São Paulo (Piracicaba)
Y = Ceará (Crato, Sobral, etc.)
Z = Pernambuco (Arcoverde)

* 12% of land value of area necessary to produce 1 ton.
** ((Man-days/hectare)/(tons/hectare)) × regional minimum wage. Technical input coefficients: *Insumos Físicos para Culturas Selecionadas no Região Centro-Sul do Brasil, 1965-66* and ... *Região Nordeste do Brasil, 1965-66*. Ministério da Agricultura, Rio de Janeiro. Yields per hectare: Serviço da Estatística da Produção, IBGE. 63-65 averages.
*** From Lave, R.E., and Kyle, D.W., *A Systems Study of Transportation in Northeastern Brazil, op. cit.* Transport costs for trucking, per kilometer, applied to appropriate route distances.
**** Recife (1960) and Fortaleza (1962): Banco do Nordeste do Brasil, *Suprimento de Gêneros Alimentícios* etc. Rio de Janeiro (1966): *Boletim Informativo dos Mercados Atacadistas*, Ministério da Agricultura. All prices converted to 1965 values with wholesale price index.

Maranhão probably has good long-run prospects for colonization. However, in the early 1960's, SUDENE suspended its plans to move 25,000 persons into the area yearly from the rest of the Northeast. A large, unofficial flow of migrants into Pernambuco in the late 1950's (probably 50,000 to 100,000 persons) created sufficient problems of organization and extension for the SUDENE Maranhão program that plans for further migration were postponed.[1]

In summary, for the one aspect of colonization examined here – transport cost – the prospects for frontier settlement are bleak for two frontier areas; a third area (Maranhão) is temporarily saturated with migrants (due to administrative difficulties), but transport costs are sufficiently low to make it a feasible colonization area in the long run. If one were to consider the other costs of settlement as well – moving and social overhead costs – the 'colonization alternative' would become even more questionable.

---

[1] Grupo Interdepartamental de Povoamento do Maranhão (GIPM), *Relatório* (Recife: SUDENE, 1963), typed.

APPENDIX B

NOTES ON THE SAMPLE DATA USED

B.1. Survey methods of the samples

The data used in chapter 3 come from three sources, which will be designated as FGV, IAA, and IRGA. Chapters 4 and 5 use only the FGV and IAA data.

The first source, FGV,[1] is a sample of 2500 farms in seven principal agricultural states in Brazil in 1963. (The states were: Ceará, Espírito Santo, Minas Gerais, Pernambuco, Rio Grande do Sul, Santa Catarina, and São Paulo.) The Getulio Vargas Foundation conducted the survey, with field assistance from local extension agents, and with partial financing from the United States Department of Agriculture. The sample was a 'cluster' sample: in each stage, a number of 'conglomerates' or regional areas were chosen, at random, in the first stage; then, a number of farms from each conglomerate were chosen at random. The sample was designed on a basis of 1960 census questionnaires. These were examined for one state (Espírito Santo). The 'census sectors' were used as conglomerates. Farm income was examined for variance. Variance of farm income was found to be much greater among census sectors than within them; the variance within sectors was thus ignored and the sample was dimensioned on a basis of variance among census regional sectors. The final sample was designed so as to attain an error of 20%[2] (of the income mean) at a significance level of 10%. For the state of Espírito Santo, this meant a sample of 48 out of 480 census sectors, with five observations per sector – a sample size of 240. For other states, a similar design was

---

[1] The information from this survey has not been published in its final form. It was used, however, for estimation of sectoral production functions, reported in Fundação Getulio Vargas, *Projeções de Oferta e Demanda de Produtos Agrícolas Para o Brasil. Texto Preliminar, op. cit.* The production functions estimated are of questionable value, since they include often up to ten independent variables (and thus often have low significance) and often enter a redundant land variable (using both area cultivated, physical, and value of land cultivated).

[2] Due to loss of some 15% of the sample observations' questionnaires, the error was increased to some 30% – according to the chief statistician involved in the survey.

immediately undertaken, without preliminary examination of census questionnaires for farm income variance information. The sample size for other states was roughly the same as for Espírito Santo, except for São Paulo which had some 700 observations.

The second source of data (IAA)[1] was a sample survey of sugar farms, conducted by the Getulio Vargas Foundation. One survey was made of sugar cane 'suppliers' *(fornecedores)* in 1963, and a survey using identical methodology was made of 'mill' *(usina)* sugar cane farms, in 1965. Roughly one hundred suppliers in each of five states were surveyed, and between 17 and 30 mills were surveyed in each of the same five states (Alagoas, Minas Gerais, Pernambuco, Rio de Janeiro, and São Paulo.) The total population of suppliers in the five states was 22,773. The population of mills was 209.

The two samples were each stratified according to production volume. The samples were designed at size to yield a confidence level of 95% and a relative error around the mean of less than 6%.

The third source of data (IRGA) was a sample, made by the author, of questionnaires in the yearly 'census' of the roughly 5000 rice farms that belong to the Rio Grande do Sul rice institute. The sample was taken from the 1963–64 crop year data. A sample size of 200 was decided on; it was then attempted to minimize sample error by stratifying the sample. The sample was stratified by size of planting, in hectares. The hypothesis was then used, that minimum sample variance is attained when the number of observations in each stratum is determined by weighting the stratum on a basis of the size of the population in that stratum, and the standard deviation of the variable investigated, in that stratum. Thus,

$$\frac{n_i}{n^*} = \frac{N_i \sigma_i}{\sum_{i=1}^{L} N_i \sigma_i}$$

where
n_i = number of observations in stratum i;
n^* = total number of sample observations (=200);
N_i = population in stratum i;

---

[1] See results published in Fundação Getulio Vargas, *Pesquisa Sobre Condições e Custos de Produção da Lavoura Canavieira* (Rio de Janeiro, 1965), and in Fundação Getulio Vargas, *Pesquisa Sobre Condições e Custos de Produção da Lavoura Canavieira – Usinas* (Rio de Janeiro, 1966).

σ_i = Standard deviation of the variable of interest, in stratum i;
L = total number of strata.

Since the standard deviations of the variables examined were unknown, the assumptions were made that: (a) the characteristics of the farms depended on the size group; (b) therefore the standard deviations of the relevant variables were proportional to the width of the size group, i.e. the ceiling of the size group minus the floor. Thus, the above formula was computed with the σ_i set equal (as a proxy) to W where $W =$ (size group ceiling − size group floor). (However, for very large size groups, complete enumeration was used, since there were very few observations.)

A test of the sample technique was made through prediction of rice production for all 5000 farms. This was done by multiplying the sample average rice production for each stratum by the number of farms in the population in that stratum, and summing. This test predicted production which was 92% of the actual production of the universe.

B.2. Size-distribution bias of the FGV sample

Cluster sampling is done as follows: the total sample number is divided into a given number of 'clusters', each consisting of a certain (equal) number of members. For each cluster, one farm is chosen at random from among the population. Then the other members of that cluster are simply the first n farms immediately adjacent to the chosen farm, where n is the number in the cluster. This method attempts to achieve random sampling, while reducing the transport cost of actually visiting farms – by obtaining random spread of clusters rather than a random spread of individual farms.

There is a reason to expect cluster sampling to produce a sample population with a greater incidence of large farms than occurs in the population of the universe. Since the probability is higher that a large farm will be contiguous with any other farm in the population than that probability for a small farm, sampling which is based on adjacency will have a biased distribution in favor of large farms.

In the Getulio Vargas Foundation survey of 1963, the bias toward large farms seems to have occurred. (The sample was on a 'cluster' basis.) Table 32 shows the percentage distribution of numbers of farms and total area, by size group, in the 1960 census, in comparison with the FGV survey. (Data for the whole sample are available to the author for only Pernambuco and Rio Grande do Sul.)

TABLE 32

Percentage distribution of number and area of farms among various size groups. 1960 census versus Getulio Vargas Foundation survey sample

Size group (ha)	1960 census % area	1960 census % number	FGV sample % area	FGV sample % number
A. Pernambuco				
<10	9.4	76.6	1.3	44.0
10 to <100	24.3	19.5	7.4	34.3
100 to <1000	43.3	3.6	50.4	18.6
1000 to <10000	17.8	0.2	41.1	3.2
>10000	5.2	0.01	0	0
	100.0	100.0	100.0	100.0
B. Rio Grande do Sul				
<10	2.3	26.3	0.7	24.9
10 to <100	30.3	66.4	9.7	54.9
100 to <1000	31.1	6.4	29.0	16.9
1000 to <10000	30.1	0.8	60.6	3.3
>10000	6.2	0.03	0.0	0.0

B.3. Weighting of sample data for land reform calculations

To transform the sample data into data that would be 'representative' of the actual size distribution of farms, the sample data were weighted. Each variable for an observation was multiplied by the factor A_i/a_i where A_i was the percent of total farm area in the universe's group i, and a_i was the same percent for the sample. A set of these weights was derived for each of the 17 product sectors of this study. Farm area distribution by farm size was available by product sector in the 1960 census. However, the census material was only available to the author for five of the seven states of the study: Alagoas, Espírito Santo, Pernambuco, Rio Grande do Sul, and São Paulo. For product sectors in these states, the A_i was found from the census and A_i/a_i was calculated directly.

For sectors in Ceará and Minas Gerais, no 'universe' farm size distribution was available, by product sector. It was therefore assumed that the average amount of size distribution distortion of the sample compared to the universe, known from the sectors of the four states for which the census was available, would accurately represent the same distortion of sample sectors in Minas Gerais and Ceará from their universes. Thus, average 'generalized weights' were calculated from the size group weights of the sectors for which census information was available. One set of average weights was calculated for crop sectors, another for cattle sectors, on grounds that since cattle sectors tend to have concentration in large farms, the degree of sample distortion might be different (less) from the degree of distortion in crop sectors.

For the sugar cane sectors, a third method was used. The census size distribution information was available for all three relevant states – Alagoas, Pernambuco, and São Paulo. However, this information was rejected. The IAA sample itself had an enumeration of roughly one-half the universe of very large farms *(usinas)*, and the sample showed more total absolute area in farms over (for example) 10,000 hectares than did the census. The problem appeared to be that the census registered as separate farms the sub-farms *(fundos)* comprising single sugar mill estates *(usinas)*, thus understating drastically the number of farms with very large area. For the sugar sectors, therefore, the size distribution of the universe was constructed. For Pernambuco, this process was facilitated by information in J. M. Rosa e Silva Neto,[1] which permitted direct calculation of the size distribution of Pernambuco sugar farms. This distribution, as had been suspected, showed much higher concentration of area in very large farms than did the census.

For Alagoas and São Paulo, an indirect method was used for each state. Sugar farms are of two types: suppliers *(fornecedores)* and mills *(usinas)*. The total area and size distribution of suppliers was found as follows. First, official IAA data showed the 1963–64 sugar cane produced by suppliers (Q_s). Second, the IAA sample data used in this study permitted an estimate of the ratio of sugar cane output to total farm size for suppliers (r_s).[2] Thus, an estimate of total area of supplier farms was arrived at $(A_s = Q_s/r_s)$. Third, the number of suppliers in each production quota bracket (in tons of sugar cane) was known, from official IAA data. This distribution was used to

---

[1] J. M. Rosa e Silva Neto, *Contribuição ao Estudo da Zona da Mata em Pernambuco* (Recife: Instituto Joaquim Nabuco de Pesquisas Sociais, 1966), pp. 21, 24, 25.

[2] For data on the sugar sectors, heavy reliance was made on two publications based on the IAA sample data used in this study. These were: Fundação Getulio Vargas, *Pesquisa sobre Condições e Custos da Produção da Lavoura Canavieira*, 1965, *op. cit.*, and Fundação Getulio Vargas, *Pesquisa Sobre Condições e Custos da Produção da Lavoura Canavieira – Usinas*, 1966, *op. cit.*

arrive at a size distribution for suppliers, as follows.[1] The floor and ceiling of each quota bracket were divided by average supplier sugar cane output per farm area (r_s) to find a floor and ceiling farm size corresponding to each production bracket. At this point, therefore, the universe number of farms in each derived size group was known. To convert this information to size distribution by desired size groups (different from the derived size groups), a rectangular distribution within each derived size group was assumed. Thus, to find the supplier farm area in the desired size group with floor X_L hectares and ceiling X_H hectares, when the 'derived' size group had floor S_L and ceiling S_H, with n farms, it was assumed that there were $n/(S_H - S_L)$ farms per hectare-step in the derived size group. Thus, to find the area of farms between size X_L and X_H where there were $M = n/(S_H - S_L)$ farms per hectare-step, the formula:

$$\text{Area} = M \left[\frac{X_H(X_H+1)}{2} - \frac{X_L(X_L+1)}{2} \right]$$

was used. This represented the summed area of M farms of size X_L, $+M$ farms of size X_L+1, ...$+M$ farms of size X_H. (The bracketed expression is the value for the sum of the integers from X_L to X_H.) Thus, area by desired size groups was known.

For *usinas*, farm size distribution was calculated as follows. Total sugar mill production of sugar cane was known from IAA data (Q_m). The IAA sample data gave an average ratio of output per farm size for sugar mills (r_m). Total sugar mill area was thus estimated (Q_m/r_m). The IAA listing of sugar mills by industrial sugar production quota was available. These sugar production quotas were converted to farm area, through assumed average relations of industrial sugar to sugar cane; of total sugar cane to 'own supply' from the mill (roughly 50%); and of 'own supply' sugar cane to farm area. The estimated farm area of each sugar mill was thus known, and total area within desired size groups was calculated directly. The *usina* data, finally, were added to the supplier data to get total size distribution for the sugar sector. Again, this procedure was used only for Alagoas and São Paulo sugar.

---

[1] It should be mentioned that direct conversion of production distribution to farm size distribution understates the variation of farm size, thus overstating the area of farms in middle size groups and understating the area in the lowest and highest size groups. It is not felt that this distortion is serious here.

TABLE 33

Sample weighting factors for simulated universe sectors

Sector	Size groups (ha)											
	<5	5–10	10–20	20–50	50–100	100–200	200–500	500–1000	1000–2000	2000–5000	5000–10000	10000–infin.
Cea. cot.	12.58	12.58	8.84	3.68	3.21	2.83	1.06	0.91	0.62	0.42	0.42	0.42
Per. cot.	16.65	16.65	4.31	1.46	1.75	1.12	0.60	0.68	0.14	0.14	0.14	0.14
S.P. cof.	13.00	13.00	13.00	3.81	2.10	2.11	1.80	0.84	0.84	0.26	0.26	0.26
E.S. cof.	10.58	10.58	3.22	1.78	1.06	1.30	0.81	0.32	0.32	0.32	0.32	0.32
Per. sug. F	17.40	17.40	17.40	5.16	5.16	2.35	0.59	1.01	1.01	1.01	1.01	1.01
S.P. cerls.	7.75	7.75	7.75	2.51	1.82	1.82	1.47	0.89	0.89	0.26	0.26	0.26
Al. sug.	81.10	81.10	81.10	13.81	13.81	5.41	4.25	1.68	2.76	1.68	0.45	0.23
P. sug. I	64.40	64.40	64.40	50.80	50.80	12.40	3.16	4.00	1.23	1.99	1.11	0.56
S.P. sug.	74.27	74.27	74.27	48.67	28.68	22.56	10.08	3.05	0.30	0.30	0.30	0.30
R.G. rice	10.10	10.10	7.34	7.34	7.34	8.38	1.08	1.73	0.53	0.53	0.53	0.53
M.G. corn	12.58	12.58	8.84	3.68	3.21	2.83	1.06	0.91	0.62	0.42	0.42	0.42
S.P. cat./gen.	8.13	8.13	8.13	4.52	3.08	3.08	2.92	1.49	0.78	0.41	0.31	0.31
Cea. cat.	5.40	5.40	5.40	5.40	2.49	2.49	2.25	1.31	0.81	0.67	0.60	0.60
E.S. cat.	6.13	6.13	6.13	6.13	1.22	1.22	0.90	0.76	0.76	0.76	0.76	0.76
M.G. cat.	5.40	5.40	5.40	5.40	2.49	2.49	2.25	1.31	0.81	0.67	0.60	0.60
R.G. cat.	4.20	4.20	4.20	4.20	2.04	2.04	1.63	1.07	0.97	0.68	0.68	0.68
S.P. cat.	5.88	5.88	5.88	5.88	4.21	4.21	4.21	2.11	0.70	0.56	0.36	0.36

Table 33 shows the weights by which sample observations in the relevant size groups were multiplied.

B.4. Imputed wages

The FGV sample data give labor in value terms. For farms using family labor, the value is imputed at regional wages for equivalent work. Some of the analysis of this study requires conversion of labor value data to 'adult worker equivalents'. The imputed yearly wage for an adult worker, at which this conversion was made, was based on a sample of the sample data. The imputed wages for all sectors of each state are shown in table 34.

It may also be noted that the IAA labor data were in man days. Thus, conversion to number of yearly workers was made by dividing the labor quantity, in man days, by 300.

TABLE 34

Imputed wage, per year, FGV sample,
adult equivalent worker

State	100 cruzeiros	Year
Ceará	897	1962
Espírito Santo	900	1962
Minas Gerais	1400	1963
Pernambuco	684	1962
Rio Grande do Sul	835	1962
São Paulo	1400	1963

APPENDIX C

STATISTICAL APPENDIX

TABLE 35

Percentage composition of land use by farm size group

	Cultivated* (1)	Planted pasture (2)	A. Percent of area used in					B. Percent of total farm area in size group
			Natural pasture (3)	Planted forest (4)	Natural forest (5)	Idle, fallow (6)	Not usable (7)	
Brazil (a)								
I	66.5	3.8	12.7	0.6	5.5	8.2	2.7	2.4
II	27.8	8.2	26.0	1.2	17.1	14.9	4.8	19.0
III	10.3	10.2	42.8	0.9	18.4	11.9	5.5	34.4
IV	3.4	8.5	52.0	0.7	20.3	9.8	5.3	28.6
V	0.6	2.9	39.0	0.5	43.9	8.6	4.6	15.6
Ceará (b)								
I	34.1	0.6	7.8	0.4	8.1	41.0	8.0	0.9
II	15.8	0.6	16.6	0.6	19.3	39.3	7.7	18.0
III	7.8	0.8	22.5	0.5	27.5	33.1	7.7	48.0
IV	3.9	0.8	28.8	0.5	34.8	23.4	8.0	27.6
V	2.3	0.5	16.7	0.0	47.3	25.5	7.8	5.5
Espírito Santo (a)								
I	63.5	5.5	11.0	0.6	9.8	7.4	2.2	1.4
II	31.8	8.9	15.4	0.8	26.7	12.7	3.7	53.3
III	18.4	14.0	22.0	1.0	30.6	10.3	3.7	37.6
IV	12.9	17.0	20.7	1.4	40.5	4.7	2.8	6.0
V	1.9	0.1	10.1	0.0	80.8	7.2	0.0	1.7
Minas Gerais (b)								
I	43.5	5.0	25.5	0.2	2.3	12.6	10.9	0.8
II	19.6	10.1	38.1	0.4	7.6	15.5	8.7	16.1
III	8.2	13.2	49.9	0.4	8.3	12.0	7.9	44.7
IV	2.7	12.3	58.5	0.3	9.9	8.8	7.4	29.7
V	0.4	3.2	58.0	0.1	14.0	14.5	9.6	8.6

Table 35 continued

	Cultivated* (1)	Planted pasture (2)	A. Percent of area used in			Idle, fallow (6)	Not usable (7)	B. Percent of total farm area in size group
			Natural pasture (3)	Planted forest (4)	Natural forest (5)			
Pernambuco (a)								
I 69.1	1.9	16.6	0.4	2.4	7.6	2.0	9.9
II 27.0	3.9	30.9	1.2	14.2	19.0	3.8	25.3
III 19.1	2.9	27.2	0.9	23.4	22.3	4.2	43.8
IV 9.4	1.8	37.7	1.1	23.7	22.7	3.7	16.2
V 1.4	0.1	54.8	0.0	29.4	7.0	7.3	4.7
Rio Grande do Sul (a)								
I 67.2	2.0	14.8	1.4	5.3	6.9	2.5	2.4
II 35.2	2.3	27.2	1.8	14.2	14.3	4.9	31.2
III 11.0	1.3	73.2	0.8	7.6	3.1	3.1	32.1
IV 3.6	1.1	84.8	0.6	5.5	1.4	2.9	30.6
V 1.6	3.7	65.6	0.2	22.7	0.4	5.8	3.7
São Paulo (a)								
I 84.1	3.6	5.8	0.5	1.7	2.8	1.5	4.0
II 39.1	18.1	23.0	1.7	8.1	6.9	3.2	23.6
III 20.5	25.1	30.8	2.3	11.6	5.9	3.9	41.9
IV 12.0	32.0	25.9	2.9	17.1	5.4	4.7	26.4
V 8.9	32.9	24.0	4.2	19.1	6.5	4.5	4.1

* Including fallow land intended for cultivation in subsequent year.
Source: (a) Instituto Brasileiro de Geografia e Estatística, Serviço Nacional de Recenseamento, *Censo Agrícola de 1960. VII Recenseamento Geral do Brasil* (Rio de Janeiro, 1967).
(b) Instituto Brasileiro de Geografia e Estatística, Serviço Nacional de Recenseamento, *Censo Agrícola de 1950. VI Recenseamento Geral do Brasil* (Rio de Janeiro, 1957).
Size groups (ha):
I – <10; II – 10-100; III – 100-1000; IV – 1000-10000; V – >10000.

TABLE 36

Percentage of inputs and production in each farm size group – simulated universe

Sector variable	I	II	III	IV	V	VI
Ceará cotton						
L	7.5	24.0	28.4	30.4	4.6	5.1
N	21.4	35.3	23.9	16.8	0.9	1.6
K	10.8	25.6	31.6	26.5	2.9	2.6
S	8.9	15.2	33.9	35.1	5.1	1.8
X	3.5	13.8	31.8	31.8	6.7	12.4
Y	3.8	25.9	24.2	33.4	9.6	3.0
Q	12.1	21.2	28.1	31.1	5.3	2.1
Pernambuco cotton						
L	47.2	25.7	15.0	4.6	7.5	0.0
N	51.3	25.7	14.0	4.2	4.7	0.0
K	38.0	24.8	19.2	9.8	8.2	0.0
S	50.9	30.3	12.1	5.1	1.6	0.0
X	16.0	17.3	24.0	20.8	22.0	0.0
Y	39.5	19.4	17.2	14.2	9.7	0.0
Q	51.9	22.2	15.5	2.9	7.4	0.0
Espírito Santo coffee						
L	14.3	11.1	45.5	15.3	13.8	0.0
N	17.2	18.1	46.9	10.3	7.4	0.0
K	6.8	10.8	42.4	19.2	20.8	0.0
S	15.2	21.3	44.9	10.6	8.0	0.0
X	5.3	10.6	48.8	20.5	14.8	0.0
Y	2.6	28.4	46.9	11.8	10.3	0.0
Q	9.8	13.4	50.2	10.4	16.2	0.0
São Paulo coffee						
L	14.3	15.1	11.6	14.2	25.4	19.4
N	40.8	17.6	7.3	8.3	17.4	8.7
K	13.0	12.3	10.7	19.1	28.9	16.0
S	5.0	7.1	6.9	13.3	40.2	27.5
X	8.6	12.0	9.2	18.3	18.1	33.9
Y	5.5	10.2	8.9	12.1	29.8	33.5
Q	8.5	12.2	8.4	14.3	30.3	26.2

Table 36, continued

Sector variable	I	II	III	IV	V	VI
Pernambuco sugar FGV						
L	0.0	6.5	8.1	6.4	58.6	20.4
N	0.0	6.5	6.2	7.7	47.7	31.9
K	0.0	7.5	9.1	10.4	53.7	19.3
S	0.0	5.7	10.5	4.2	60.3	19.4
X	0.0	3.5	6.8	5.4	55.0	29.3
Y	0.0	4.3	15.0	5.4	56.1	19.2
Q	0.0	6.7	10.1	6.6	47.8	28.8
São Paulo cereals						
L	5.0	25.3	38.6	13.0	9.0	9.1
N	10.5	39.3	31.7	11.8	4.0	2.7
K	3.2	37.4	36.0	6.6	9.6	7.1
S	2.2	27.8	45.6	12.1	5.5	6.8
X	3.0	16.3	28.6	16.8	14.6	20.7
Y	2.3	17.1	34.3	18.6	13.3	14.5
Q	6.3	27.3	37.4	14.0	10.0	5.0
Rio Grande do Sul rice FGV						
L	3.8	6.8	18.7	37.3	14.3	19.1
N	9.0	12.2	23.5	33.2	12.2	9.9
K	2.0	4.9	24.4	30.1	20.4	18.2
S	2.4	7.4	20.5	29.7	15.7	24.2
X	1.3	2.7	17.9	18.8	19.0	40.3
Y	1.3	3.6	13.4	16.5	22.1	43.2
Q	2.8	8.7	17.3	37.7	12.8	20.7
Minas Gerais corn						
L	19.9	22.8	26.5	25.6	5.1	0.0
N	46.8	25.9	13.2	12.2	2.0	0.0
K	26.5	17.2	26.6	25.7	4.0	0.0
S	22.3	33.7	21.2	20.6	2.1	0.0
X	5.0	9.7	25.4	37.7	22.1	0.0
Y	11.0	13.1	21.7	50.0	4.1	0.0
Q	37.0	18.0	24.5	18.9	1.6	0.0
São Paulo cattle/general						
L	2.0	6.2	5.9	58.0	18.8	9.1
N	16.4	8.0	6.8	56.5	7.8	4.7
K	2.9	7.2	4.4	66.4	10.9	8.2
S	4.1	7.3	4.2	69.6	12.5	2.4
X	1.9	5.9	5.6	57.0	19.4	10.1
Y	3.0	6.1	5.0	69.9	11.1	5.9
Q	7.0	7.4	3.5	71.3	8.3	2.4

Table 36, continued

Sector variable	size group					
	I	II	III	IV	V	VI
Alagoas sugar						
L	0.0	1.6	6.6	8.7	24.3	58.8
N	0.0	1.4	6.5	8.3	22.7	61.1
K	0.0	0.6	3.6	5.8	21.6	68.3
S	0.0	1.3	5.2	9.0	25.3	59.3
X	0.0	2.5	5.5	7.6	28.5	55.9
Y	0.0	2.3	5.4	7.2	28.6	56.4
Q	0.0	1.3	6.2	9.2	25.3	58.0
Pernambuco sugar IAA						
L	0.8	1.7	7.2	10.3	26.5	53.4
N	0.8	1.4	6.0	9.2	24.7	57.8
K	0.6	1.3	4.3	6.3	27.8	59.8
S	0.4	0.7	5.6	16.4	22.3	54.5
X	0.4	1.5	3.6	8.1	22.3	64.0
Y	1.7	2.3	3.0	12.6	23.1	57.4
Q	1.2	2.0	7.4	7.5	24.2	57.7
São Paulo sugar						
L	1.0	5.0	9.5	14.0	43.5	27.0
N	0.8	3.8	9.3	12.7	48.6	24.9
K	0.7	5.0	6.9	13.7	43.3	30.2
S	0.5	4.2	4.8	12.4	45.0	33.1
X	0.9	3.5	9.3	15.5	44.4	26.3
Y	1.0	3.6	8.8	12.9	43.3	30.4
Q	0.8	4.6	10.3	13.0	46.5	24.6
Ceará cattle						
L	1.5	4.0	13.4	49.8	23.9	7.5
N	14.1	10.2	25.4	37.2	10.5	2.6
K	4.4	6.4	23.4	40.5	20.0	5.2
A	5.0	7.9	23.7	45.7	12.1	5.5
V	6.5	7.7	20.5	56.0	8.6	0.6
X	1.6	4.2	13.6	47.5	22.5	10.6
Y	2.8	7.0	13.1	38.0	12.2	26.9
Q	5.4	15.1	16.3	50.6	10.1	2.5
Espírito Santo cattle						
L	0.0	4.8	24.8	35.5	34.8	0.0
N	0.0	19.7	34.8	38.5	7.0	0.0
K	0.0	5.5	43.5	35.1	16.0	0.0

Table 36, continued

Sector variable	size group					
	I	II	III	IV	V	VI
A	0.0	14.0	33.3	34.6	18.1	0.0
V	0.0	7.9	31.5	38.5	22.1	0.0
X	0.0	5.8	22.3	34.4	37.6	0.0
Y	0.0	17.2	28.4	29.3	25.2	0.0
Q	0.0	7.4	33.8	39.0	19.8	0.0
Minas Gerais cattle						
L	0.0	4.0	10.3	23.1	15.2	47.4
N	0.0	19.5	21.3	34.7	12.3	12.3
K	0.0	15.4	26.3	28.3	18.5	11.6
A	0.0	5.7	17.5	29.8	17.9	29.1
V	0.0	16.2	25.5	30.2	12.7	15.5
X	0.0	3.4	10.0	19.1	20.9	46.6
Y	0.0	6.2	15.4	30.0	37.4	11.0
Q	0.0	25.2	23.7	26.7	9.8	14.6
Rio Grande do Sul cattle						
L	0.2	3.4	5.2	19.0	28.2	44.0
N	10.3	15.7	10.0	29.1	15.7	19.2
K	4.7	9.8	6.7	42.3	12.4	24.2
A	1.1	8.5	4.7	20.8	23.0	41.9
V	15.7	17.7	1.1	37.9	16.4	11.2
X	0.3	4.1	4.0	16.9	23.0	51.6
Y	0.8	5.9	2.6	20.7	22.4	47.6
Q	8.4	13.8	3.2	33.1	14.1	27.5
São Paulo cattle						
L	0.8	5.2	7.4	21.2	20.2	45.2
N	6.8	13.9	12.7	38.2	19.7	8.6
K	1.5	13.8	9.2	29.2	21.8	24.5
A	2.3	8.1	6.1	32.0	10.8	40.8
V	3.2	15.0	8.7	45.4	18.1	9.6
X	0.9	4.9	7.5	19.7	24.7	42.2
Y	1.3	11.4	13.1	20.7	21.2	32.4
Q	3.1	10.6	8.8	33.5	15.5	28.5

Size groups: see table 12.
A = animal capital; K = capital; L = land input; N = labor; Q = production; S = seeds, fert., insecticide; V = feed, vaccines; X = farm area; Y = farm land value.

BIBLIOGRAPHY

1. Books and pamphlets

Andrade, Manoel Correia de, *A Terra e o Homem no Nordeste* (São Paulo: Editôra Brasiliense, 1963).

Baer, Werner, *Industrialization and Economic Development in Brazil* (Homewood, Illinois: Irwin, 1965).

Callado, Antônio, *As Indústrias da Sêca e os 'Galileus' de Pernambuco: Aspecto da Luta Pela Reforma Agrária no Brasil* (Rio de Janeiro: Ed. Civilização Brasileira, 1960).

Chayanov, A. V., *The Theory of Peasant Economy*, Ed. by D. Thorner, B. Kerblay, R. E. F. Smith (Homewood, Ill.: Richard D. Irwin, 1966).

Cleophas, João, *Reforma Agrária no Brasil* (Recife: Instituto Joaquim Nabuco de Pesquisas Sociais, 1960).

Confederação Nacional da Indústria, *Seminário Para o Desenvolvimento do Nordeste: Anais*, Vols. 1 and 2 (Garahuns, Pernambuco: Serviço Social da Indústria, 1959).

Cox, Roy Raymond, *Análise da Distribuição dos Recursos Através da Função de Produção da Região Cacaueira do Estado da Bahia, Safra 1963/64*, M.S. Thesis (Vicosa, Minas Gerais: Univ. Rural, 1965).

Dantas, Bento, *A Recuperação da Lavoura Canavieira de Pernambuco com Base no Aumento da Produtividade e Intensificação da Policultura* (Recife: Estaçã Experimental dos Produtores de Açúcar de Pernambuco, 1965).

Diegues, Manuel Junior, *Populaço e Propriedade da Terra no Brasil* (Washington, D.C.: União Pan-Americana, 1959).

Dumont, Rene, *Tierras Vivas: Problemas de la Reforma Agraria en el Mundo* (Mexico: Ediciones ERA, 1963).

Eicher, Carl, and Witt, Lawrence, *Agriculture in Economic Development* (New York: McGraw Hill, 1964).

Fei, J. C. H., and Ranis, G., *Development of the Labor Surplus Economy: Theory and Policy* (Homewood, Ill.: Richard D. Irwin, 1964).

Flores, Edmundo, *Tratado de Economia Agrícola* (Mexico: Fondo de Cultura Económica, 1962).

Fonseca, Gondin da, *Os Gorilas, O Povo, e A Reforma Agrária. Manifesto dos Bispos de Brasil* (São Paulo: Ed. Fulgor, 1963).

Franco, Alberto, *Nature and Conditions Associated with the Existence of Latifundia in Southern Brazil*, 'Teaching Materials on Agrarian Reform No. 3' (Rio de Janeiro: Inter American Center of Agrarian Reform, 1965).

Fundaçao para Desenvolvimento Industrial do Nordeste, *Recife e Salvador: Frigorificação, Consumo de Carne, e Outros Dados* (Recife, 1966).

Fundação Getulio Vargas, Instituto Brasileiro de Economia, *Contas Nacionais* (Rio de Janeiro, 1966). Mimeographed.

Fundação Getulio Vargas, Instituto Brasileiro de Economia, *Pesquisa Sobre Condições e Custos de Produção da Lavoura Canavieira* (Rio de Janeiro, 1965).
Fundação Getulio Vargas, Instituto Brasileiro de Economia, *Pesquisa Sobre Condições e Custos da Produção da Lavoura Canavieira – Usinas* (Rio de Janeiro, 1966).
Fundação Getulio Vargas, Instituto Brasileiro de Economia, *Projeções de Oferta e Demanda de Produtos Agrícolas para o Brasil. Texto Preliminar* (Rio de Janeiro, 1966).
Furtado, Celso, *Dialética do Desenvolvimento* (Rio de Janeiro: Editôra Fundo de Cultura, 1964).
Furtado, Celso, *A Pre-Revolução Brasileira* (Rio de Janeiro: Editôra Fundo de Cultura, 1962).
Gonçalves, Fernando Antonio, *Condições de Vida do Trabalhador Rural da Zona da Mata do Estado de Pernambuco – 1964* (Recife: Instituto Joaquim Nabuco de Pesquisas Sociais, 1965), Mimeographed.
Hagen, Everett, E., *Planning Economic Development* (Homewood, Ill.: Richard D. Irwin, 1963).
Hagen, Everett, E., *The Economics of Development* (Homewood, Ill.: Richard D. Irwin, 1968).
Hapgood, David, and Millikan, Max F., eds., *Policies for Promoting Agricultural Development. Report of a Conference on Productivity and Innovation in Agriculture in the Underdeveloped Countries* (Cambridge: M.I.T. Center for International Studies, 1965).
Harris, Marvin, *Town and Country in Brazil* (New York: Colombia Univ. Press, 1956).
Hauser, Philip M., ed., *Urbanization in Latin America* (New York: UNESCO, International Documents Service, 1961).
Hawaiian Agronomics International Inc., *Diversification and Modernization of Agriculture in the Sugar Cane Zone of Northeast Brazil* (Recife: U.S. Agency for International Development, 1966).
Heady, Earl O., and Dillon, John, *Agricultural Production Functions* (Ames, Iowa: Iowa State Univ. Press, 1961).
Heady, Earl O., *Economics of Agricultural Production and Resource Use* (New York: Prentice Hall, 1952).
Heady, E. O., Johnson, G. L., and Hardin, L. S., *Resource Productivity, Returns to Scale, and Farm Size* (Ames, Iowa: Iowa State Univ. Press, 1956).
Hirschman, Albert O., *Journeys Toward Progress: Studies of Economic Policy Making in Latin America* (New York: Twentieth Century Fund, 1963).
Huss, Donald L., *A Glossary of Terms Used in Range Management* (Portland: American Society of Range Management, 1964).
Instituto Brasileiro de Ação Democrática, Artur Rios, et al., *Recomendações Sobre a Reforma Agrária* (Rio de Janeiro: Edição do IBAD, 1961).
Instituto Joaquim Nabuco de Pesquisas Sociais, *As Migrações Para o Recife*, Vols. 1–4 (Recife: Ministério da Educação e Cultura, 1961).
Instituto Joaquim Nabuco de Pesquisas Sociais, *Problemas do Abastecimento Alimentar no Recife* (Recife: Ministério da Educação e Cultura, 1962).
Instituto de Pesquisas e Estudos Sociais, C. J. de Assis Ribeiro, et al., *A Reforma Agrária: Problemas, Bases, Solução* (Rio de Janeiro: IPES, 1964).
Lave, R. E., and Kyle, D. W., *A Systems Study of Transportation in Northeast Brazil* (Stanford: Institute in Engineering-Economic Systems, 1966).
Maciel, Telmo Frederico do Rêgo, *Nível de Vida do Trabalhador Rural da Zona da Mata – 1961* (Recife: Instituto Joaquim Nabuco de Pesquisas Sociais, 1961).

Mayer, Dom Antônio de Castro, et al., *Reforma Agrária: Questão da Conciencia* (Rio de Janeiro: Ed. Cruz., 1960).
Nerlove, Marc, *Estimation and Identification of Cobb Douglas Production Functions* (Chicago: Rand McNally Co., 1965).
Nerlove, Marc, *The Dynamics of Supply* (Baltimore: Johns Hopkins Univ. Press, 1958).
Netto, Antonio Delfim, Pastore, Affonso Celso, and Carvalho, Eduardo Pereira, *Agricultura e Desenvolvimento no Brasil*, Estudos ANPES No. 5 (São Paulo: ANPES, 1966).
Netto, Antonio Delfim, *Problemas Econômicas da Agricultura Brasileira* (São Paulo: Faculdade de Ciencias Econômicas e Administrativas, Univ. de São Paulo, 1965).
Pessoa de Morais, *Sociologia da Revolução Brasileira: Análise e Interpretação do Brasil de Hoje* (Rio de Janeiro: Ed. Leitura, 1965).
Price, Robert E., *Rural Unionization in Brazil* (Madison, Wisconsin: Land Tenure Center, 1964). Mimeographed.
Rangel, Ignacio, *Questão Agrária Brasileira* (Rio de Janeiro: Presidência da Republica, Conselho do Desenvolvimento, 1961).
Raposo, Ben-Hur, *Reforma Agrária Para o Brasil* (Rio de Janeiro: Ed. Fundo da Cultura, 1965).
Rask, Norman, *Tamanho da Propriedade e Renda Agrícola. Santa Cruz do Sul* (Pôrto Alegre: Faculdade de Ciencias Econômicas, IEPE, Univ. de Rio Grande do Sul, 1965). Mimeographed.
Rask, Norman, *Tamanho Mínimo e Combinação de Atividades para Pequenas Propriedades* (Pôrto Alegre: Faculdade de Ciencias Econômicas IEPE, Univ. de Rio Grande do Sul, 1965). Mimeographed.
Robock, Stefan H., *Brazil's Developing Northeast: A Study of Regional Planning and Foreign Aid* (Washington, D.C.: Brookings Institution, 1963).
Rosa e Silva Neto, J. M., *Contribuição ao Estudo da Zona da Mata em Pernambuco: Aspectos Estruturais e Econômicos da Área de Influência das Usinas de Açúcar* (Recife: Instituto Joaquim Nabuco de Pesquisas Sociais, 1966).
Rosa e Silva Neto, J. M., *Estimativa do Custo da Produção da Cana de Açúcar (Safra 1965/1966)* (Recife: Conselho de Desenvolvimento de Pernambuco, 1966).
Sá, José Itamário, *Utilização da Mão de Obra e Níveis de Renda em Pequenas Propriedades Rurais. Santa Rosa, Rio Grande do Sul* (Pôrto Alegre: Fac. de Ciencias Econômicas, IEPE, Univ. de Rio Grande do Sul, 1965).
Schultz, Theodore W., *Economic Crises in World Agriculture* (Ann Arbor: University of Michigan Press, 1965).
Schultz, Theodore W., *Transforming Traditional Agriculture*, Studies in Comparative Economics, No. 3 (New Haven: Yale University Press, 1964).
Seers, Dudley, ed., *Cuba: The Economic and Social Revolution* (Chapel Hill: Univ. of North Carolina Press, 1964).
Simonsen, Mário Henrique, *A Experiência Inflacionária no Brasil* (Rio de Janeiro: Instituto de Pesquisas e Estudos Sociais, 1964).
Singer, H. W., *Estudo Sobre o Desenvolvimento Econômico do Nordeste* (Recife: Comissão de Desenvolvimento Econômico de Pernambuco, 1962).
Smith, T. Lynn, *Agrarian Reform in Latin America* (New York: Alfred Knopf, 1965).
Smith, T. Lynn, *Brazil: People and Institutions* (Baton Rouge: Louisiana State Univ. Press, 1963).
Southworth, Herman M., and Johnston, Bruce F., eds., *Agricultural Development and Economic Growth* (Ithaca, New York: Cornell Univ. Press, 1967).

Stein, Stanley J., *Vassouras: A Brazilian Coffee County, 1850–1900* (Cambridge: Harvard Univ. Press, 1957).
Vilaça, Marcos Vinicius, and Albuquerque, Roberto C., *Coronel, Coroneis* (Rio de Janeiro: Editôra Tempo Brasileiro, 1965).
Wald, Haskell P., *Taxation of Agricultural Land in Underdeveloped Economies: A Survey and Guide to Policy* (Cambridge: Harvard University Press, 1959).
Wolf, Eric R., *Peasants*, Foundations of Modern Anthropology Series (Englewood Cliffs: Prentice Hall, 1966).

2. Articles: periodicals, journals, and collections of essays

Accioly Borges, Thomas Pompeu, 'Relationship between Economic Development, Industrialization and the Growth of Urban Population in Brazil', in: Philip M. Hauser, ed., *Urbanization in Latin America* (New York: UNESCO, International Documents Service, 1961), pp. 149–169.
Arrow, K., Chenery, H. B., Minhas, B., and Solow, R., 'Capital–Labor Substitution and Economic Efficiency', *Review of Economics and Statistics*, 43 (August 1961), pp. 225–250.
Bachman, K. L., and Christensen, R. P., 'The Economics of Farm Size', in: H. M. Southworth and B. F. Johnston, eds., *Agricultural Development and Economic Growth* (Ithaca: Cornell University Press, 1967), pp. 234–257.
Barraclough, Solon L., and Domike, Arthur L., 'Agrarian Structure in Seven Latin American Countries', *Land Economics*, (November 1966) pp. 391–424.
Bonilla, Frank, 'Rural Reform in Brazil', *Dissent*, 9 (Autumn 1962), pp. 373–382.
Brewster, J. M., 'The Machine Process in Agriculture and Industry', *Journal of Farm Economics*, 32 (Feb. 1950), pp. 69–81.
Caio Prado, Jr., 'Nova Contribuição a Análise do Problema Agrária no Brasil', *Revista Brasiliense*, 43 (Set.-Out. 1962), pp. 11–55.
Chacel, Julian, 'Land Reform in Brazil: Some Political and Economic Implications', *Proceedings of the Academy of Political Sciences*, 27 (May 1964), pp. 56–77.
Chenery H. B., 'Comparative Advantage and Development Policy', *American Economic Review*, 51 (March 1961), pp. 18–51.
Chenery, H. B., 'Patterns of Industrial Growth', *American Economic Review*, 50 (September 1960), pp. 624–654.
Chonchol, Jacques, 'Análisis Crítico de la Reforma Agraria Cubana', *Trimestre Económico*, 30 (Enero-Marzo 1963), pp. 69–143.
Cline, William R., 'Influencia das Dimensões e Relações Jurídicas na Eficiência Produtiva do Estabelecimento Agrícola', *Revista Brasileira de Economia*, 21 (Março 1967), pp. 45–60.
Conjuntura Econômica, Rio de Janeiro, monthly, Various Issues.
Delgado, Oscar, 'Revolution, Reform, Conservatism: Three Types of Agrarian Structure', *Dissent*, 9 (Autumn 1962), pp. 350–363.
Freebairn, Donald K., 'Relative Production efficiency between Tenure Classes in the Yaqui Valley, Sonora, Mexico', *Journal of Farm Economics*, 45 (December 1963), pp. 1150–1160.
Furtado, Celso, 'Development and Stagnation in Latin America: A Structuralist Approach', *Studies in Comparative International Development*, 1 (1965), pp. 159–175.
Galenson, W., and Leibenstein, H., 'Investment Criteria, Productivity, and Economic Development', *Quarterly Journal of Economics*, 69 (August 1955), pp. 343–370.

Georgescu-Roegen, N., 'Economic Theory and Agrarian Economics', *Oxford Economic Papers*, 12 (February 1960), pp. 1–40.
Greenfield, Sidney M., and Edgard de Vasconcelos Barros, 'Rural Labor and Economic Development in Brazil', *Interamerican Economic Affairs*, 19 (Summer 1965), pp. 75–82.
Griliches, Zvi, 'Sources of Measured Productivity Growth: United States Agriculture, 1940–1960', *Journal of Political Economy*, 71 (August 1963), pp. 331–346.
Junquéira, Antonio Augusto B., 'Cana de Açúcar: Custo de Produção e Análise da Renda, Safras de 1962–63 e 1963–64', *Agricultura em São Paulo*, 2 (Junho 1964), pp. 40–56.
Leeds, Anthony, 'Brazil and the Myth of Francisco Julião', in: J. Maier and R. W. Weatherhead, eds., *Politics of Change in Latin America* (New York: Praeger, 1964), pp. 190–204.
Lewis, W. Arthur, 'Economic Development with Unlimited Supplies of Labor', *The Manchester School*, 22 (May 1954), pp. 139–91.
Long, E. J., 'The Economic Basis of Land Reform in Underdeveloped Economies', *Land Economics*, 37 (May 1961), pp. 113–23.
Mellor, John W., 'Toward a Theory of Agricultural Development', in: H. M. Southworth and B. F. Johnston, eds., *Agricultural Development and Economic Growth* (Ithaca: Cornell University Press, 1967), pp. 21–60.
Nicholls, W. H., and Paiva, Ruy Miller, 'Desenvolvimento Técnico da Agricultura Brasileira', *Revista Brasileira de Economia*, 19 (Setembro 1965), pp. 27–63.
Nicholls, W. H., and Paiva, Ruy Miller, 'Estrutura e Produtividade da Agricultura Brasileira', *Revista Brasileira de Economia*, 19 (Junho 1965), pp. 5–28.
Nicholls, W. H., and Paiva, Ruy Miller, 'The Structure and Productivity of Brazilian Agriculture', *Journal of Farm Economics*, 47 (May 1965), pp. 347–361.
Paglin, Morton, 'Surplus Agricultural Labor and Development: Facts and Theories', *American Economic Review*, 55 (September 1965), pp. 815–834.
Pazos, Felipe, 'Comentarios a dos Artículos sobre la Revolución Cubana', *Trimestre Económico*, 29 (Enero-Marzo 1962), pp. 1–13.
Raup, Philip M., 'The Contribution of Land Reforms to Agricultural Development: An Analytical Framework', *Economic Development and Cultural Change*, 12 (October 1963), pp. 1–21.
Rios, José Arthur, 'O Estatuto da Lavoura Canavieira como Instrumento de Reforma Agrária', *Jurídica*, 27 (Abril-Junho 1962), pp. 6–20.
Schaedel, Richard P., 'Land Reform Studies', *Latin American Research Review*, 1 (Fall 1965), pp. 75–122.
Schattan, Solomão, 'Estrutura Econômica da Lavoura Paulista', *Revista Brasiliense*, 26 (Nov.-Dez. 1959), pp. 21–34.
Schickele, Rainer, 'Obstacles to Agricultural Production', *Journal of Farm Economics*, 24 (May 1942), pp. 447–462.
Seers, Dudley, 'A Theory of Inflation and Growth in Under-developed Economies Based on the Experience of Latin America', *Oxford Economic Papers*, 14 (June 1962), pp. 173–195.
Sen, Amartya K., 'Peasants and Dualism With or Without Surplus Labor', *Journal of Political Economy*, 74 (October 1966), pp. 425–450.
Sen, Amartya K., 'Some Notes on the Choice of Capital Intensity in Development Planning', *Quarterly Journal of Economics*, 71 (November 1957), pp. 561–584.
Smith, Gordon W., 'A Agricultura e o Plano Trienal', *Revista Brasileira de Economia*, 16 (Dez. 1962), pp. 113–122.

De Souza, Janes Angelo, 'A Dimensão Ótima da Propriedade Agrícola em São Paulo', *Revista Brasileira de Economia*, 16 (Junho 1962), pp. 35–42.
Sunkel, Osvaldo, 'Inflation in Chile: an Unorthodox Approach', *International Economic Papers*, 10 (1960), pp. 107–131.
Walters, A. A., 'Production and Cost Functions: An Econometric Survey', *Econometrica*, 31 (Jan.-April 1963), pp. 1–66.
Wolf, Eric R., and Mintz, Sidney W., 'Haciendas and Plantations in Middle America and the Antilles', *Social and Economic Studies*, 37 (September 1957), pp. 380–412.

3. Official publications

Banco do Nordeste do Brasil, S.A., *Abastecimento de Generos Alimentícios da Cidade do Recife* (Fortaleza, 1962).
Banco do Nordeste do Brasil, S.A., *Suprimento de Generos Alimentícios Para a Cidade de Fortaleza* (Fortaleza, 1964).
Banco do Nordeste do Brasil, S.A., *Suprimento de Generos Alimentícios Para a Cidade do Salvador)* (Fortaleza, 1964).
Comissão Executiva do Plano de Recuperação Econômica-Rural de Lavoura Cacaueira, *Relatório de 1963–64* (Rio de Janeiro, 1964).
Comissão Nacional de Alimentação, *Balanço Alimentar do Brasil* (Rio de Janeiro: Ministério de Saúde, 1959, 1962, 1964).
Commissão Nacional de Política Agrária, *Os Problemas da Terra no Brasil e na America Latina: Documento e Conclusões do Seminário Sobre o Problema da Terra* (Rio de Janeiro: Ministério da Agricultura, 1954).
Comité Interamericano de Desarrollo Agrícola, *Chile: Tenencia de la Tierra y Desarrollo Socio-económico del Sector Agrícola* (Santiago: Talleres Graficos Hispano Suiza, 1966).
Comité Interamericano de Desarrollo Agrícola, *Inventário da Informação Básica Para a Programação do Desenvolvimento Agrícola na América Latina. Brasil* (Washingon, D.C.: Unión Pan Americana, 1964).
Comité Interamericano de Desarrollo Agrícola, *Land Tenure Conditions and Socio-Economic Development of the Agricultural Sector. Brazil* (Washington, D.C.: Pan American Union, 1966).
Comité Interamericano de Desarrollo Agrícola, *Tenencia de La Tierra y Desarrollo Socio-Económico del Sector Agrícola: Argentina* (Washington, D.C.: Pan American Union, 1965).
Conselho de Desenvolvimento de Pernambuco, Grupo de Trabalho, *Plano de Melhoramento da Alimentação e do Manejo do Gada Leiteiro* (Recife, 1964).
Departamento Nacional de Obras Contra as Sêcas, *Primeiro Plano de Obras e Estudos. 1965–1968* (N.P., N.D.).
Escritório de Pesquisa Econômica Aplicada, *Diagnóstico Preliminar do Setor de Agricultura* (Rio de Janeiro: Ministério de Planejamento e Coordenação Econômica, 1966). Mimeographed.
Escritório de Pesquisa Econômica Aplicada, *Situação Monetária, Creditícia, e do Mercado de Capitaes: Diagnóstico Preliminar* (Rio de Janeiro: Ministério de Planejamento e Coordenação Econômica, 1966).
Escritório de Pesquisa Econômica Aplicada, *Programa de Ação Econômica do Govêrno 1964–1965 (Síntese)* (Rio de Janeiro: Ministério de Planejamento e Coordenação Econômica, 1964).
Estados Unidos do Brasil, *Estatuto da Terra: Lei No. 4504 de 30 de Novembro de 1964* (Rio de Janeiro: Departamento de Imprensa Nacional, 1965).

Grupo Executivo da Racionalização da Agroindústria Açúcareira do Nordeste (GERAN), *Programa Estadual de Pernambuco* (Recife: SUDENE, 1966).

Grupo Executivo de Racionalização da Cafeicultura (GERCA), *Relatório, 1965* (Rio de Janeiro: Instituto Brasileiro do Café, 1965).

Grupo Interdepartamental de Povoamento do Maranhão (GIPM), *Relatório* (Recife: SUDENE, 1963). Typed.

Groupe d'étude du Val du Jaguaribe (GEVJ), *Mise en Valeur du Bassin du Jaguaribe. Etudes General de Base (1962–64). Tome VIII. Possibilités et Orientations Hydroagricoles.* (Recife: SUDENE, 1964).

Hilton, Norman, *Interim Economic Report: Survey of the São Francisco River Basin (Brazil)*, U.N. Special Fund Project No. 18, (Recife: F.A.O. – SUDENE, 1963).

Instituto Brasileiro de Geografia e Estatística, Conselho Nacional de Estatística, *Anuário Estatístico do Brasil* (Rio de Janeiro: Yearly Issues).

Instituto Brasileiro de Geografia e Estatística, Serviço Nacional de Recenseamento, *VI Recenseamento Geral do Brasil – 1950* (Rio de Janeiro, 1954).

Instituto Brasileiro de Geografia e Estatística, Serviço Nacional de Recenseamento, *Censo Agrícola de 1960. Brasil. VII Recenseamento Geral do Brasil. Série Nacional, Volume II, 1. Parte* (Rio de Janeiro, 1967).

Instituto Brasileiro de Geografia e Estatística, Serviço Nacional de Recenseamento, *VII Recenseamento Geral do Brasil – 1960. Sinopse Preliminar do Censo Agrícola* (Rio de Janeiro: 1964).

Instituto Brasileira de Reforma Agrária, *A Estrutura Agrária Brasileira: Dados Preliminares, Volume I* (Rio de Janeiro, 1967).

Instituto Brasileira de Reforma Agrária, *Ante Projeto do Plano de Reforma Agrária da Area Prioritária de Emergência do Nordeste* (Rio de Janeiro, 1966). Mimeographed.

Instituto Brasileira de Reforma Agrária, *Instrução Especial IBRA No. 1* (Rio de Janeiro: Dept. de Imprensa Nacional, 1965).

Instituto Brasileira de Reforma Agrária, Delegacia Regional do Nordeste, *Anteprojeto de Quatis* (Recife, 1966). Typed.

Instituto Brasileira de Reforma Agrária, *Unidade Agro-Indústrial de Caxangá. Levantamento Socio-Cultural* (Recife, 1966). Typed.

Instituto Gaucho de Reforma Agrária, *Socio-Economic Survey of Tapes* (Pôrto Alegre, 1966). Typed.

Instituto Rio Grandense do Arroz, *Anuário Estatístico do Arroz* (Pôrto Alegre: Yearly Issues).

Interdepartmental Committee on Nutrition for National Development, U.S. Department of Defense, *Northeast Brazil Nutrition Survey, March-May 1963* (Washington, D.C., 1965).

Lucena, Vinicius G. de., *Os Resíduos e Sub-Produtos da Agro-Indústria Açúcareira como base para o Forrageamento de Bovinos e Suínos em Pernambuco* (Recife: Conselho de Desenvolvimento de Pernambuco, 1964).

Ministério da Agricultura, Dept. Econômico, *Insumos Físicos para Culturas Selecionadas na Região Centro-Sul do Brasil 1965–66* (Rio de Janeiro, 1966).

Ministério da Agricultura, Dept. Econômico, *Insumos Físicos para Culturas Selecionadas na Região Nordeste do Brasil 1965–66* (Rio de Janeiro, 1967).

Ministério da Agricultura, Dept. Econômico, Serviço de Informação de Mercado Agrícola, *Boletim Informativo dos Mercados Atacadistas. Guanabara, São Paulo, Minas Gerais* (Rio de Janeiro, 1966). Mimeographed.

Newberg, R., and Miller, E., *Aspects of Frontier Settlement in Northern Brazil: Report of Interagency Reconnaissance Team* (N.P.: United States Agency for International Development, 1964). Mimeographed.

Superintendência do Desenvolvimento do Nordeste, *Bases da Política de Desenvolvimento do Nordeste do Brasil e Esquema do Plano Qüinqüenal da Sudene* (Recife, 1964).

Superintendência do Desenvolvimento do Nordeste, *Third Master Plan for the Social and Economic Development of the Northeast 1966–68*, English Translation (Recife: U.S.A.I.D., 1965).

United Nations, Department of Economic Affairs, *Progress in Land Reform* (New York, 1954).

United Nations, Department of Economic Affairs, *Progress in Land Reform. Third Report* (New York, 1962).

United Nations, Department of Economic Affairs, *Progress in Land Reform. Fourth Report* (New York, 1966).

United Nations, Economic Commission for Latin America, *The Economic Development of Latin America in the Postwar Period* (New York, 1964).

United Nations, Food and Agriculture Organization, *Coffee in Latin America: Productivity Problems and Future Prospects. Vol. 2. Brazil. State of São Paulo. Parts 1 and 2* (Mexico, 1960).

United Nations, Food and Agriculture Organization, *Food Composition Tables for International Use* (Rome, 1949).

United Nations, Food and Agriculture Organization, *Livestock in Latin America: Status, Problems, and Prospects 2. Brazil* (New York, 1964).

United States Department of Agriculture, Economic Research Service, *The World Food Budget, 1970*, Foreign Agricultural Economic Report No. 19 (Washington, D.C., 1964).

United States Department of Commerce, United States Bureau of Census, *Historical Statistics of the United States: Colonial Times to 1957. A Statistical Abstract Supplement* (Washington, D.C., 1960).

4. Unpublished theses and manuscripts

Barraza, Luciano, and Solis, Leopoldo, 'Notes on Land Reform'. Mimeographed, n.p., n.d.

Cline, William R., *Economic Considerations for a Land Reform in Brazil*, Ph.D. Thesis (Yale University, 1969).

Leeds, Anthony, *Economic Cycles in Brazil: the Persistence of a Total Culture-Pattern: Cacão and Other Cases*, Ph.D. Thesis (Columbia Univ., 1957).

Pastore, Affonso Celso, 'A Resposta da Produção Agrícola aos Preços no Brasil', Unpublished paper (São Paulo, 1966: Universidade do São Paulo).

Sund, M. D., *Land Tenure and Economic Performance of Agricultural Establishments in Northeast Brazil*, Ph.D. Thesis (University of Wisconsin, 1965).

INDEX

Agrarian Fund Bonds, 5
Agricultural growth rates, 1–2
Albuquerque, Roberto C., 42
Animal units, grazing requirements, 82n

Bachman, K. L., 10
Barazza, Luciano, 38n
Barraclough, Solon L., 8n, 18n
Brewster, J. M., 20n

Cadastral survey, 7
Caio Prado Jr., 28n
Callado, Antonio, 43n
Capital market, 33, 168
Carvalho, Eduardo Pereira, 3n
Cattle ranch land use, 106, 108, 134n
Chayanov, A. V., 9n, 24n
Chenery, H. B., 3n, 18n
Christensen, R. P., 10
Cobb–Douglas production function
    estimates for Brazil, 64–65, 68–69
    estimates for other countries, 70–71
    form, 66–67
    possible bias, 59
Colonization, 182–186
Comité Interamericano de Desarrollo Agrícola (CIDA), 9
Concentration of land ownership, Brazil, 126–127
Cooperativas Integral de Reforma Agrária, 6
Costs of land reform, 162
Credit, 168, 170

Dillon, John, 73
Domike, Arthur L., 8n, 18n

Entrepreneurial ability, 20, 74–76
Escritório de Pesquisa Econômica Aplicada (EPEA), 33n
Estatuto da Terra, 4–6
Excess labor on small farms, 153
Exports of agricultural goods, 1
Expropriation, 4–5, 7

209

Extension, 170
External economies, 21

Factor combinations, 9, 12, 31–32, 47–48, 116–122
'Family farm' behavior, 24–29
'Family property', 5
'Farm-efficiency', 19, 22, 80
Fei, J. C. H., 23
Flores, Edmundo, 41
Franco, Alberto, 34n, 44
Furtado, Celso, 14n

Galenson, W., 18n
Georgescu-Roegen, N., 9n, 24n
GERAN plan, 7
Getulio Vargas Foundation, 61, 187n, 188n, 191n
Goulart, 172n
Greenfield, Sidney M., 42
Grupo Interdepartamental de Povoamento do Maranhão (GIPM), 186n

Hagen, Everett E., 10
Hapgood, David, 21n
Heady, Earl O., 73
Hirschman, Albert O., 43n, 172n
Huss, Donald L., 82n

Income on land reform parcel, 150–151
Income redistribution, 13–14
Inflation, 33n
Innovation, 14–15
Input use by farm size, 109–115
Instituto Brasileiro de Reforma Agrária (IBRA), 4–5, 36n
Instituto Joaquim Nabuco de Pesquisas Sociais, 15n
Instituto Riograndense de Arroz (IRGA), 34, 61, 188
Institute of Sugar and Alcohol, 61
Inter-American Committee for Agricultural Development, *see* Comité Interamericano de Desarrollo Agrícola (CIDA)

Kyle, D. W., 182n

Labor absorption, 14
'Labor-market dualism', 22–32, 116–117, 121–125
Land market imperfections, 36, 121–122
Land prices, 34–36, 91, 94
Land quality, 43–45, 85, 94
Land reform
   Brazilian experience, 7
   law, 4–7
   previous literature, 8–10

Land tax, 6, 32–33n, 167, 171
Land use intensity
  empirical tests, 80–115
  theory, 11n, 22–47
Latifúndio, 5, 41–42, 97, 106–108
Lave, R. E., 182n
Leibenstein, H., 18n
Letras de Câmbio, 33
Lewis, W. Arthur, 23
Linear programming, 163–164
Long, E. J., 20n
Long run growth, 16–19

Mechanization in agriculture, 7
Mellor, John W., 9n, 24n
Migration, 15n
Miller, E., 182n
Millikan, Max F., 21n
Minifúndio, 5
Minimum wage, 168
Mintz, Sidney W., 41
Modern inputs, 169
Módulo, 5
Monopsony, 38–41, 126–127

Nerlove, Marc, 59
Netto, Antônio Delfim, 3n
Newberg, R., 182n
Nicholls, W. H., 17n
Non-maximization by large farms, 41–42, 125–126
Northeast, 7, 106–107
Nutrition, 3

Optimal farm size, 51
'Own consumption', 36–38

Paglin, Morton, 22n
Paiva, Ruy Miller, 17n
'Partial reform' calculation, 153–161
Pastore, Affonso, 3n
Pazos, Felipe, 16n
Pernambuco
  land expropriation, 7
  land quality, 43
Political likelihood of land reform, 172
Portfolio asset, land as, 32–35
Price supports, 169, 171
Priority areas for land reform, 4
'Production-efficiency', 19–21

Ranis, G., 23
Raposo, Ben-Hur, 4n
Rask, Norman, 10n
Raup, Philip M., 10
Rent control, 6, 168
Returns to scale
  empirical tests, 62–74
  theory, 19–21
Rice prices, 34
Rio Grande do Sul
  land quality, 43
  rice land prices, 34
Rosa e Silva Neto, J. M., 191
Rural enterprise, 5

Sample
  design, 187–188
  expansion, 138–140, 193
São Paulo coffee land quality, 44
Savings, 16–18
Schaedel, Richard P., 8n
Schattan, Solomão, 9n
Schickele, Rainer, 9n, 52n
Sen, Amartya K., 9n, 18n, 24–25
Shadow prices, 48–50
Sharecropping, 6, 52
Simonsen, Mario Henrique, 33n
Smith, Gordon W., 2n
Smith, T. Lynn, 43n
Social efficiency, 48–52, 128–130
Solis, Leopoldo, 38n
Souza, Janes Angelo, 9n
Sternberg, Marvin, 18n
Sund, M. D., 10n
Supply elasticity of agriculture, 3
Surplus labor, 23n, 154, 161

Tenure
  controls, 6, 36
  economic effect, 52–53, 78, 85, 94
Terms of trade, agriculture vs. industry, 2, 180
'Total reform' calculation, 140–153
Transport costs, colonization zones, 182

Variables, definitions, 60–61
Vasconçelos Barros, Edgard de, 42
Vilaça, Marcos Vinicius, 42

Wald, Haskell P., 33n

Wheat imports, 1, 2
Wolf, Eric R., 41